Early Praise for *Agile Retrospectives, Second Edition*

Even if you think you know "everything" about retrospectives, you'll learn something new in this book. If you only read the sections on remote teams and how to change, you'll gain insights you did not consider before. A must for every team member who wants to support their team's improvement—agile or not.

➤ **Johanna Rothman**
Consultant and author of *Modern Management Made Easy*

As someone who frequently coaches and trains others, I found the second edition of *Agile Retrospectives* to be an excellent resource. It provides practical advice for both beginners and experienced retrospective facilitators, addressing common questions and challenges. I highly recommend this book as a valuable planning tool that you will refer to time and time again.

➤ **Joanne Perold**
Director, Faethm

I facilitated my first retrospective back in 2006 after reading the first edition of this book. It gave me the information that made that retrospective, and many others, a success. I'm glad to see that this edition still contains what a newcomer needs to facilitate their first retrospective. Yet I'm delighted to find so much more in this book. I learned new things, and suspect I'll be even more effective in the future.

➤ **George Dinwiddie**
  Author, *Software Estimation Without Guessing*

This book is an essential aid for a beginner retrospective facilitator and moreover provides deep insights and the right amount of theoretical foundation for an advanced facilitator. In general, the book equips all facilitators to improve continuously and thus ensuring the retrospectives they're leading are getting more effective.

➤ **Jutta Eckstein**
  Author, *Retrospectives for Organizational Change: An Agile Approach*

The single most valuable resource for helping people learn together.

➤ **Tricia Broderick**
  Leadership Advisor, Ignite Insight + Innovation

Agile Retrospectives, Second Edition

A Practical Guide for Catalyzing
Team Learning and Improvement

Esther Derby

Diana Larsen

David Horowitz

The Pragmatic Bookshelf

Dallas, Texas

When we are aware that a term used in this book is claimed as a trademark, the designation is printed with an initial capital letter or in all capitals.

The Pragmatic Starter Kit, The Pragmatic Programmer, Pragmatic Programming, Pragmatic Bookshelf, PragProg and the linking *g* device are trademarks of The Pragmatic Programmers, LLC.

Every precaution was taken in the preparation of this book. However, the publisher assumes no responsibility for errors or omissions, or for damages that may result from the use of information (including program listings) contained herein.

For our complete catalog of hands-on, practical, and Pragmatic content for software developers, please visit *https://pragprog.com*.

The team that produced this book includes:

Publisher: Dave Thomas
COO: Janet Furlow
Managing Editor: Tammy Coron
Development Editor: Adaobi Obi Tulton
Copy Editor: Corina Lebegioara
Indexing: Potomac Indexing, LLC
Layout: Gilson Graphics

For sales, volume licensing, and support, please contact *support@pragprog.com*.

For international rights, please contact *rights@pragprog.com*.

ISBN-13: 979-8-88865-037-0
Book version: P1.0—February 2024

For all those retrospecting, wherever you are.

Contents

Part II — Selecting Activities

Part III — Considerations

Foreword

To boil agile down to one practice, I choose this one. The retrospective creates space for reflective practice and continuous small improvements, the two habits at the core of agile work.

The second edition of this book embodies both. The authors' reflective practice of facilitation informs every piece of information here. Their continual improvement at teaching this facilitation informs which pieces of information are here. The pandemic changed how we work together, and this new book supports that.

There's a lot of reality in this book. Esther, Diana, and David do not assume that every team is excited to retrospect. They do not believe that every organization will make this smooth, or that each situation can be easily resolved.

Instead, this book sets *you* up to set *a team* up to develop a shared sense of their work. For collaborative practice, we need shared reflection.

The recommendations here focus on the team's needs and on strengthening the interactions between people who participate. This book does not center you, the retrospective leader. It will not bring you glory. It will make you and everyone you help more effective.

As the retrospective is the central agile practice, it is also the most portable. Advice here is useful outside software and outside work. Making sense of a situation together, collectively changing ourselves and our surroundings—this is what forms human society.

Thank you for contributing to the world by running effective retrospectives.

Jessica Kerr
Symmathecist, in the medium of software

Acknowledgments

Like many projects, this one didn't go quite as planned.

As we wrote, we discovered some of our initial assumptions were incorrect. In talking with our potential readers, we found they wanted things we hadn't initially planned to include. The more we collaborated, the more we unearthed additional topics we wanted to include.

We eliminated some material, too. We inspected, adapted, and worked incrementally.

And the end product, we believe, is much better for it.

Nevertheless, the book-writing process wasn't without its challenges. Between us, we had five surgeries, several injuries, three bouts of Covid, many miles of travel, schedule challenges, urgent priorities, and some major life changes. We are each grateful for the support and grace we extended to each other during these difficulties.

We are thrilled that so many people came forward to share their experiences with retrospectives with us. We couldn't include all the stories and examples. We do want to acknowledge all of those who offered. We learned something from each of you. Our sincere appreciation goes out to (in alphabetical order by first name):

Aldo Barbara, Allison Pollard, Anne Riley, Anthony Santos, Anthony Bonfante, Anthony Coppedge, Ben Ziskoven, Chokchai Phatharamalai, Dana Pylayeva, Daniela Malqui, David Rabinek, David Whitlock, Dhaval Panchal, Ed Rowand, Eleanor Bennett, Elisabeth Keuschnigg, Emily Webber, Enrico Teotti, George Dinwiddie, Gregor Streng, Helen Garcia, Horia Slușanschi, Ines Garcia, Inês Matos, Irene Asay, Jeanice Wong, Jeff Kosciejew, Jenny Tarwater, Joanne Perrold, Judy Graham, Lalitkumar Bhamare, Lauren Maffeo, Lemont Chambliss, Mark Kilby, Markus Wessjohann, Martin West, Marty Bland, Melinda Harrington, Narayanarao Thota, Ola Ellnestam, Rhys Jacob, Rickard Jones, Ritu Gaur, Ron Lichty, Ruud Rietveld, Sam Huang, Sam Roychowdhury,

Sarah O'Brien, Scott Ferguson, Steve Brown, Tobias Anderberg, Veit Richter, Viktor Cessan, Wim Van Nieuwenhoven, and Yves Hanoulle.

We were very lucky to have the able assistance of Jessica Parker. Jessica was our research assistant and general wrangler of details that we likely would have otherwise missed. She did all of the practitioner interviews, transcriptions, and coordinated permissions. Her assistance was invaluable.

Alecia Nippert and Luis Fleitas created most of the graphics. Their work was a huge step up from the "sharpie on index card" style used in the first edition. The book wouldn't be the same without their contributions.

On many occasions we found ourselves with questions about writing and publishing a successful book. We came to rely on Erika Brooks for her knowledge, expertise, and insights in the area. We owe her a great deal.

Adaobi Obi Tulton and Tammy Coron aided us in navigating the ins and outs of working with The Pragmatic Bookshelf.

Thank you to our reviewers—Astrid Claessen, Enrico Teotti, George Dinwiddie, Joanne Perold, Johanna Rothman, Jutta Eckstein, Malte Sussdorff, Sebastian Eichner, and Tricia Broderick—each of whom provided insights that caused us to rethink and rework certain parts of the book. Okay, it didn't always feel wonderful to realize we had to make significant changes, but it was always worthwhile doing so in the end. This is something to keep in mind as you lead or participate in retrospectives.

If we've missed acknowledging someone who contributed to the book, it was unintentional and the mistake is ours. We appreciate you nonetheless.

Not least, we all had support from the loved ones in our lives. They sustain us.

Introduction

Agile Retrospectives: Making Good Teams Great [DS06] has been an enormously influential and popular book. It has sold over 60,000 copies and regularly shows up as a top recommendation for agile books. Scrum Masters, agile coaches, and team members have relied on the book as the guide to retrospectives for years.

Why would we mess with a good thing?

Two big reasons:

- The world has changed. Agile software development and agile retrospectives are no longer novel.

- Sadly, we've observed that for some teams and organizations, retrospectives still fail to deliver much in the way of useful results.

This second reason breaks our hearts!

So if you are a retrospective skeptic, or haven't gotten the results you desire, we feel you. That's why we've pooled our collective experience together in this second edition to share new ideas, approaches, and solutions with you.

Speaking of collective experience, we're thrilled that David Horowitz, CEO and co-founder of Retrium, an online platform for effective retrospectives, has joined us as a co-author. In fact, it was our conversations with David that pushed us over the edge to write this second edition. While we aren't endorsing any particular tool in this book, David and Retrium have been contributors to the retrospective community for many years and David's experiences with retrospectives have greatly enhanced the book.

This second edition includes a significant amount of new material. We've added more depth to existing chapters based on what we've learned since we published the first edition. We've also added brand-new chapters that expand the scope of the book. And interspersed throughout, we've included new stories from other practitioners—people who are out there holding retrospectives every couple of weeks. These individuals have faced situations we haven't and come up with great ideas we didn't think of. They have generously shared their experiences, tips, and exercises with us, and by extension with you. Be on the lookout for them.

The rest of this introduction will provide an overview of what to expect in each chapter of the book.

In the updated and expanded Chapter 1, Help Your Team Inspect and Adapt, on page 3, we'll go over the fundamentals of retrospectives by describing the five phases of a retrospective from Set the Stage to Close the Retrospective. We'll show how a well-designed retrospective encourages participation. In the new edition, we've added depth about choosing data and choosing how to decide what to do.

In Chapter 2, A Retrospective Custom-Fit to Your Team, on page 23, we'll help you to ensure that your retrospectives match what your team needs right now.

For anyone who isn't an experienced "professional facilitator," check out Chapter 3, Leading Retrospectives, on page 49, for ideas on how to prepare for your role as a facilitator.

Chapter 4, Managing Group Dynamics, on page 63, dives deeper into the challenges of facilitating groups—so that people feel safe to participate creatively.

Chapters 5 through 9 describe various activities for each of the five phases of a retrospective. As compared with the first edition, we've added some activities and removed others. In particular, pay attention to the new activities in Chapter 7, Activities to Generate Insights, on page 115, which help you to identify small changes and experiments that the team can do without a lot of overhead.

In the new Chapter 10, Retrospectives for Common Scenarios, on page 161, we explain how we might design a retrospective in response to ten common scenarios teams face. Perhaps even more importantly, we explain the rationale behind our decisions. We hope that thinking aloud in this way will help you choose activities that best support your teams, too.

Chapter 11, Retrospectives When the Team Isn't Colocated, on page 183, deals with the reality that many teams aren't colocated. Unlike in 2006 when the first edition was released, colocation is neither assumed nor expected for many teams. We now know that excellent collaboration is possible with remote and distributed teams. This new chapter talks about the challenges of remote retrospectives and how to overcome them.

One of the most common challenges teams face is how to follow through on their retrospectives. We've written another new chapter, Chapter 12, Catalyzing and Sustaining Change, on page 201, to help teams catalyze change after the retrospective is over. It is not enough to say "make it so."

When teams struggle with problems they believe are outside of their control, helplessness can ensue. In the new Chapter 13, Elevating Issues Beyond the Team's Control, on page 219, we give you strategies to address these issues in a more productive manner.

If you face resistance to retrospectives from individuals on your team or in your organization, you will find the advice in the new Chapter 14, Overcoming Objections, on page 235, helpful. This chapter talks about how to graciously invite these individuals to give retrospectives another try.

Finally, Chapter 15, Continuing the Learning Journey, on page 247, provides additional resources and an invitation to join the broader retrospective community.

So, dive in! No more learn-nothing, do-nothing, change-nothing retrospectives. Join us in helping teams think, learn, decide, and act together.

Part I

Nuts and Bolts

The first four chapters in this book reinforce retrospective basics. These foundational elements will assist you in both designing and facilitating retrospectives. They form the essentials for getting the most out of the time and effort the team expends.

CHAPTER 1

Help Your Team Inspect and Adapt

Retrospectives help teams—even great ones—get better.

During a retrospective, teams examine the way they're working. They look at data to find patterns and identify influencing factors. They come up with potential experiments or actions to work on based on what they found. Then they choose one—maybe two—to focus on for the next period of work. Throughout, they learn together.

That may mean discovering how to improve technical skills or unearthing new ones. It may mean rebuilding or enhancing collaboration within the team. It could entail examining assumptions about practices, processes, or products. It might even involve working with other groups to address issues that span beyond the team.

Retrospectives that accomplish these things have several important benefits.

First, they help teams surface problems early while they are still small, have less emotional weight, and are easier to deal with.

Second, they foster a sense of agency by encouraging teams to take responsibility for their own improvement. Teams discover that, in many cases, they don't have to wait for others to fix problems. This contributes to engagement, which translates into creativity and investment in the organization.

And third, they increase the speed of learning, which is a great advantage in a fast-changing world. In fact, teams that hold regular retrospectives *learn how to learn* together, which has benefits that extend far beyond the retrospective itself. These teams are able to respond to changing conditions and novel problems more rapidly and gracefully.

If you've struggled to hold effective retrospectives in the past, these claims may seem far-fetched. But your team can achieve these results, too.

To do so, it's not enough to show up at the retrospective and hope for the best. Nor is it enough to have an open-ended conversation without guardrails or guidance. It's not even enough to ask "What's going well? What's not going well?"

To hold truly effective retrospectives, you will need to introduce more structure than is required in simple conversations.

Our five-phase retrospective format is specifically designed to help your team do just that.

Five Phases of a Retrospective

Our format helps groups process information and think more deeply about a particular topic.

These are the five phases of a retrospective:

1. Set the Stage
2. Gather Data
3. Generate Insights
4. Decide What to Do
5. Close the Retrospective

Each of these phases has a specific purpose. Set the Stage gets the team ready for the retrospective. Gather Data helps the team develop a shared mental model of what happened. Generate Insights enables the team to build a deeper understanding of their context and the problems at hand. Decide What to Do prompts the team to take action. And finally, Close the Retrospective brings the conversation to its conclusion.

The five-phase structure can fit into a few minutes or expand to fill several days. Regardless, stick to this outline—this structure does what a retrospective needs to do.

Retrospectives can happen after any period of work: an iteration, an ensemble session, a pomodoro, a project, a release, a week, a month, or a year. Some teams continuously pull work, pick a span of time for their retrospectives, and create their own cadence. Other teams hold retrospectives after outages or production issues. Some of the most high-performing teams use a mixture of these approaches based on their ever-evolving needs.

Good retrospectives become part of the natural rhythm of work. The "infinity loop" diagram in the figure on page 5 shows the flow between product development work and retrospectives. During the time of development work, the team incorporates insights, improvements, and experiments, while building and

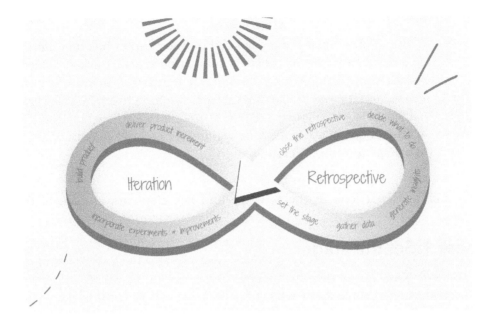

delivering an increment of software. During the retrospective, the team sets the stage, gathers data, generates insights, decides what to do, and closes the retrospective. Rinse and repeat!

A Little History

In 2001, seventeen software developers drafted the Agile Manifesto, which laid out four key values and twelve principles designed to help teams develop software better.[1] The twelfth principle states: "At regular intervals, the team reflects on how to become more effective, then tunes and adjusts its behavior accordingly."

The term retrospective predates the Manifesto. Norm Kerth first used the term to describe learning and improvement sessions held at the end of projects.

Well before the Agile Manifesto was developed, we held project retrospectives, problem-solving sessions, and working sessions of all sorts. We learned that when people have a process that helps them think, learn, and decide together, they come to better outcomes with more engagement and more ownership.

---

1. https://agilemanifesto.org/

> **A Little History**
>
> The five-phase process introduced in this chapter has its origins in a facilitation method called *Focused Conversation* that's designed to help groups think, learn, and decide together. It helps teams to consider data and perspectives before jumping to superficial conclusions. The structure itself helps to build safety by creating clarity about how the meeting will unfold and by encouraging participation from everyone.

Let's take a deeper look at the purpose and key elements of each of the phases.

Phase 1: Set the Stage

The Set the Stage phase prepares people for the work they will do in the retrospective. It lets people know what to expect, gets every voice in the room, and helps to create safety.

Start with a simple welcome and appreciation for people's investment of time. Restate the purpose and focus of the retrospective. (For more on shaping the focus of the retrospective, see Chapter 2, A Retrospective Custom-Fit to Your Team, on page 23.) Share the timebox and agenda. These simple gestures acknowledge that people's time is valuable and that you're treating it that way.

Then ask everyone in the room to speak. You can do this with a short check-in—a word or two. You might ask everyone to share a hope for the retrospective or a word that describes the previous week. We've been saying for years that when someone doesn't speak at the beginning of the retrospective, it's easier for them to remain silent for the remainder of the retrospective. Research supports our lived experience.[2]

Allison Pollard, leadership and team coach at Helping Improve, LLC, points out, "If you don't get everyone speaking early, the extroverts will take over. Getting everyone involved at the start encourages engagement throughout the meeting, instead of relying on the same few people to talk."

Send the message that everyone's input is expected and valued.

---

2. https://www.researchgate.net/publication/260038654_Personality_and_Participative_Climate_Antecedents_of_Distinct_Voice_Behaviors

Create Safety

Our brains are primed to detect and avoid threats. As David Rock mentions in *Quiet Leadership: Six Steps to Transforming Performance at Work [Roc22]*, threats don't come only from physical danger. They can also be social or psychological.

In an organization where blame is the norm, people will expect the same in a retrospective. Participants might worry that they'll be blamed for mistakes. They might worry the session will deteriorate into a gripe session. They might fear having to admit they don't know something or that they screwed up. Or, as Allison Pollard said, they might anticipate being excluded from the conversation.

Whatever the reason, people who feel threatened are on guard, and cannot participate fully.

In contrast, when people feel safe, they're more likely to be open to new information and more willing to share ideas, insights, and feelings. In fact, effective retrospectives require psychological safety.

Amy Edmondson, a renowned researcher and professor at Harvard Business School, describes psychological safety this way:

"Psychological safety is a belief that one will not be punished or humiliated for speaking up with ideas, questions, concerns or mistakes." (*The Fearless Organization: Creating Psychological Safety in the Workplace for Learning, Innovation, and Growth [Edm18]*)

Group safety affects actions and interactions at all times. But it's not something most teams articulate. When there is safety, people often don't notice it. When safety is absent, there might be a sense of wariness, or physical discomfort. Obviously, you can't turn safety on like a switch for retrospectives. But you can create the conditions where safety can grow over time.

The way you start a retrospective—a welcome, sharing purpose, focus, agenda, and hearing from everyone—all contribute to safety in indirect ways. You can create safety more directly by identifying team values, developing working agreements, and then sticking to them.

Team values and working agreements are both social contracts that describe acceptable behavior and interactions. Team values represent what people hold as important—for example, *Courage, Collaboration, Respect.* Team values *may* guide behavior, but aren't, in themselves, actionable.

Working agreements are protocols that the group develops and agrees to follow. The protocols aim to forge commitment and a shared approach that will help the team meet their goal.

An example of a working agreement might be: *We each speak from our own perspective, and don't assume we speak for others in the group, or the whole group.*

For more on developing working agreements, see Chapter 4, Managing Group Dynamics, on page 63.

Some people are tempted to skip the Set the Stage phase to quickly get to the "meat" of a retrospective. But setting the stage *is* real work—creating clarity, setting boundaries, and getting every voice into the room support safety. We never regret spending time setting the stage and neither should you. "Saving" time by skipping this part costs time later.

Don't skip setting the stage, and don't skimp on it either.

Phase 2: Gather Data

Why gather data? After all, we're only talking about a short period of time. Everyone will remember, right? Ummm, no. Following are the four big reasons to gather data before you start generating ideas on what to do differently:

- Even when people are all present, even for a short period of time, they don't see everything. Further, different people can have wildly different perspectives on the same event.

- When someone misses just one day in a weeklong timebox, they've already missed 20% of the events and interactions.

- When all or part of the team is working remotely, their contexts aren't the same.

- You can't make headway on some topics *without* data. Imagine trying to have a conversation about household spending without looking at expenditures and a bank statement. Or imagine a conversation about the quality of your development process without understanding how customers respond to the software and talking about defects.

Gathering data creates a shared picture of what happened. Without a common picture, individuals tend to verify their own opinions and beliefs. Gathering data expands everyone's perspective. Data can make the difference between quick fixes that don't work and developing a deeper understanding that leads to more effective action.

Which data will be useful in your retrospective depends on what you're choosing to focus on for this retrospective at this time. Choose data that helps the team consider and understand the topic under discussion.

Sometimes, choosing what data to bring to the retrospective is obvious. For example, if the team is looking at patterns of defects, you need the defect data. If you're looking at teamwork, you need to know people's perceptions about how they collaborate. Other times, choosing which data to bring into the retrospective is a bit of a judgment call.

Two Types of Data

There are two broad categories of data: objective and subjective. Sometimes you need one kind. Sometimes you need the other. Often you need both.

Objective Data

Objective data represents things that you can see, hear, count, measure, or verify in some way. Objective data can be counts, ratios, or trends.

The focus of your retrospective determines which data might be useful in exploring patterns and/or influencing factors. The following table shows some examples of objective data a team might examine during a retrospective, depending on the focus. This is by no means an exhaustive list!

Retrospective Focus	Potentially Useful Objective Data
Development process	Number of stories completed
	Number of stories started
	Number of stories that bounce back for revision
	Number of stories added during the iteration
	Number of stories with dependencies on other teams
Quality issues	Number of defects
	Point at which defects are discovered
	Categories of defects (or you might categorize them in the retrospective)
Missed iteration commitments	Number of interruptions during the iteration
	Number of stories added during the iteration
	Number of—or amount of time spent on—support requests
	Number and source of other ad hoc requests

Retrospective Focus	Potentially Useful Objective Data
Customer satisfaction	Number of support calls for new features
	Number of positive or negative comments on new features
	Number of sales following a new feature release
	Number of customers who recommend the product to others
	Number of customers who find the product through recommendation
	Number of new subscriptions or cancelled subscriptions
Collaboration with other parts of the organization	Lead time to schedule meetings
	Number of contacts with customers or teams you coordinate with
	Number of informal interactions

A good rule of thumb is that if you can say "number of" in front of a noun, you're talking about objective data. Sometimes that number is one. Whether something happened or not is also objective data.

Often, the absolute number isn't informative, but a ratio or trend is. Ratios show the relationship of two discrete factors—for example, stories started versus finished, or the ratio of positive to negative review comments. Both are bits of information that could lead to an interesting conversation. Trends show how a particular factor has changed over time. Is the number of defects going up or down?

Subjective Data

Subjective data is information from a personal perspective, such as feelings, perceptions, or concerns.

There are people who don't want to talk about their feelings. Some people believe emotions have no place at work. So in retrospectives, we usually don't ask people how they feel.

But emotions are important information! They tell us what matters and help us make decisions. They have a place—as subjective data—in analysis.

Knowing how team members feel can be important to the retrospective, but people may be put off by being asked directly. So ask the question a different way:

- When were you excited to come to work? When was coming to work "just a job"? When did work seem like a grind?

- What were the high points? What were the low points? How was it to be on this iteration?
- When were you [fill in an emotion, for example mad, sad, or surprised]?

Questions like these let people talk about how they experienced the iteration without using the word "feelings." How people respond to objective data and events indicates importance.

You may focus on perceptions within the teams—how people are working together, with other groups, or their satisfaction with their process:

- Satisfaction with the pairing schedule
- Team happiness or morale
- Perceptions about some aspects of the team's work—for example, technical practices, collaboration, or meeting effectiveness.

Teams often use a radar chart to gather perception data on some aspect of the team's work—technical practices, collaboration, their interface with other groups, or so on. The overall focus is the exploration of that facet of the work. However what shows up on the radar may lead the team to narrow their focus based on what they discover. An interesting outlier, a cluster of low ratings, or a dramatic difference in ratings all point to something worth exploring. Learn more about radar charts in Chapter 6, Activities to Gather Data, on page 103.

At some point, you'll want to look at perceptions *outside* the team. External feedback helps ensure the team meets organizational needs. What are customers saying about the team's work? What sort of support calls come in about your features? Often the company already collects data that can inform the team about their work:

- Metrics that measure customer satisfaction, such as Net Promoter Score (NPS), Customer Satisfaction Score (CSAT), or Customer Effort Score (CES)

- Customer rating of support calls

- Customer health scores

- Sentiment analysis of textual or voice data

Subjective data is *potentially* measurable, though it's not always easy to do so with scientific accuracy. You probably don't need scientific accuracy for a retrospective. You need information that will lead to a discussion and insights. Scales are a common and useful way to gather perception data about quality, intensity, or frequency. A traditional Likert scale has a declarative statement and a numerical range that balances the number of negative and positive responses with a neutral choice in the middle. Likert scales usually have an odd number of choices, with five being the most common.

It's also possible for people to feel differently about the same objective event or information. Someone might be elated that the team reduced defects by 50% and another disappointed that it wasn't 100%. This divergence is often useful information and worthy of discussion, as happened in a retrospective where the team members' perceptions of an event were dramatically different.

Carly's Card

A team created a timeline (objective events) and then color-coded their response to those events (subjective perception). Green dots indicated high-point events, and blue, low points.

When all the dots were in place, one card stood out—Carly's card, shown in the following image. The card had seven light dots and one dark dot.

Carly confessed that the card and the blue dot were hers. "I felt like I had hijacked the planning session. I can't believe anybody thought that was good."

"Carly, we knew you were upset, but it wasn't until you spoke up that we were able to fix the problem," one of her teammates responded.

Several team members revealed they had concerns similar to Carly's. But because no one was talking about it, no one could solve the issue. Carly's "outburst" was the key to solving an ongoing problem.

Hearing other points of view helped Carly feel better, but it also highlighted the consequences of team members keeping concerns to themselves. Without subjective data, this conversation probably wouldn't have happened.

Having a structured way for people to talk about perceptions and feelings makes it more comfortable to raise topics that have an emotional charge. When people avoid emotional content, it doesn't go away. It goes underground and may flare up in anger or other unpredictable ways.

Data Collection Guidelines

In some cases, the team can gather data during the retrospectives, especially when the data is about the team and their own perceptions. But, if you require hard data, have it ready prior to the retrospective. Depending on how much data there is, you may need to give people time to absorb it. In that case, distribute it beforehand.

You don't need a formal measurement program or a tracking tool to have useful data. You can obtain useful, "good enough" data without formal programs, advanced tools, or huge effort. Here are three guidelines for collecting data outside the retrospective:

1. Make It Easy to Collect Good Enough Data

One team noticed that they usually didn't finish the stories they pulled into a sprint. The problem wasn't the way the stories were written. Plus they were convinced they weren't being overly optimistic when they committed to stories.

It turned out they were right. And they were wrong. They weren't being unrealistic when they sized stories, but they were optimistic in judging how much time they spent actually working on stories.

For one iteration, each team member tracked how often they were interrupted. For each nonstory-related interruption, they glanced at their watch, and when the interruption was over, they made a note about the duration and the nature of the interruption. They didn't count conversations with other devs, testers, or the product owner because those were directly related to finishing stories. They did count impromptu conversations that caused context-switching. So when their manager stopped by to chat about an upcoming vacation, they logged it. When they got a support call, they logged it. Likewise with random visits from the VP, HR announcements, and so forth.

All it took was a piece of paper and agreement on what they would and wouldn't track.

If you're using either a physical or virtual task board, you may already have access to useful information. Many popular tools track how long stories take, when stories are in a wait state, and estimated versus actual time.

2. Make It Safe

Sadly, many employees have the experience of data being misused. Make the purpose of collecting the data clear, and make it clear it is only for the team. And then keep it for the team, unless they agree to share the data with others.

Guard against blame when gathering individual data. In the previous example, the team tracked interruptions, which has to happen on an individual basis. It might be useful to know if one team member experiences more interruptions than others, because it influences the solution. Be wary of collecting individual data about group responsibilities such as code quality, number of stories completed, defects introduced, number of commits, or who broke the build. The goal is to optimize team performance, not to shine the light on individual members. If people fear that data might be used against them, they may not report accurately. Then the data won't be worth much and may be misleading.

3. Stop When the Need for the Data Has Passed

One of the ways that formal measurement programs become bloated is that people keep thinking of new useful things to track (or notice new things that would be easy to track). They keep adding, but never stop collecting. Collect data to serve a purpose, and when that purpose is complete, stop.

It's much easier to stop if your data collection method is informal and not automated. You simply stop because no permission is needed. And remember the old saying, "Not everything that counts can be counted, and not everything that can be counted counts."

Consider the Best Way to Present Data

Now that the team has data, think about how to present it. The way the data is visualized can illuminate or obscure.

Say the team wants to analyze customer calls by feature. To understand which features are generating the most customer calls, you need more than a gut feeling. The team needs facts. A pie chart would show the proportion of calls for each feature for all feature-related customer calls. But a pie chart won't tell you whether calls increased or decreased after the latest release.

Determine whether understanding the number of occurrences for a category or changes over time will be more useful. The following table shows various ways to display objective data and the table on page 16 shows various ways to display subjective data. Each shows different data graphics along with the benefit of the different emphases and examples of when they'd be a good fit.

Objective Data

Presentation	Emphasis	Examples
Pie Charts	Shows frequency distribution Obscures changes over time	Defects by type, module, source Severity of issues
Bar Charts	Frequency distribution, especially when there is more than one group of things to compare Similar to histograms, but typically used for quantitative data	Bugs found in testing by module, bugs found by customers by module
Histograms	Frequency of continuous data (not categories)	Distribution of length of outages
Trends	Shows movement over time. Often trends are more significant than absolute numbers in spotting problems.	Defects Outages Stories Completed Stories accepted/rejected
Scatter Plots	Shows the relationship between two variables	Size of project and amount over budget
Time Series	Shows patterns and trends over time. Use when the temporal order of data might be important, e.g., to see the effects of events	Outage minutes over a period of time Through-put
Frequency Tables	Shows how often events occur. May be a preliminary step for other charts, or stand on its own.	Defects Stories accepted on first, second, third demo
Data Tables	Shows how often events occur. May be a preliminary step for other charts, or stand on its own.	Impact of not-ready stories

Subjective Data

Presentation	Emphasis	Examples
Spider and Radar Charts	Shows clusters and spreads Highlights areas of agreement/disagreement Points towards areas for improvement	Use of XP practices Adherence to team working agreements Levels of various factors (e.g. training, satisfaction, independence)
Leaf Charts	Use a pre-defined rating scale to show frequency distribution in the group Similar to bar charts, but typically used for qualitative data	Satisfaction, motivation, safety Severity of issues Anything with a rating scale
Timelines	Shows patterns of events that repeat over time (objective) Reveals pivotal events with positive or negative effects	Project, release, iteration Events over time
Tables	Shows patterns and relationships between two sets of information	Team skills profile (who has certain skills, where there are gaps, etc.)
Trends	Changes over time	Satisfaction, motivation, safety Anything with a rating scale

Before proceeding to the next phase of the retrospective, do a quick review of the data with the entire team. Ask the team to scan the data you've gathered and comment on patterns, shifts, and surprises.

Phase 3: Generate Insights

Many business cultures value quick solutions and rapid action. Sometimes, both are called for. When a site that handles 30,000 visitors per minute goes down, you move fast. That habit of lightning-quick response can permeate a culture. People develop an (often unspoken) assumption that *all* decisions are urgent. It's easy for people to jump to immediate solutions as soon as problems emerge. First solutions *may* be correct, but often they're not. Slow down and think!

To solve problems and make improvements, you need two sorts of insights: those that relate to the nature of the issue and those that might resolve the issue.

Understanding potential contributors and devising potential solutions or experiments are two different mental processes. The first is analysis, whereas the second is idea generation. Separating the two leads to better outcomes.

The Rule of at Least Three

When it comes time to generate options for action, help the group get beyond the usual solutions.

Aim for at least three options before you choose—both for what contributes to the issue and what might improve the issue.

We find that if a group can think of three options, they can usually think of many more—and in the process, think about the issue in fresh ways and understand it more deeply.

The work of this phase is to consider additional possibilities, look at how causes and effects intertwine, and think about them analytically. The point is to think deeply, not to rush into action.

To make timely decisions that the group can support, teams need to do three things, according to the *Facilitator's Guide to Participatory Decision-Making* [KLTF14]:

- Diverge by including and considering multiple points of view, data, and ideas.

- Converge by finding common threads or areas of common interest and concerns.

- Agree on what they will do.

Without a sufficient variety of thought, input, and perspectives, the result is superficial solutions and habitual thinking. Variety can lead to novel thinking, emergent solutions, and creativity, but only when there's a way for the group to converge. Without convergence, you have a heap of ideas and no clear direction forward.

That point between divergence and convergence is often uncomfortable and messy, and people often attempt to avoid it. When it comes to finding insights in your retrospective, you need to keep the ideas flowing long enough to get past the familiar and push into the creative. This is where structure is helpful.

Structure helps people hang in there and ensures that everyone has a chance to contribute. You'll find structures that help people converge and diverge in Chapter 7, Activities to Generate Insights, on page 115.

The following image depicts divergence and convergence in the phases of a retrospective, using Kaner's "Diamond of Participation."

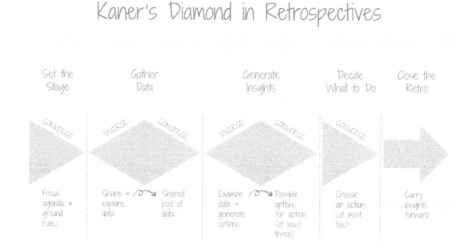

When you skip generating insights, your team may not understand how events, behaviors, and circumstances affect their ability to develop software. Time spent generating insights helps ensure that when your team plans an improvement, it's one that will make a positive difference.

Phase 4: Decide What to Do

At this point, the team has a list of potential actions. Now is the time to pick one or two and plan what to do. Your primary job is to provide structure and guidance for your team to plan experiments and actions. After considering an issue and potential actions, the team may determine that they don't know enough about a problem yet—further investigation is a valid action. So are exploration, research, group learning activities, and influencing someone outside the team.

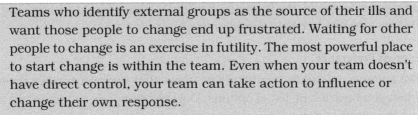

Avoid the Do-Nothing Retrospective

Teams who identify external groups as the source of their ills and want those people to change end up frustrated. Waiting for other people to change is an exercise in futility. The most powerful place to start change is within the team. Even when your team doesn't have direct control, your team can take action to influence or change their own response.

Change happens in the course of normal work. Teams who believe their retrospectives are a waste of time often keep their improvement plans completely separate from their daily work plans. When the plans are separate, no one finds time to do the "extra" work.

For more on avoiding do-nothing retrospectives, see Chapter 12, Catalyzing and Sustaining Change, on page 201.

How the team chooses depends on the nature of the proposed action.

If the team has identified a *specific problem* along with candidate solutions, *compare or evaluate* those options based on how well they address the problem and which has the fewest undesirable aspects.

If there are many *general* possibilities for improvement, gauging the *preferences or energy* of the team is sufficient.

Compare or Evaluate

When we see teams get stuck evaluating alternatives, it's usually for one of two reasons: either people don't have a common definition of the options under discussion or the group is talking about all the options at the same time.

To ensure everyone is working from the same definition, write the key points of each alternative down and post them where everyone can see them during the evaluation step. Review each alternative and clarify as needed before starting the evaluation. As for the issue of trying to discuss all options at once, apply some discipline. Discuss each option on its own before comparing options to each other. This is much easier when each option is written down and visible. Then point everyone to the first option and discuss that option. Move on to the second, and so forth. Decide only after discussing all the options.

One way to evaluate options is to list the upsides and downsides of each option and make a note of anything particularly interesting about that option. Complete the analysis for one alternative before moving on to the next. (See "Evaluating Options" in Chapter 8, Activities to Decide What to Do, on page 131.)

Generally, the group won't apply formal criteria to a candidate option in a retrospective. Focus the group on how each option would address the problem they've identified or help the team improve.

Express Preference

Dot voting is useful to identify a few items that warrant further development when you have a long list of options. Dot voting expresses *preference* for items, not the merit of items. Use dot voting to identify the most popular item or to winnow options to a shorter list. (See "Dot Voting" in Chapter 8, Activities to Decide What to Do, on page 131.)

Energy

"Go with the energy" is an important principle for any group endeavor. People may recognize something is important, but if they don't have any enthusiasm for the work, it probably won't get done.

You may get better follow-through by having the group rate candidate options based on impact, effort, and energy. (See the full activity description in Chapter 8, Activities to Decide What to Do, on page 131.) Get a quick estimate of whether the impact on the team will be high, medium, or low. Estimate effort in the same way. Then dot vote on energy. Following is an example of a flip chart after the team indicates their responses. It's pretty clear which action the team wants to pursue. The third option on the list will have a big impact, won't take much effort, and has the most votes of all the options.

Sometimes teams come up with long lists of candidate improvements, but too many initiatives can overwhelm your ability to change. Pick one or two experiments for the next iteration. Help your team choose items that they can commit to and that will have a positive effect. If your team is recovering from a stressful change, choose something less complex this time.

One way to plan for experiments and changes is to create story cards or backlog items. This makes it easier to incorporate improvement plans into the work plan for the next iteration. Some teams like to do their retrospective right before planning.

Reflecting and planning are different modes of thought, so it's best not to run them together. If your team works that way, take a break—even if it's only lunch—between the retrospective and the planning session. Allowing time for retrospective insights to sink in for a while might actually improve the planning.

If the action the team chooses is straightforward, they may be able to complete it during the retrospective. Taking action during the retrospective builds momentum. For example, one team created a new working agreement, "Everyone will pair program at least four hours a day," to address the need to share knowledge of the code base across the team. Another team redesigned their lab and created new check-in procedures.

Some actions and experiments require more planning or research. Add those to the team's backlog. You may finish them in your planning session or create a story to work on them during the iteration. Retrospective actions are real work and should be part of the real plan, not some separate "improvement" plan. Separate plans too often fall by the wayside.

For more on this, see Chapter 12, Catalyzing and Sustaining Change, on page 201.

Phase 5: Close the Retrospective

When you get to the end, close the retrospective decisively. Decide how to document the experience and plan for follow-up. Help your team decide how they'll retain what they've learned from the retrospective. Create a record—whether you use high- or low-tech means.

This doesn't necessarily mean the person who leads the retrospective has to do this work. The learnings belong to the team and its members—not the coach, not the team lead, and not you as the retrospective leader. The team needs to own them, and having the team create the record and reminders helps establish that.

Before you end, take a few minutes to perform a retrospective on the retrospective. Look at what went well and what you could do differently in the next retrospective. The concept of "inspect and adapt" applies to retrospectives, too. Close the retrospective with an appreciation for the hard work everyone did during both the iteration and the retrospective.

Summing Up the Benefits of This Structure

Using this structure—Set the Stage, Gather Data, Generate Insights, Decide What to Do, and Close the Retrospective—will help your team do the following:

- Understand different points of view.

- Follow a natural order of thinking.

- Take a comprehensive view of the team's current methods and practices.

- Allow the discussion to go where it needs to go, rather than predetermining the outcome.

- Leave the retrospective with insights, concrete actions, or experiments for the next iteration.

The structure gives you, as the retrospective leader, a tried-and-true process to help your team inspect and adapt. In Chapter 2, "A Retrospective Custom-Fit to Your Team," we'll proceed step-by-step through using this structure to create a retrospective that will work for your team.

A Retrospective Custom-Fit to Your Team

In the previous chapter, we introduced the five-phase structure for retrospectives. In this chapter, we'll explore how to customize your retrospective. Why customize? Every team is unique. So your retrospective needs to be unique, too. For each phase, choose an activity that will help your team explore their recent work.

Let's get started!

Tips for Larger Groups

 This book primarily addresses retrospectives at the team level (which we assume has five to ten members).

However, larger groups can benefit from retrospectives, too. For example, teams that worked together on a single release may benefit from reflecting together on their experience.

Interspersed throughout this chapter, we'll offer tips on how to adapt retrospectives for larger groups. You can find these tips in sidebars such as this one with a title starting with "Tip for Larger Groups."

Design a Retrospective for Your Team's Needs

Before you jump into choosing activities, you need to make several important decisions about logistics:

- *What topic area should the retrospective focus on?* A focus places attention on one aspect of the team's work. It could be technical practices, collaboration, or intra-group conflict. Having a retrospective topic can make the difference between a scattershot conversation that leads to shallow answers and a focused discussion that leads to significant improvement.

- *Who should be included?* The focus tells you who should be included in the retrospective. Most of the time, it will be only the team. But if the focus involves people outside the team, you will want to involve them, too.

- *How much time is needed for the retrospective?* If the retrospective is only for the team, the topic is fairly straightforward, and you're retrospecting on a one-week timebox, an hour may be enough. But if the timeframe is longer, another team is involved, or the topic is complex or controversial, it may require more time to have a robust exploration of the focus.

- *What venue will be most conducive for the retrospective you want to create?* The team room is probably the default location (or the team's retrospective or collaboration platform if the team isn't colocated). But sometimes it makes sense to choose an alternative venue.

The answers to these questions depend on the context. So that's where we'll start.

Tip for Larger Groups: Bring a Co-Facilitator

You'll see many of the same behaviors in a large group as in a small group. But in larger groups, the effects are more pronounced. Between the process and the people, there's a lot to keep track of. So for a large retrospective, you might find it useful to team up with a co-facilitator.

Consider the Team's Context

There's a lot you could take into account when you design a retrospective. At a minimum, consider these:

- *What is the morale of the team?* If morale is low, focusing on a big problem might not be the best fit right now. Think about how the team might get some small wins out of the retrospective.

- *What happened during the previous period of work?* Unusual events or patterns of events can both be fruitful topics in a retrospective.

- *Are there conflicts or controversies that the team needs to address?* Sometimes the subject of the conflict needs to be the topic for the retrospective. Other times, it's not the main topic, but may influence the activities you choose to keep discussions productive.

- *What external factors might be influencing the team's work?* Exploring these can lead to identifying cross-organizational issues. (See Chapter 13, Elevating Issues Beyond the Team's Control, on page 219.)

- *What is their experience with retrospectives?* If the team has a negative impression of retrospectives, check out Chapter 14, Overcoming Objections, on page 235, for help on gently addressing this issue. Aim for an area where the team has control in the retrospective.

- *What is the larger organizational context?* Layoffs, cancelled products, new leaders, and reorgs can all impact a team's mood and concentration. Think about what might help the team feel agency and purpose in the face of external turmoil.

Tip for Larger Groups: Introducing Retrospectives

Your agile team may know and love retrospectives, but the broader organization may not. They may be skeptical, overscheduled, or unaware of what to expect.

If people aren't familiar with retrospectives, it's worth your time to introduce the concept and answer questions.

People you invite may push back against full-day or multi-day retrospective events. They may feel pressured to accomplish daily work and may want to drop by the retrospective when they don't have another meeting scheduled. Even with the best intentions, drop-ins slow down the process; at worst they derail it. Dropouts send a different, often puzzling, message.

Set the expectation for full-time attendance by explaining that the retrospective follows a structure and each part builds on the next.

See Chapter 14, Overcoming Objections, on page 235, for ideas on helping folks get on board with the improvement effort.

Shape the Focus

Focus implies that you will give attention to some topics and not to others, at least for now. It provides a sense of why people are investing their time. The focus might be a pattern over time, an unusual event, an improvement goal, interactions within or outside the team, the flow of work, a technical practice, or any other topic that's specific enough to provide a lens for the conversation.

More Than One Focus?

 Can you have more than one focus in a retrospective? Yes, of course. We'd still advise following the same flow: attention, data, insights, and decisions. Finish one topic before you start another. Talking about multiple topics at the same time reduces the chance of making progress on any of them, and often it simply leaves people confused.

Methods to Pick a Focus

You have several ways to choose a focus. You can either choose a focus yourself as the retrospective leader or you can ask the team to choose a focus. In either case, it's best to work on topics where the team expresses energy for improving. This is true even if the topic doesn't seem like the most important topic to you.

The following table describes the various methods of picking a focus:

Who picks the focus	When	Method
The retrospective leader (you)	Before the retrospective	Propose a focus based on your own observations.
		Or, ask the team a day or two prior to the retrospective for ideas and make the decision yourself.
The team	Before the retrospective	Keep a running list of potential topics during the iteration. Then ask the team to vote a day or two before.
The team	During the retrospective	Have your team brainstorm a list of potential topics and ask the team to vote on the one they want to focus on.
		Or, pick a few candidate topics, place them on a Team Radar, and use the resulting data to pick a focus. See the Team Radar activity on page 81.

All of these methods can work. We generally recommend having the team choose during the retrospective only after the team has some experience with retrospectives and has learned how to have productive discussions.

Choosing the focus at the beginning of the retrospective implies that you can't prepare up front, and it might require more facilitation skill on your part, at least until the team is in the groove and essentially self-facilitates.

Tip For Larger Groups: Discovery Questions

More preparation is needed for a larger group retrospective than for a typical team retrospective. Consider interviewing participants ahead of time to understand their perspectives as you shape the focus.

For a list of potential interview questions, see Appendix 1, Potential Prework Questions, on page 251.

If you do interviews, be aware that some participants may believe that once they've written the issue down or mentioned it in a conversation or prework, it's no longer their job to bring it up. Make it clear that issues belong to the people who have them, and you're relying on them to raise topics in the retrospective.

Broad or Narrow Focus?

Retrospectives with a broad focus allow a team to explore, identify trends, and surface issues for future consideration. Those with a more narrow focus enable the team to dive deeper into a specific topic or concern. Either can be valuable, and some teams alternate between the two.

In general, start with a narrow focus when tangible progress is both necessary and possible until possibilities for progress are exhausted (or people need a break), then go broad. You will probably discover something new to focus on!

Writing a Useful Focus

Once you have a potential focus, ask yourself whether the focus follows these four criteria:

1. *Explore the issue with a systems mindset*, rather than restrict thinking to a single part of the problem.

2. *Stay curious and open to learning*, rather than blame a person or a group.

3. *Consider all possible causes and solutions*, rather than assume the source of the problem.

4. *Focus on a small enough topic such that action becomes likely*, rather than broaden the lens so wide that focus is difficult.

To better understand how to apply these criteria in the real world, let's look at some examples. For each example, we'll describe the scenario, share the team's retrospective focus, and describe how the focus could be improved.

Example 1: A Team That Struggled with Testing

One team was working for a while on integrating more tests into its development process. Despite their focus on testing, the team hadn't yet seen a positive impact on the quality or efficiency of its work. When it came time for the team's next retrospective, the retrospective leader picked the following focus:

Determine what we are doing wrong with testing

What are the issues with the way this focus is written?

First, this focus asks the team to look exclusively at itself ("what *we* did wrong"), in contrast with criteria 1 which promotes systems thinking.

Second, this focus biases the team toward looking for blame since it asks what the team "did wrong," whereas criteria 2 encourages openness. Perhaps no one did anything wrong at all!

We'd suggest rewriting the focus as follows:

Find ways to improve our testing practices

This version of the focus is blame-free and helps the team to broaden its perspective.

Example 2: A Team That Missed Its Iteration Goals

For the past few iterations, this team had been missing its goals. The team decided to focus its next retrospective on this problem. The team wrote its focus as:

Determine how to meet iteration goals

What are the issues with the way this focus is written?

This focus assumes the team *should have* met its iteration goals in the first place. Perhaps...but perhaps not! In contrast, criteria 3 asks us to consider all possibilities.

We'd suggest rewriting the focus as follows:

Understand the reasons behind missed iteration goals

Notice how this focus primes the team to have a systems mindset. Could the issue be the work itself? Could it be how the team is setting its goals? Or could it be something about the way work is structured in the organization more broadly? The team doesn't know ahead of time, and that's the point.

Example 3: A Team Whose Stories Were Getting Rejected

Another team had a recurring issue that was causing plenty of frustration: towards the end of many iterations, the product manager would reject the work being done with feedback such as, "The quality just isn't there!" A lot of time, energy, and effort was being wasted on work that would never be released, and the team was growing resentful. The retrospective leader wrote down this focus:

> *Improve the quality of our work*

What are the issues with the way this focus is written?

This focus is so broad it's unlikely to lead to learning and action, while criteria 4 encourages us to focus on smaller topics. "Improving quality" is an admirable goal, but it presents too wide of a lens to enable a focused conversation.

We'd suggest rewriting the focus as follows:

> *Increase our understanding of the product manager's needs*

Notice how this rewritten topic encourages the team to have a focused conversation. At the same time, it's not so restrictive that it discourages curiosity and creativity.

Determine Duration

How long should your retrospective last? It depends. There's no set formula, but there are things to consider. Remember, shortcutting time means cheating results!

Base the length of your retrospective on these factors:

- *Length of the block of work the team will consider.* A five-minute retrospective might be the perfect length for an ensemble session or a pomodoro (in which case you probably aren't going through the exercise of choosing activities). An hour-long retrospective can be enough for a one-week iteration. A half day may be enough time for thirty days' worth of work. Release and end-of-project retrospectives last longer. Plan for at least one day and up to four days in some cases.

- *Complexity.* Complexity can be about the technical environment or about relationships. Add more time when there's bound to be lots of discussion.

- *Size of the team or the number of people in the retrospective.* More people means more time. Everything will take longer.

- *Level of conflict or controversy.* Watch out for projects that fail and for products beset by politics. Plan on more time to Set the Stage and more time to allow team members to vent or work through issues.

- *Team setting.* Remote meetings usually require more structure to manage communication, which means more time. See more about this in Chapter 3, Leading Retrospectives, on page 49 and Chapter 11, Retrospectives When the Team Isn't Colocated, on page 183.

- *The focus.* A focus that's simple and familiar will require less time than one that's challenging or unfamiliar.

Too much time is rarely the problem. If people identify meaningful improvements and finish their implementation plans before the scheduled end, you can end the retrospective early. If your team consistently produces superficial insights and shallow plans, it's likely that you need more time, not less.

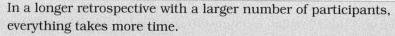

Tip for Larger Groups: Longer Duration

In a longer retrospective with a larger number of participants, everything takes more time.

Remember to allow time for everyone to split into smaller groups, time for each group to find its discussion location, time for the discussion itself, and then time for each group to report out its findings.

Select a Location and Setting

Look for these characteristics in a retrospective space:

- Everyone has the ability to see each other.
- The setup encourages participation (or can be altered to do so).
- There's room to move about if you will be using breakout groups.
- There's space to post the agenda and any collateral materials needed for activities during the retrospective.

If your typical retrospective location interferes with these conditions, find a different place to meet.

Another reason to find a different location is when you need a fresh perspective. For example, consider a change in venue if the team is dealing with an abnormal iteration termination, missing a goal, or when there's an unproductive conflict within the team. Events like these aren't business as usual (at least we hope not). Moving to a different setting makes that clear symbolically.

Changing location can even help when your retrospectives have gone stale. A new venue can help people notice different things.

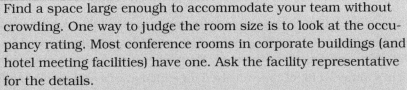

Tip for Larger Groups: Room to Move

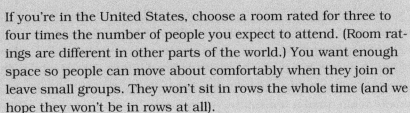

Find a space large enough to accommodate your team without crowding. One way to judge the room size is to look at the occupancy rating. Most conference rooms in corporate buildings (and hotel meeting facilities) have one. Ask the facility representative for the details.

If you're in the United States, choose a room rated for three to four times the number of people you expect to attend. (Room ratings are different in other parts of the world.) You want enough space so people can move about comfortably when they join or leave small groups. They won't sit in rows the whole time (and we hope they won't be in rows at all).

The space you're in will, by definition, constrain your retrospective design. Ideally, you will have a space with the flexibility to arrange and rearrange tables and chairs to suit the activities in your design.

A circle or semicircle of chairs encourages participation because people can see each other. Classroom and theater-style arrangements stifle participation. It's hard to have a conversation while looking at the back of someone's head. Tables can be a physical barrier that becomes a psychological barrier—however some activities are easier with tables.

Whatever furniture arrangement you choose, a room that has one long blank wall (or lots of windows) is a bonus. You'll appreciate it for posting timelines, charts, and loose flip chart pages. If you can't find a room with a blank wall, look for alternate ways to hang flip charts. In a pinch, you can turn tables on their sides (*Improvising Space for a Timeline [Dav05]*) or hang a clothesline (*Re: Improvising Space for a Timeline [Hin05]*). You can also use the open floor spaces to spread out flip pages so people can walk by and view them.

For remote teams, see Chapter 11, Retrospectives When the Team Isn't Colocated, on page 183, for ideas on how to set up a space conducive to effective retrospectives.

Allocate Time Within the Retrospective

In general, plan on spending the bulk of your time on the Gather Data and Generate Insights phases (roughly two thirds of the retrospective in aggregate).

Assuming the team explores things thoroughly in these two phases, the Decide What To Do phase will be relatively seamless (perhaps another 15% of your time). The remainder of your time will be split between the Set the Stage and Close the Retrospective phases, each of which tends to be relatively brief.

Build in slack time in case an activity or discussion takes longer than planned. A buffer gives you breathing room. Also, consider the time needed for people to shift from one activity to the next. Even when people aren't physically moving, there's always a bit of time involved for explanations and mental shifts.

If you're planning on a retrospective longer than one hour, build in extra time in case there is a need to break. Take breaks when there is a logical stopping point, when energy drops, or when people express a need. For retrospectives longer than two hours, build time for breaks into the schedule. Our rule of thumb is a ten-minute (minimum) break every ninety minutes or so. For a remote team, plan a ten-minute (minimum) break after every fifty minutes.

Example of the Decisions Covered So Far

Here's how one retrospective facilitator thought about designing a retrospective for a team of nine programmers, two testers, and a sec-ops specialist.

The scenario:

While the team is using some Extreme Programming practices, team members haven't been pair programming. They have yet to hold their first retrospective. It's a large team and information flows sluggishly among them. A few team members complain of being in the dark about decisions. The team is in their sixth two-week iteration. In this iteration, they met their planned work but only by working overtime. They violated their agreement to work at a sustainable pace. On top of that, their build system broke during the second week of the iteration.

Given how the iteration went, a team member suggested that they'd do better if they examined what happened. Then they could try making changes in the next iteration. The rest of the team agreed. They want to use their first retrospective to learn from the mishaps and mistakes of the iteration.

The retrospective leader made notes about the following design decisions:

- What is the focus? Learn from mishaps on the previous iteration, uncover contributing factors, and choose a way forward.

- Who will attend? Everyone who works daily on the team's purpose and shared goal.

- How long? Three hours. Why so long? The first retrospective may take longer since the team is unfamiliar with this style of discussion. They'll need breaks. Also, the team has been working for twelve weeks. Given the focus, the team will have to look back over the entire twelve-week period, which takes longer than a retrospective looking at a shorter timespan.

- Where shall we hold the retrospective? Given the size of the team involved (twelve people), an open conference or training room that comfortably can hold twenty-five people will fit well. People need to be able to move around for small-group work.

- How will we set up the room? Move the tables to the side of the room. Start seated in a semicircle facing the long wall and then move to the corners of the room for small-group work. We don't want people seated around a conference table. The semicircle will allow everyone to see each other for the initial discussion. We'll need variety and space for people to move around.

Select Activities

After you've decided on the focus, duration, attendees, venue, and setup, it's time to think about activities. The goal is to move the group in a smooth, logical flow through the phases of the retrospective. Activities support that purpose while encouraging relatively equal participation and deeper thinking. The structure provided by activities helps the team think together.

Activities do the following:

- *Encourage equal participation.* With five or more people it's hard for everyone to participate in a conversation. Working in smaller groups makes it more likely that people will hear each other and feel heard.

- *Focus the conversation.* Activities have a particular focus that frames the conversation. That reduces (but doesn't eliminate) the chance of tangential drift.

- *Encourage new perspectives.* Activities bring people outside their day-to-day modes of thinking. They encourage the team to consider new ideas. Activities don't have to be elaborate or involved to be effective.

Select activities to reinforce focus. If there's no way to connect the activity with the work, leave it out. Make sure the activities you choose engage attention, are relevant to the task at hand, and can be accomplished by the group. It's especially important to choose activities that won't make people feel foolish, inept, or set up.

We include many examples of group process activities in Part II, Selecting Activities, on page 77. A full list of the activities mentioned in this book is available in Appendix 2, Activities Reference Sheet, on page 253.

Games, Icebreakers, and Energizers

Beware the trap of games, icebreakers, and energizers that don't relate to the work. They don't fit in retrospective meetings.

Games, icebreakers, and energizers become a trap when they have no particular learning value and don't help the team with its focus on improvement. They contribute to a perception that retrospectives are time wasters as opposed to serious work.

There's only so much time, so don't waste it with a game, icebreaker, or energizer that is "just for fun." Have fun, but have a purpose!

Vary activities to keep your team engaged. Follow a paired activity with one that involves a small group or the whole group. Alternate sedentary activities with ones in which people move.

After a while, the same old activities can lose their zest. If you're bored with an activity, chances are your team is too. Find new activities to keep your team (and yourself) interested. When people stay interested, they're less likely to fall into habitual thinking.

After you've facilitated retrospectives for a while, you may discover the desire to start designing your own activities. You can find many sources of inspiration to develop new activities for your retrospectives. Start with existing activities for generating ideas, analyzing problems, or identifying novel solutions and iterate from there.

Have a Backup Activity

When you select activities to fit into your plan, hold them lightly. Sometimes things happen during the retrospective that cause you to change your plan. You might need to respond to the immediate needs of the team, rather than follow your plan. See more about this in Chapter 4, Managing Group Dynamics, on page 63.

Or you could find your schedule isn't going quite as planned. Then it's useful to have two activities for each stage: one short and one long. Use the shorter activity if time is tight or the longer one when you have the luxury of time to devote more attention to it.

Guidelines for Selecting Activities by Phase

Keep the above general guidelines in mind as you consider each phase.

Set the Stage

When there's low controversy and the team is functioning well, it won't take much to set the stage. You may review the focus, share the agenda, point to existing working agreements, do a quick check-in, and leave it at that.

When safety is low or the topic is controversial, you'll need to spend more time in this phase. Look for activities that will bolster safety and shape positive interactions.

Gather Data

In Chapter 1, Help Your Team Inspect and Adapt, on page 3, we shared a table that listed topics and the sort of data that might be relevant. If you're gathering subjective data, consider activities that ask people to rate or categorize their perceptions.

If you're sharing objective data, you may not need an activity. It might be enough to simply present the data (perhaps as a chart or graph).

Generate Insights

Generating insights involves the problem space and the solution space. Choose an activity that helps people understand the issue and then another activity that will support developing potential actions.

Objective data calls for a more analytical approach during the Generate Insights phase. For example, if the team is looking at defects, you may choose an activity suited to looking at contributing factors such as Fishbone, which we describe on page 117.

Some activities involve subjective responses to objective data—for example, exploring how people perceive (subjective) events (objective). Color coding, categorizing, and energy lines all address the interplay of objective and subjective data.

Decide What to Do

What people are deciding on influences how to support team decision-making.

When the team has a list of potential actions, you might want to evaluate which are the best fit for the issue by looking at the pros and cons of each option, or test them against criteria. Criteria can be objective (for example, if it fits within a budget or standard) or somewhat subjective (such as a gut feeling about impact and effort).

When there isn't an obvious set of criteria to test against, go with preference.

Close the Retrospective

It always makes sense to review actions or conclusions and thank people for their hard work.

In choosing activities to close the retrospective, we go more by the "feel" of the group. If it's been a tough topic, consider an activity that invites the group to focus on the positives.

As a backup, it never hurts to ask the group for feedback on the retrospective and collect ideas to improve it next time.

Choosing Small Group Work

Group size is another consideration for selecting and managing activities.

The activities included in this book assume a team size of five to ten people.

Many of the activities suggest breaking into small groups for all or part of the activity. If your group is only five people, you may choose to do the activity with your entire (small) group.

Tip for Larger Groups: Breakout Groups

If you have a large number of participants, consider splitting into smaller groups so that people can converse rather than attempt to discuss with the entire group (or plenary).

Small groups of four to seven people make it more possible, and even encouraging, for everyone to contribute their views and engage in discussion. Small groups of eight to twelve collaborate well in more physically active activities.

When small groups come back together into the plenary, request that each group select a spokesperson to represent its intent and observations.

Be intentional about forming small groups. Random selection works when you want cross-pollination and perspective sharing. Functional groups are useful for clarifying different perspectives and interests.

Example of Selecting Activities

Now, we'll look at selecting activities for each phase. We'll pick up the scenario from earlier in the chapter that focused on a remote extreme programming team. (We have included a number of additional retrospective designs based on common scenarios in Chapter 10, Retrospectives for Common Scenarios, on page 161.) Because of the length of time (twelve weeks) and seriousness of the topic, the facilitator plans this retrospective for three hours, from 9:00 a.m. to 12:00 p.m., followed by a team lunchtime together.

Pay attention to how each activity flows easily out of the one before it and sets up the context for the one that comes after. Activities that have no relationship to one another make the retrospective feel choppy and inhibit the team's ability to learn and think.

Phase: Set the Stage (10 minutes)

Activity: Share the Agenda (2 minutes)

Instructions: See this activity on page 81.

Show team members the focus topic and schedule—that is, how you'll use the time. Let them see that you've prepared for the meeting. It communicates respect. Post and review team working agreements as a reminder.

Focus: Learn from mishaps on the previous iteration, uncover contributing factors, and choose a way forward.

Tip for Larger Groups: Socialize Working Agreements

 People in the broader organization may not be familiar with working agreements. They might not view developing or using them as "real work."

Take time to socialize the idea of working agreements when doing outreach.

Activity: Focus On/Focus Off (8 minutes)

Instructions: See this activity on page 87.

After the opening, this activity will help establish a mindset of looking at the issues without assigning blame. You want to foster open discussion. After introducing the agenda, emphasize the need for honest, nonjudgmental conversation. Focus On/Focus Off helps to set that tone.

Phase: Gather the Data (45 minutes)

Activity: Review Objective Data Related to Focus (15–20 minutes)

Instructions: See this activity on page 104.

Pulling together the data related to hours and pattern of overtime vs. sustainable pace will underscore the impact of the team's experience. Look for data about the number and topics of team members' complaints. Consider data about the length of time for important information to circulate among all team members. Add some of this data to prepopulate the timeline. Display the rest on flip charts so team members may easily reference the data when working on the next activity.

Activity: Timeline with Color Code Dots (25–30 minutes)

Instructions: See this activity on page 114.

The team is looking at a fairly long period of time and this will help them remember the objective factual events that happened in earlier iterations. It will help people see connections between events and how the data emerged. Color coding will help the team see subjective data. This is the start of revealing divergent views and perspectives from team members. This would be a good time for a break (10 minutes).

Phase: Generate Insights (45 minutes)

Activity: Patterns and Shifts or Pattern Spotter Questions (15 minutes)

Instructions: See this activity on page 116.

Building on the objective and subjective data, guide the group to recognize and name patterns and significant events contributing to our current problems. Look for generalized patterns as well as significant details. Discuss the implications of continuing to work in the same way. This will have been a long time spent in larger group work. The team may be experiencing some clash of perspectives. Next, assess the implications in small groups first to begin converging toward a decision.

Activity: Circles and Soup (20 minutes)

Instructions: See this activity on page 120.

Give small groups an opportunity to identify the parties who have control over various issues, and begin to consider ideas for action.

If the underlying issues can't be solved in the team, create an influence strategy to show the manager why it's important to fix the problem.

Activity: Report Out and Synthesis (10 minutes)

Instructions: Share the work from small groups and create a smaller subset of action ideas to consider in the decision phase. This will move a step closer toward converging on the team's shared action. This would be a good time for a break (10 minutes).

Phase: Decide What to Do (30 minutes)

Activity: Impact/Energy Decision Criteria (10 minutes)

Instructions: See this activity on page 139.

Identify the top one or two actions to work on starting in the next iteration. People can't absorb a long list of changes. The team needs to work on the things that will make the biggest difference.

Activity: Begin the Action (20 minutes)

The next step depends on what the team identifies as the most important thing to work on. Keep several options in mind and use the one that will best help the team.

Option 1: Write Story Cards (Retrospective Planning Game)

Instructions: Ask the group to write down potential actions and then have them establish an order for performing the tasks.

You can carry the story card items into your next iteration planning meeting and incorporate them into the rest of your work.

Option 2: Add Working Agreements

Instructions: See this activity on page 89.

The team may need at least one more relevant working agreement (since they have been violating the one they have now). The team creates a new agreement during the session.

Option 3: Define a Hypothesis

Instructions: See this activity on page 142.

If the next step is too difficult to identify, clearly note that. Then the team can take the time to formulate a hypothesis. The action becomes creating an experiment.

Tip for Larger Groups: System Problems

The problems identified in multi-group retrospectives often cross organizational boundaries—they are system problems.

The people in the room may not be able to fix system problems, but they can influence and make proposals. For more on how to do this, see Chapter 13, Elevating Issues Beyond the Team's Control, on page 219.

Phase: Close the Retrospective (10 minutes)

Activity: +/Delta (5 minutes)

Instructions: Ask your team what worked during the retrospective (+) and what could be improved (Delta).

Learn areas to improve the retrospective, and begin the transition to action.

Activity: Appreciations (5 minutes)

Instructions: See this activity on page 151.

Provide an opportunity for people to acknowledge each other's contributions. Team members may need a lift after a tough iteration and hard work in the retrospective. Remember to thank the team for their hard work.

Slack/Shuffle Time (20 minutes)

Sometimes a discussion needs more time than expected or the team needs extra time to shift to small groups or for extra breaks. Be sure to set aside some extra time to cover these possibilities.

Tip for Larger Groups: The Group Owns the Report

 The person sponsoring the large group retrospective may want a written report. The report should come from the group, not from the retrospective leader. As part of the closing, decide who will create the report on behalf of the group. When a retrospective leader writes the report, it reduces group ownership.

Suppose This Design Was for Your Retrospective

You know the focus for the retrospective. You know how long it will be. It's clear where the session will be and who will attend. You've outlined the activities you'll use to help the group think and solve problems together.

Now, prepare notes that will help you stay on track while you lead the retrospective meeting. Your outline notes might look something like the figure on page 41.

Make sure you have all the supplies and items to share with the team. Create an agenda to circulate ahead of time and share as you set the stage for your retrospective. The agenda isn't the same as your notes. The agenda is aimed at the team. It lets the team know that you've prepared and plan to use their time well. You don't need to list the details of how the activities will flow. Cover all five phases of a retrospective in terms the team will understand.

Retro Design Outline

9:00am – 12:00pm

~Time	Retro Step	Notes
9:00am	Set the Stage	Welcome everyone! Activity: Share agenda. Emphasize focus and schedule with breaks. Refer to working agreements (plan to highlight "sustainable pace" again in Gather Data. Activity: Focus On/Focus Off to check in.
9:10am	Gather Data	Activity: Review objective data. Relate to Focus. Activity: Timeline with Color-Code Dots.
9:55am	Break	
10:05am	Generate Insights	Activity: Pattern + Shifts or Pattern Spotters Activity: Circles and Soup Activity: Report Outs + Synthesis
10:50am	Break	Determine which decision action to use during this break
11:00am	Decide	Activity: IEIEC Decision Criteria Activity: Begin the Action - Implement Option 1, 2, or 3
11:30am	Close	Activity: Plus/Delta Activity: Offer Appreciations
11:40am	Slack Time	For any activity that needs more time, unexpected tech issues, or extra breaks. Must end no later than noon!

The following example shows the retrospective agenda poster example previously discussed.

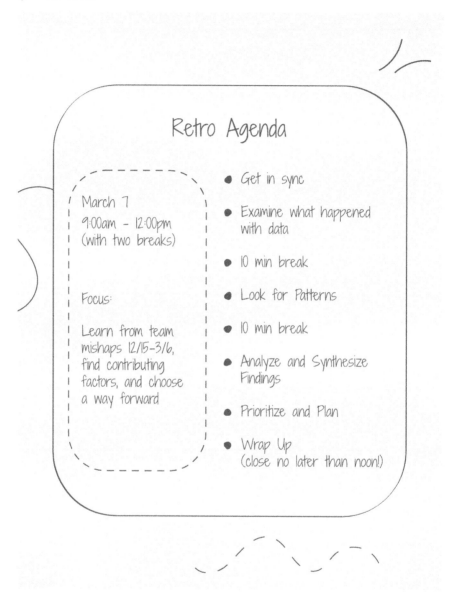

Decide on the objective data sources and how to display them best during the retrospective. Will you share them online ahead of time? Will you create posters? Or will you ask the team members to bring their data to the retrospective?

See the following example of a typical poster to display (in person or virtually) that shows a team's working agreements.

Our Team Working Agreements

developed v1 11/10, 2020; v2 1/23;

We work best together when...

1 We communicate team blockers quickly and crisply to the appropriate people, in or outside the team.

2 All team members are available for meetings and communication during our six core hours of 9am – 3pm, US Central Time Zone. We commit to a sustainable pace for all team members.

3 We plan better and strategize better every 2 weeks.

4 We cast no silent vetoes; we speak up if we disagree with the action or direction the team is moving.

5 We define "done" for our work as: code complete unit tested, code deployed to staging, and functional testing complete.

6 We enjoy working together, and we joke. This is one.

DIY Activities

We've included tried-and-true activities for every phase of a retrospective in this book. If you're starting out as a facilitator, these will serve you well for a long time. But, as you gain more experience and confidence, you may want to branch out. There will come a time when you can't find an activity that fits the needs of your group and your retrospective. What to do? Do what we do: modify an activity you already use or make one up!

Most of the time, when we design new activities, we want to create an experience based on what is happening for *this* team examining *this* focus in *this* retrospective. Some of these activities live for only one retrospective. Others become part of our toolbox. A smaller number even get shared widely.

The following are some examples of situations when you might want to create DIY activities for a given phase:

- For the Set the Stage phase, we may want to perfectly set the tone for the retrospective for a team that's facing a specific challenge or disappointment.

- For the Gather Data phase, it might be useful to shape the area of consideration by emphasizing past or future events, insights, emotional responses, or some other factor.

- For the Generate Insights phase, the data we gather might indicate an alternate approach to analyzing it.

- For the Decide What to Do phase, you might observe the team struggles to pick a course of action and devise an activity that eases that process.

- For the Close the Retrospective phase, it may be helpful to emphasize a sense of purpose or reinforce the fabric of the team, especially when they've had to deal with difficult issues.

To get you started with designing your own activities, let's look at some variations on column-based activities for the Gather Data phase to expose the thought process.

One of the early retrospective activities for gathering data was Mad/Sad/Glad. Participants write down events from the previous period of work and put them in the column that reflected their reaction to the event.

There are dozens of variations such as Prouds and Sorries, Loved and Lacked, and the 4Ls (aka Liked, Learned, Lacked, and Longed For by Mary Gorman and Ellen Gottesdiner), to name a few.

These activities have three main things in common.

1. Collect subjective and/or objective information—events and how people respond to them.

2. Ask for contrasting perceptions: negative (such as Lacked and Sorry) and positive (such as Loved and Learned).

3. Highlight that different people may have different perceptions of the same event.

While they have commonalities, each of these activities will nudge conversations and analysis in distinctly different directions.

In our experience, it's less common to need new activities for the Generate Insights or Decide What to Do phase. However, sometimes an insight gained from working with teams prompts a new activity for these phases as well.

For example, Learning Matrix came about as a quick way for people to summarize their insights. The categories flow nicely into both the Decide What to Do and Close the Retrospective phases.

Start/Stop/Continue is a common activity for the Generate Insights phase. This also has variations, such as What Worked Well/What to Do Differently, More Of/Less Of/New, Keep/Drop/Add, and others. The subtle difference in language matters. Start/Stop/Continue and Keep/Drop/Add lean toward quick decisions. What Worked Well/What to Do Differently might lead to a more thoughtful response.

Two by Two boxes, like Learning Matrix, invite people to categorize items based on multiple dimensions, rather than just listing items. If you're designing your own activity, the dimensions you choose for your two by two box will depend on context. For example, if the team is struggling to find things they can take action on, you might create a matrix like the one in the figure on page 46 that compares the level of control and size of the task.

Our friend Mike Lowery noticed that when deciding what to do, some people tried to swing the results in dot voting. He devised a way to make it less obvious how people were using their votes. His solution involved putting chips in cups with slotted covers rather than posting dots.

At some point, we noticed that the importance of a proposed retrospective action didn't correlate with the follow-through for that action. Many important things feel too big or too daunting. So they don't get done, starting a cycle of disillusionment.

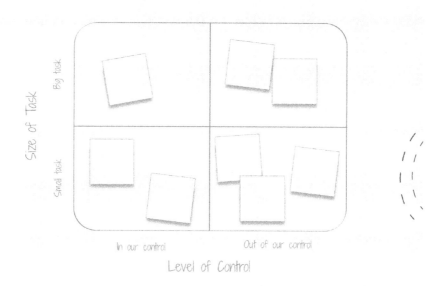

Asking about energy for a retrospective action was a much better predictor of future actions. Thus the activity Effort/Impact/Energy (and its variants) came to be.

For the Close the Retrospective phase, the biggest consideration is the mood you want the team to leave with. Often this is a response in the moment, based on your observation of team sentiment. A common solution is to come up with a future-oriented question that team members can answer with one or two words.

The thought process is similar to creating or modifying an exercise for any of the phases:

- Consider the context and focus of the retrospective.

- Consider the phase and the mental work the team needs to do in that phase.

- Consider the experience you want for the team.

- Consider how the activity flows with what came before, and how it will set up and flow into the next phase.

Remember, you likely don't need a brand-new activity. You can thoughtfully modify one you already know.

What Could Possibly Go Wrong?

In this chapter and the previous one, we've looked at the flexible framework and how to design a retrospective to fit your team's context. Now all you have to do is show up and lead the group. We've got lots of guidance on how to do just that in Chapter 3, Leading Retrospectives, on page 49.

Leading Retrospectives

In the previous chapter, we walked through the thought processes and considerations for designing a retrospective. Now, it's time to talk about leading or facilitating the group through the process you've outlined.

This can feel a bit intimidating. But don't worry, leading a typical team retrospective doesn't require advanced skills. It's helpful to understand the concepts of facilitation and have basic facilitation skills.

So what does facilitation involve? The word *facilitate* means to make something easy. For leading retrospectives, that means making it easier for the group to examine data, generate ideas, converge on options, and make decisions. There are dozens upon dozens of activities for each of the five phases of the retrospective. We've included a collection of these activities for each of the five phases of a retrospective in Part II, Selecting Activities, on page 77.

In this chapter, we'll talk about what it means to facilitate a retrospective. We'll cover how to manage activities, time, and yourself.

What Is Your Title When You Lead a Retrospective?

Are you a facilitator? A host? A guide? A retrospective leader? Something else?

Throughout this book, we use these terms interchangeably. Whatever you call the role, the responsibilities are the same:

- Provide a process that will help the group achieve an outcome.
- Create an environment for full participation.
- Guide the group through the process.
- Manage activities.
- Manage how time is used.
- Manage yourself.

The Facilitator's Role

Process is about *how* the group is talking. Content is *what* people are talking about. As the retrospective leader, you're responsible for the *process*. The group is responsible for the *content*. Maintaining this distinction helps the team trust that the leader is neutral and serves the group.

When we talk about processes, we don't mean a heavyweight methodology. Group processes include activities, techniques, methods, exercises, or any means of participation that help the group work together in a meeting or event.

Guiding the process means managing activities, time, and yourself (*The Skilled Facilitator* [Sch94]).

When you're involved in (or knowledgeable about) the content, you will likely follow the conversation. It's almost unavoidable. The good news is this can be very useful. It allows you to summarize the discussion and notice when the group is venturing off-track. The risk is that you will get caught up in the discussion, at the expense of your responsibility as a facilitator.

In these situations, it might be tempting to jump into the conversation, especially when you care about the topic. But when you're immersed in the content, it's difficult to pay full attention to your primary responsibility: the process. Take a moment to determine whether your thoughts are necessary. Most often, your team will make progress without your input.

When the leader jumps in too soon or too often, it squashes group discussion. Even worse, getting involved in the content risks the group feeling the facilitator is actually trying to use their power to steer the discussion, favor certain points of view, or lead people to a particular decision.

When and How to Participate as the Facilitator

There are situations in which you have important content to offer that no one else in the group has.

In these cases, *not* sharing your thoughts would actually be doing a disservice to your team!

But tread carefully—it's important to be explicit when you step out of the facilitator role.

One of our favorite ways to do this is to put on a hat (yes, a real physical hat!) whenever you stop facilitating and start participating.

When and How to Participate as the Facilitator
We love this approach because it injects a bit of playfulness that can contribute to maximum learning. But be careful! If the mood is somber because the topic is heavy, playfulness might seem inappropriate or dismissive.

George Dinwiddie, agile coach at iDIA Computing LLC, shared a story about a time when he was a facilitator and also needed to share content. "I've always tried to avoid playing both a facilitator role and a contributor role in the same meeting. It's an inherent conflict of viewpoints. Sometimes, though, it's hard to avoid."

As he was facilitating a retrospective, a team member brought up an issue that concerned George. In this case, George himself *was the content* and he wanted to apologize for his part in the team issue.

"Time out. I'm stepping out of the facilitator role for a moment," he said, then walked to a different place in the circle. "Now I'm speaking for myself."

He explained the intent behind his part of the problem. He took responsibility for not knowing he had been working on the same thing as the other team member. He apologized to the team for contributing to the issue. George asked the other team member what he would like to have happen next. Once the team concluded with that issue, George resumed his role as facilitator. He walked back to his original place in the circle and the retrospective continued.

Other Considerations

Some groups divide the work of facilitation among group members. Barbara Hui from Frameshift Consulting devised a way to distribute facilitation responsibilities by splitting the role into four separate components:

- The *facilitator* structures and guides the activities.

- The *notetaker* records the discussion. They may keep their notes visible during the meeting or share them afterward.

- The *moderator* redirects discussion when topics have gone off track or when someone takes too much "airtime." They invite comments and make space for those who haven't had a chance to contribute.

- Finally, the *timekeeper* watches the team's progress on the agenda and speaks up as needed.

You can learn more on Frameshift Consulting's website.[1]

---

1.   https://frameshiftconsulting.com/resources/meeting-skills/

When working with a larger group, it can be helpful to have more than one facilitator. One person can keep their attention on guiding activities. At the same time, another observes the group's dynamics. Then they can switch roles with each other. It takes coordination and planning beforehand, but it can work well.

On many teams, members rotate retrospective leadership from one retrospective to the next. Some companies even have a process in which teams can choose to bring in someone from another team in their organization to facilitate their retrospective. This allows the person who typically would be leading the retrospective to become a full participant instead. This may also help to reveal patterns of impediments and issues that affect more than one team. If that happens, it's a good idea to hold a cross-team retrospective to find out more. See Chapter 13, Elevating Issues Beyond the Team's Control, on page 219, to learn more about how to handle these situations.

On some occasions, the leader might realize that another team member has organically picked up the role of the facilitator in the middle of the retrospective and is doing just fine. When this happens, sit back and enjoy! It's wonderful for your teams to self-facilitate when they can.

During a recent retrospective, Elisabeth Keuschnigg, Scrum Master for a team, noticed that "one team member was facilitating just fine," and so Elisabeth "chose to sit down in silence and observe." After about half an hour the team member turned to Elisabeth: "What's with you today, why are you not doing anything?" She replied: "Why would I? You're doing just fine!" The team member stood there in revelation: "Oh, you are right, I didn't even realize I was facilitating!" That led to the whole team having "a good laugh about facilitating while not facilitating."

Manage Activities

Every retrospective design includes activities that help teams collaborate on problems or issues. Activities may include any process or exercise that moves the team through to the end. In Part II, Selecting Activities, on page 77, we describe a variety of activities for each phase of a retrospective. In Chapter 10, Retrospectives for Common Scenarios, on page 161, we offer retrospective designs in response to common scenarios that teams tend to face.

As the facilitator, you'll need to introduce each activity, monitor progress, and encourage the team to capture learnings or conclusions. Then you move on to the next activity and so on through the end of the retrospective.

Most people want to know something about the purpose of an activity before they begin. A good introduction provides purpose. Give a broad sense of the territory the team will explore. Hold back on revealing the details of what will happen or specifying what the team will learn. While writing this book, we asked people in our networks to submit stories of retrospectives. We got scores of responses. We noticed that practically everyone who submitted a favorite activity or facilitation technique enjoyed telling us about why it worked well for them and their teams.

Introducing Activities

The first time you use an activity, write a simple script. It will ensure you remember what to say and that you don't garble the instructions or leave something out.

Once you have your script, practice saying it aloud. Saying the words is different from reading them or thinking about them. Listen as you hear yourself give the instruction. Notice where you stumble and where even you can't follow the instructions. Then refine your script and practice again.

Listen to yourself:

- Are your instructions clear?
- Do you state the purpose of the activity?
- Do you give an overview of the activity?
- Do you break the steps down into chunks?

You may not follow the script in the end. In fact, you probably won't. However, preparing and practicing will help you describe each activity clearly and concisely.

Here's a sample introduction for the Timeline activity, which we describe on page 112.

> To understand our iteration, we need to tell the whole story from everyone's perspective. We'll create a timeline that shows events that happened during the project. After we have a timeline as complete as it can be for now, we'll look for interesting patterns and explore puzzles.

This short description tells the team a lot about the territory of the activity. The group will collaborate to "understand our iteration." It lists the steps at a high level. First, "create the timeline." Second, "look for interesting patterns." Third, "explore puzzles." It doesn't give too many details for instruction yet. It doesn't tell your team exactly what the outcome will be. That's for the team to discover.

Most people can't absorb detailed instructions for a multipart activity. Give the details for each part at the last responsible moment, just in time.

For example, when it's time to dive into the Timeline activity previously mentioned, the details of the first steps are as follows: "Let's get into groups of two or three. In your group, brainstorm all the events that took place during the release. An event doesn't have to be a milestone—it can be anything that happened on the project. Write each event on a sticky note." (Notice this works for both in-person and remote team retrospective settings.) After giving the instructions, ask whether anyone has questions about the task. Pause. Slowly count to ten in your head. Someone will have a question—wait for it.

Instructions for Remote Retrospectives

With remote teams, it's even more important to have clear instructions for activities. Give instructions for short chunks of work and ask for questions. Have the instructions written down and available so people can refer to them while they are in breakout rooms.

As the facilitator, you have two tasks during the activity: 1) to be available to answer questions about the activity and 2) to monitor the room.

When you're in the same physical room, the level of "buzz" is a useful indicator of how the group is doing. Even when you don't hear the words, the tone can tell you whether people are engaged, confused, or moving on. If it sounds like there's still lively conversation at the end of a discussion activity, check to see whether people need more time. For quieter activities, like individual writing, increased conversational buzz means the opposite. It tells you that people have stopped writing and started talking to their neighbors. Check in to learn whether the conversation still has relevance to the activity. Then you can decide whether to let it go on or move on to the next part.

Monitoring How the Group Is Doing During Remote Retrospectives

If you're a remote team that utilizes breakout rooms, you have no way to listen to the buzz. Instead, you will use other techniques to gain a sense of how things are going. Watch the movement of virtual sticky notes or other activity to gauge engagement and whether people are done. When the typing becomes less frequent, it's time to move on.

Some platforms allow the moderator to drop into the breakout rooms. This isn't as subtle as walking by and noticing if a group seems stuck or on the wrong track. It's actually rather intrusive and often stops the conversation entirely. Be sure to let people know in advance if you plan to suddenly appear in their breakout room while they're working.

If your platform supports it, remind people they can always raise a virtual hand if they need assistance.

For more tips, see Chapter 11, Retrospectives When the Team Isn't Colocated, on page 183.

Move Through the Diamond

Leading the group through their collective learning and thinking requires a trip (or two) through the "Diamond of Participation" (see *The Facilitator's Guide to Participatory Decision-Making [KLTF96]*), which we initially referenced in Chapter 1, Help Your Team Inspect and Adapt, on page 3.

You might recall that Kaner's model says that when any group is dealing with a complex situation where there are no easy answers, they will tend to *diverge*. They will bring in different perspectives, ideas, and opinions. If they are able to work through these differences (Kaner calls this sometimes difficult process the "groan zone"), they will converge, integrating new information and generating new ideas.

The prospect of the groan zone can deter people from divergence. People may stick to what's safe and familiar, in which case the discussion is unlikely to result in deep thinking. Without divergence, you're left with habitual thinking and business as usual. On the other hand, if the team doesn't have a way to converge, they will struggle to reach a decision that all can support.

Most retrospectives take two trips through the "diamond."

First, in the Gather Data phase, the group diverges. They explore different data, perspectives, and responses. When they can absorb different responses and views, they converge on a shared pool of data. Without shared data, the Generate Insights and Decide What To Do phases get "groany" because people have different mental models of what happened.

The group again diverges in the Generate Insights phase as they explore a wide range of possible causes and potential actions. Once the group agrees on a cause or path forward, it converges once again.

The challenge for the facilitator lies in keeping the group engaged with activities that move the group through the diamond.

Manage the Unexpected

Sometimes something unexpected happens and you roll with it. Ruud Rietveld, agile coach at Trailblazers B.V., had chosen activities for each of the five phases of the retrospective. For the Set the Stage phase, he picked an activity that involved choosing and discussing images from a collection he provided.

As the activity began, one team member explained the picture he chose. He had a role in information security that kept him separate from the rest of the team. He said the picture showed that he was unhappy with his contribution to the team. In addition, the situation left him feeling alone.

Ruud realized this activity, which was intended to serve as an easy way into the rest of the meeting, had instead surfaced an important, yet hidden, problem. He decided to abandon his original plan. He shifted his approach to the remainder of the retrospective by picking a focus that was devoted to that team member's contributions and how they affected the whole team.

The team discussed their experiences and insights. They found "good, concrete actions" that would help to integrate this team member's work into the whole team's work. They examined similar solutions for all members of the team and defined a much finer line for when to work separately.

In essence, Ruud threw his other preparations for a well-planned design out the window. As an experienced retrospective leader, he had the flexibility and versatility to replan quickly when the team encountered an unexpected moment for learning. Ruud reflected that shifting the focus to what was going on in the moment had a "much more meaningful impact" than his original plan would have.

Reflecting as You Go

Sometimes it's helpful to reflect on activities within the retrospective. This can help the group identify key points and insights, make connections, and form new ideas. Pay particular attention to check-ins, data-gathering exercises, and interpretation activities.

Start by asking for observable events and sensory input. "What did you see and hear in that last activity?"

Ask how people responded to those events and inputs. "What surprised you about it? Where were you challenged? What made you uncomfortable? When did you feel satisfied with your response? When did you have fun?"

Reflecting as You Go

Ask for insights and analysis. "What insight do you have about the activity?" followed by, "How did this activity connect to our retrospective topic?" These questions help people form their ideas and connect the activity to the rest of the design flow.

After you've established the link between the activity and topic, complete the learning cycle. Ask group members how they will apply the insights from their reflections. Consider a question like, "What's one thing you might want to remember for our next step?"

As with the five-phase format, you will gather objective and subjective data, generate insights, and decide what to do.

Manage Time

When you're leading a retrospective, a lot is going on. You have to respond to the needs of the group. You have to manage activities and assess whether your design is meeting the group's needs or requires adjustment. You have to pay attention to how the group uses their time well. But it's easy to lose track of time or go with the flow if the team seems to be having a useful discussion.

Let the group help you. When you introduce an activity, tell people how much time you've allotted so that they can track time. Give a warning when one or two minutes remain.

Be prepared to extend the time if everyone seems intensely engaged. Many teams use "Roman voting" to choose whether to extend the time. In Roman voting, participants give a thumbs up to mean "yes," thumbs down to mean "no," and thumbs sideways to mean "meh" or "I'll support the group."

An alternative is to use the Lean Coffee protocol and ask if the group wants to continue the current topic for five more minutes. For more about Lean Coffee, see *How To Have Great Meetings: A Lean Coffee Book [Yur16]* by Adam Yuret.

An Unanswerable Question

Avoid asking the question, "Is everyone ready to move on?" This question not only results in unreliable answers, it's also unanswerable by any individual. People know whether they themselves are ready to move on, but cannot answer for others.

You will have to gauge whether letting the conversation continue will serve the team better than moving on. If you give the conversation or activity more time, what's the trade-off? Will there still be time to converge on team insights or actions?

Usually, it's pretty clear. When it's not, look for a compromise. Suggest time-boxing the discussion to leave time for the original intent. Agree to revisit the topic later (in the retrospective or afterward). Use a "parking lot" (or "bike rack") to keep a list of topics to come back to later. Ask the team to remind you to return to the topics they want to deal with soon.

Situations like these are when having a backup activity comes in handy. Swap to a shorter activity if time is running short. As the facilitator, you still have the responsibility to address the focus of the retrospective (and sometimes shift it, as Ruud did). The retrospective is not over until the team has a chance to identify and plan for actions, experiments, learning, or improvements. The team may even decide that the best way forward is to "wait and see" to learn more or conduct additional research. As long as it's a conscious, explicit whole team decision, it moves them together in collaboration.

Joanne Perold, agile coach at Faethm, was working with a cross-organization group that worked in two-week iterations. At the end of the iteration, Joanne scheduled the retrospective and prepared a ninety-minute design for their in-person meeting. Everyone arrived on time for the retrospective—a good sign! Several of the team leaders told Joanne, "We only have thirty minutes for this." Joanne had to adapt her plan, fast. But she didn't know exactly what was going on, so she involved the group.

Joanne outlined what had been intended and shared her view of what might be possible. Since they were familiar with our retrospective framework, she suggested they go through all five steps, but at a high level. Given the new time constraint, they didn't have time to go deep. "I was quite explicit about it," Joanne related. "I set up a quick frame about what we were going to do, then I did a One-Word Check-in to get all the voices in the room. Then I did a very fast Mad/Sad/Glad to gather data." The activity yielded interesting data. Given the constraints, they only had time to briefly discuss one topic. Even so, they took those insights and came up with a few possible changes. In the end, they chose one action. Joanne thanked everyone and closed their short retrospective.

Joanne had the experience, willingness, and toolbox to respond to a last minute request. But it was a *choice*, and you don't have to make the same decision Joanne did. Rescheduling is a completely valid option in such situations. If you believe you cannot do the topic justice in a constrained timeframe, postpone the retrospective. If you feel flustered and unable to bring your best thinking—which would be completely understandable—postpone it.

You may also want to consider whether this is a sign some people think it's OK to blow off a retrospective on short notice. See Chapter 14, Overcoming Objections, on page 235, for ideas on how to best handle these types of situations.

Cue the Group

At various times during your retrospective, you will need to alert the group that a transition is about to occur. This might be when it's time to move on to a new topic of discussion or when people need to return from their breakout rooms to a full-group setting.

In these situations, you have two approaches to get your team's attention.

First, you can make a sound that alerts your team that it's time to transition. You can use a bell or a chime. Other music cues can work as well. To reduce confusion, make sure the sound is distinctive from the sounds that mobile phone notifications tend to make.

Alternatively, follow the "raising hands" protocol: ask the team to raise their hands whenever they see you raise your hand at the front of the room. As more people raise their hands, others will notice and raise their hands as well. Pretty soon, the whole group will be quiet and will turn their attention to you.

A variation is to get people's attention via clapping. You can say, "If you can hear me, clap once!" A few people who are paying attention will clap. Then say, "If you can hear me, clap twice!" More people will join in. Keep this going until everyone is paying attention, the room is quiet, and people are focused on the instruction you will offer next.

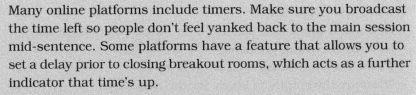

Keeping Track of Time During Remote Retrospectives

Just because your team is remote, that doesn't mean you can't use the same techniques.

Many online platforms include timers. Make sure you broadcast the time left so people don't feel yanked back to the main session mid-sentence. Some platforms have a feature that allows you to set a delay prior to closing breakout rooms, which acts as a further indicator that time's up.

You can also supplement these methods with other timing apps, as desired. For example, many online whiteboards and some retrospective tools have built-in timers. Keep a personal timer handy if you need to track smaller increments that you will share with the team.

Manage Yourself

Besides managing activities and encouraging follow-through, you need to manage yourself.

Staying aware of all these team and interpersonal dynamics may seem over-whelming. The key to managing group dynamics is not technique. (Although it helps to develop some strategies for that.) The key lies in understanding and managing your own emotional state and responses. If you are not man-aging your own state, no technique or strategy will help. When emotions are high, the team needs a steady guide who stays outside the turmoil. That guide is you, the retrospective leader.

When (not if) you feel your own anxiety or tension rising, take a deep breath. Then check in on yourself. Your anxiety is a clue that you need to sort out what to do next to serve the group. Call for a short pause. Brief stretch breaks are a facilitator's best friend. Your sensations may be a response to the emerging mood of the group. Remember, you didn't cause the emotions in the room. You don't have the responsibility to make everything and everyone happy and everything nice. You do have the responsibility to do your best to get everyone through it safe and undamaged, including you.

During the break, take a moment to release the physical tension. Invite others to do so as well. Shake out your hands and get your blood flowing again. Take three deep breaths. This may seem like superfluous advice. It's not. When people are tense and anxious, it reduces blood flow to the brain. Reduced blood flow inhibits the ability to think clearly. Cloudy thinking contributes to anxiety and tension. It's a devolving cycle. More oxygen to the brain is a good thing. It helps you think.

Once your brain has the oxygen it needs, ask yourself these questions:

- What just happened?
- How much was inside me, and how much was outside me?
- How did the group get here?
- Where does the group need to go next?
- What are three options I have for the next steps?
- What will I offer the group?

These questions will help you recenter. Then use your brain and heart to decide what to do. Taking a break and oxygenating your brain will save you from standing there frozen, not knowing what to do. It's always acceptable to say, "I'm not sure what just happened, and I don't know what to do next.

What would help the group?" Stuff happens. No one is perfect, so learn how to recover gracefully.

Over time, your comfort in dealing with charged emotional situations will grow. Find a mentor whom you have seen effectively manage emotions in groups. Work with your mentor to gain confidence. And remember to breathe.

The more you learn to manage your own internal responses, the more you will be able to serve the groups you facilitate. This doesn't mean suppressing your responses. It means being aware, knowing how to recenter yourself, and gaining time to think.

Just Add People

So far, you've learned a structure for retrospectives and how to customize a retrospective for your team. You've considered the role of a retrospective leader. Now, just add people.

Put a bunch of them together and wonderful things can happen! But so can bumps, warts, and awkward situations. We have the bruises to show for it and the stories to tell.

Some common less-than-optimal behaviors show up in groups. There are also strategies to deal with them in a way that respects the individual and creates a better experience for the group. That's what we'll cover in Chapter 4, "Managing Group Dynamics."

CHAPTER 4

Managing Group Dynamics

Simply put, *group dynamics* describe how people in a group behave and interact with one another. Creating the conditions for positive behaviors and interactions is critical. Here's just one example: the most effective teams have what researchers call "equality in distribution of conversational turn-taking."[1] In other words, over the long run, on the best teams, everybody talks about the same amount. As the retrospective facilitator, it's up to you to create the conditions that make this possible.

Yet, despite your best attempts, issues will intrude and people may behave in ways that aren't completely helpful for collaboration and learning.

In this chapter, we'll talk about how to shape the conditions for productive interactions. We'll discuss how to handle some common "not what I planned for" situations. Finally, we'll go over some of the common group dynamics we've observed and strategies to overcome them.

Let's start with working agreements.

Create Working Agreements

Working agreements are statements of aspiration adopted by a group to support their work. They clarify mutual expectations and form a social contract.

Working agreements make *everyone* responsible for civil behavior and collaboration. Without those agreements, participants tend to unconsciously transfer that responsibility to the person leading the meeting (*Helping Your Team Weather the Storm [Der05]*). Working agreements can address a variety of daily concerns about practices, communication, conflicts, decision-making, or any aspect of work and group life.

---

1. https://www.nytimes.com/2016/02/28/magazine/what-google-learned-from-its-quest-to-build-the-perfect-team.html

Many teams adopt working agreements when they first come together. If your team has working agreements that reference collaborative behavior, you can use them for the retrospective. If not, it's worth developing a set for your retrospective. They're especially important for cross-organization retrospectives or when conflicting views are likely.

For most teams, five working agreements (plus or minus two) will be sufficient. Too many and people won't be able to remember them. Too few and they won't cover enough surface area.

Working Agreements May Tell You What People Worry About

As Chris, a tech lead from outside the team, helped establish working agreements, the group identified "Everyone participates" as their first working agreement. Later as they started discussing data, Chris realized that the group had been worried about Dave, their "star" performer. Dave went on and on giving his perspective.

When other team members attempted to join the conversation, Dave dismissed them with a wave and kept talking—in spite of the new working agreement regarding participation. Chris supported the team in holding their agreement by recording Dave's comments and saying, "Thank you, Dave; now let's hear from someone else." After that, team members were more assertive with Dave. And Chris asked to go round-robin on report outs (and didn't start with Dave). Dave still had a great deal to say, but he didn't dominate the discussion.

We've included two activities, along with variations, to guide the team in developing working agreements in Chapter 5, Activities to Set the Stage, on page 79.

Violating Working Agreements

No matter how you approach developing and using your working agreements, sooner or later team members will violate one or more of them. That's normal! Be understanding—we're all humans after all. At the same time, be direct when it happens. As soon as possible, remind your team of their working agreements.

If you allow violations to continue without comment, you undermine collaboration. Team members get the message that supporting the working agreements doesn't matter. Optional working agreements have no value.

Remember, it's everyone's job to monitor working agreements!

Draw Out Quiet People

One of the responsibilities of a retrospective leader is making sure people who have something to say have the chance.

Make an opening for the quieter team members by asking to hear other opinions. Notice when someone looks as though he or she is about to speak before another team member interjects first. Create an opportunity without putting people on the spot or demanding an answer (*How to Improve Meetings When You're Not in Charge [Der03]*).[2]

You might say something like "I'd like to hear from people who did not say anything in the last five minutes. What would you add?" It's not a demand to perform, but making space for comment. Always be willing to accept a pass.

If you have one person who speaks but no one follows, try asking "What else?" As each person responds, thank them and then repeat, "What else?" If this turns into a longer discussion than you intend, switch to "Anyone else?" That signals to the group that one more answer or comment is all that's needed.

Create Space for Everyone

There are a variety of reasons why people feel they don't have the space to speak up.

Some aren't comfortable speaking in front of a group, even when the group is just the five to ten people on their team. Many of the same individuals would be more than happy to participate in small breakout groups of one to two. It's your job to make sure that happens.

Other times, a single group member might dominate the conversation. Acknowledge their contributions and then turn to others in the group and invite them to participate by saying, "What else?" or "Others?" If the behavior persists, try a gentle "stop" gesture and say, "Let's hear from someone else first this time."

Finally, consider offering feedback privately outside the retrospective. Describe the behavior and the impact on the team. There's a good chance the person either isn't aware of the behavior or doesn't see the impact.

Manage Power Differences

People recognize that power plays a part in organizations but are often reluctant to name it. Yet, power still influences behavior at work.

In "The Bases of Social Power" (an article in the book *Studies in Social Power [Car21]*), John French's and Bertram Raven's seminal research identified five sources of power. The one of most concern for retrospectives is positional power (sometimes called legitimate power).

---

2. http://www.humansystemsinaction.com/how-to-improve-meetings-when-youre-not-in-charge/

Positional power comes from being selected or appointed to a role that comes with the ability to make big decisions that affect other people's lives. In most organizations, managers have the power to hire, fire, rate, rank, and hand out assignments and other rewards.

When managers attend the retrospective, they often decrease the psychological safety of the team without meaning to. Many people are less likely to say what they truly believe in front of their manager, especially when they believe their managers will likely disagree. It's usually not the specific manager's fault. It's an artifact of positional power.

Sometimes team members hold back when a manager attends, based on past experience. Those experiences may have been with a different manager, but the impact is the same. If no one else speaks up, many managers will fill the dead air. Facilitators allow fertile silences. Managers often fill them before new ideas can grow.

For these reasons, managers shouldn't attend every retrospective unless they're specifically invited by the team. Including them is a special case, not the default.

When faced with this advice, some managers push back by claiming that they enable the team to address issues that it can't solve on its own. Perhaps, but there are other, more effective approaches to address these "beyond the team" concerns that don't reduce psychological safety. We discuss these in detail in Chapter 13, Elevating Issues Beyond the Team's Control, on page 219.

If you do plan to include a manager in the retrospective, coach them beforehand on appropriate participation. Ask them to let others talk first. Suggest they acknowledge the contributions others make. Caution them to take care how they disagree. A statement like, "I see it differently" preserves participation. Comments like, "You're wrong," "You just don't understand," "You're not listening to me," and "I disagree" quash participation. They may lead to confrontation. Both will derail the retrospective. It doesn't have to be this way.

Consider the approach Diana used. Rajiv, a project manager, was known as a high-energy, verbal guy. He felt excited about the product and the team's work. Diana met with him before the retrospective to discuss his participation. Rajiv worried he'd forget to wait for others to speak first. Diana and Rajiv agreed on a signal. If he spoke out of turn, she would walk over and stand next to him. They never used the signal. Knowing the signal might come was enough to help Rajiv pause to think before speaking and give himself a chance to hear new ideas.

Scrum Master Jeanice Wong tried another way of structuring the manager-team conversation. She told us:

"Two years ago, I witnessed my team disengaged with the ideas proposed by my manager. They commented that the proposed solutions weren't what they wanted." Eventually, people stopped caring.

The manager enjoyed participating in the retrospectives and couldn't understand why the team didn't welcome her help. So Jeanice found time for a conversation about how they could do things differently. "My manager and I decided to do dialogue sessions with the team to understand their concerns and conduct a brainstorming session together. As a facilitator, I adapted 1-2-4-All and the Fishbowl."

Jeanice asked the whole group, team members and manager, to discuss in pairs. After their first round of discussion, the paired team members continued the topic with another pair as a small group. Once the small group concluded the second round, each group shared their insights with everyone. During the sharing, everyone could ask questions to clarify their understanding before moving into decisions.

Jeanice said, "At first, it was an awkward sharing experience because my manager did most of the talking; and others acted as her audience. After some tryouts, my manager started to speak less and encouraged others to speak more. From then on, the dialogue session has become our monthly routine session with everyone."

She went on to say, "My teams are now more receptive to sharing their concerns and trying new ideas to deal with departmental problems. They also felt that their voices were heard and supported by the management team. One takeaway is that the relationship with the manager is equally important as with the customer." Jeanice emphasized the need to build two-way trust between team members and managers.

Avoid Blame

From a psychological perspective, blame is the discharge of pain, discomfort, or anger. It makes the blamer feel better. It may make the blamer feel bigger to themselves and to the people around them. However, it has a terrible effect on retrospectives (and life and work in general).

Once blaming starts, problem-solving ends. People are less likely to risk speaking up and less likely to share ideas that aren't fully formed. When blame is pervasive, people keep their heads down and focus on avoiding being the one who gets blamed. Blame starts a downward spiral of defensiveness and counter-blame. By that point, trust has disappeared.

The High Cost of Blame and What to Do About It

For a quick introduction to the cost of blame, listen to Esther's podcast, *Curiosity or Blame.*[3]

For guidance on how leaders can shift the blame dynamic, see *Lead without Blame: Building Resilient Learning Teams [LB22].*

You will know the team is in blame mode when you hear a lot of "you" language. For example, *You broke the build! You never follow through. You should have done it this way!* "You" language hurts the retrospective and distracts from real problems.

Instead, encourage your team to adopt "I" language. "I" language centers on the speaker's own observation and experience. For example, rather than saying, "*You* broke the build!," you might try, "Our build has been broken three times in the last couple of days, and I'm blocked from integrating my work." Rather than saying "*You're* always late!" you could try, "The other day we had a meeting and I waited 15 minutes."

Be careful though: even "I" language can be twisted into blame. For example, "I think the way you handled that was idiotic." Labels like "idiotic" are another form of blame. Whenever you hear personal criticism, intervene. Redirect the discussion to the content and the system.

Consider this approach to handling blaming comments. During one retrospective, one team member blamed another. James thought Vivek was at fault for breaking the build. "We'd have met our target if it weren't for you!"

"Hold on!" the retrospective leader said. "Can you say that using 'I' language?" James thought for a while. Then he said, "I am angry that we missed our target because we had so much trouble fixing the build." Then the team was able to look at bigger issues with the build without blaming one individual.

Facts vs. Stories

When you notice blame in your retrospective, describe what you've seen and heard: "I'm hearing labels and 'you' language." Describing the behavior causes people to pause and consider what they're doing.

Then ask, "What facts and stories are relevant to this topic?"

---

3.   https://changebyattraction.simplecast.com/episodes/blame-or-curiosity

Facts vs. Stories

For example, "It's a *fact* that the build broke ten times yesterday. The *story I make up* about it is that none of us cared enough to fix it."

Notice how in most cases the blame doesn't come from the facts. The blame comes from stories that may or may not be true!

Another way to discourage blaming is to incorporate Norm Kerth's "Retrospective Prime Directive" into setting the stage for your retrospective...or as a working agreement for your daily teamwork. Norman Kerth introduced the Retrospective Prime Directive in his book, *Project Retrospectives: A Handbook for Team Reviews [Ker01]*.

It states:

"Regardless of what we discover, we understand and truly believe that everyone did the best job they could, given what they knew at the time, their skills and abilities, the resources available, and the situation at hand."

This statement redirects blame from individuals toward the systemic and situational factors at play.

Team members may trip over the portion of the Prime Directive that states "and truly believe." Remind them that the agreement is only in force for the time of the retrospective or whenever the team decides it applies. It leaves the door open that a team member's best job on any given day may not have been adequate to what the team needed. However, don't focus on blaming the team member. Focus on the factors that kept the team member's best from being good enough.

Did they have the right information or knowledge available? Did we assign someone whose skills and abilities weren't a good match for the task? Did they have all the resources they needed? What else in the situation may have gotten in the way?

These are all questions about our system of work. The answers give clues about how it can be improved to keep these issues from happening again in the future. They take into account that team members may have personal issues that impact their ability to work to their own standards of personal best. We've found many instances where after understanding the situation, a team made choices to adjust their process or expectations. These choices helped the individual and the team's work.

Watch Out for Weaponizing

Watch out for "weaponizing" any of these recommendations. They all are meant to set a positive, collaborative, open tone in the retrospective. A blame-free tone.

Weaponizing happens when a person or group takes a word or phrase and uses it to attack, undermine, or hurt. For instance, the phrase "interpret generously" is intended as advice to give a potentially constructive spin to the comments of others (or at least attempt it).

We have heard it turned into a defense against being held accountable, as in, "You can't take offense at (this offensive thing I said) because you're supposed to interpret generously." One comment like this can shut down open, honest discussion.

In today's world of many virtual interactions, weaponizing or trolling has become a game to some. Unfortunately, it's a game that has unfavorable consequences for teams and collaboration.

Deal with Emergent Issues

Fidgeting and intense side conversations may signal an issue. Something's bubbling close to the surface, but it's not yet on the table for discussion. Again, ask the group what is going on. Sometimes they will tell you. Other times the issue is more apparent.

In the midst of a retrospective, Diana noticed the manager took a call. This was counter to a department-wide agreement about taking calls in meetings, so the manager's behavior surprised everyone.

Next, the manager left the room. When she came back in, she had a quiet side conversation with one person and then another. Laptops opened. Other team members continued to try to stay with the main topic. But the disruption distracted them too much to keep on track. Diana stopped the discussion and asked, "What's happening?"

Diana paused the retrospective and helped the team discuss their options. The team chose to pause the retrospective, set a timebox for problem-solving in the room, and then resumed the retrospective—all without blame. By naming the issue, she brought it into the open and shifted what could have been a difficult dynamic.

Four Steps for Handling an Emergent Issue Without Blame

When something unexpected comes up, these four steps will help you find a way forward that works for the group.

1. *Notice the behavior.* The very first thing is to notice something is happening. This isn't as easy as it sounds, given all the things a retrospective leader must attend to. It may be someone opening a laptop or a normally engaged team seeming distracted.

2. *Comment on it.* Be careful to use neutral language. If, as in Diana's story, the situation involves a working agreement, remind people of the agreement.

3. *Ask the group what is happening.* They may have a different perspective or some essential information.

4. *Help the team clarify their options.* The options will be different for every situation. It's always a good rule of thumb to have at least three.

It's impossible to predict what sort of situation will arise, but rest assured, sooner or later something surprising will happen.

Gregor Streng, an agile coach, told us he's learned that he must "facilitate the retro for success even if the team takes over...as a Scrum Master, you prepare a retro, then start facilitating it, and then it moves just in a direction you haven't thought at all."

He continued, "This has happened to me quite a few times. The first time I was a little confused. But at the end of the retrospective, the team and I were happy that it went this way because we had valuable outcomes that helped the team. I even thanked the team for going this way and not just 'enjoying the retro show.' For me, this is an indicator of teams that really live agility and use retrospectives as an important part of their work."

Emergent topics may not show up right at the beginning of the retrospective. That's why it helps to keep a few alternative activities in your facilitator's toolkit or metaphorical "back pocket." And be ready to throw things out completely and go with what's most important in the present. Stay alert to the energy of the team and move with it.

And, if you're a participant in the retrospective and become aware of a big disruptor, as the manager in Diana's retrospective did, say something!

Handle Challenging Dynamics

The vast majority of retrospectives go pretty much as planned. If you've chosen activities to equalize participation, you will most likely take on challenging topics in a pleasant way. But sometimes, chaos breaks loose.

Remember, there's a pretty good chance these issues don't have much to do with what's happening in the room but with some other deeper pattern. It's not your job to fix people's issues. If outbursts are the ongoing rule on your team, something else is happening. You will want to attend to those outside the retrospective. Retrospectives aren't appropriate venues to solve every problem. Your human resources representative or manager may be able to offer guidance.

Before you jump in to fix things, notice your own response. While it's easy to focus on comforting one person, you may lose track of the goal and needs of the team. Remember, your primary responsibility centers on healthy interactions for the whole team—not on any particular individual. That doesn't mean ignoring what ss going on with individual emotions. It means dealing with their emotions in a way that is helpful and respectful to the team and to the individual.

Strategies that have worked for us can work for you. Have a mental picture of how you'll respond. It will give you more options at the moment. Think of the outburst that scares you the most and then mentally rehearse using one of these strategies. Outbursts are unsettling, but they don't have to derail the process. If you think you could never handle interactions like this, remember that it's a skill you can build. Like any other skill, practice helps.

Handling Strong Emotions

 In general, handle strong emotions using the same four-step process as you would any other emergent issues—with some slight modifications. Notice what's happening. Comment in a neutral way. For example, "Wow, that was big." Ask, "What's happening for you?" Help clarify options, perhaps by saying, "What would you like to have happen?"

The following are some challenging dynamics we've witnessed while facilitating. Many teams (but not all) consider these behaviors to be disruptive. If it's unclear what is "within bounds" and what isn't, refer to the team's working agreements. If the working agreements don't address these behaviors and they keep popping up, consider running a retrospective on *that* instead.

Tears

For some teams, tears can feel inappropriate at work. For other teams, tears are perfectly acceptable—normal even.

No matter, if you're in person, offer a box of tissues. If you're working with a virtual team, give the team member a bit of time. Show patience. Ask if the group needs a break.

When the person is able to speak, ask, "What is happening for you? Would you feel comfortable sharing it with the group?" Pause. Give them time and understanding. A tearful person often will share a heartfelt (and very relevant) comment about the topic. Those comments may shift the thinking of the whole team.

Remember, tears may feel disruptive, but they also might be exactly what's needed. Sometimes, the best way to get past a difficult situation is to work *through* it. If you sense that's the case, invite the tears. Support the person as they feel their feelings.

Shouting

When someone starts shouting, the rest of the people often stop participating. That makes it unproductive for everyone. Intervene immediately. Hold up one hand as a stop sign and say calmly but forcefully, "Hold it." Then say, "I want to hear what you have to say. I can't when you're shouting. Can you tell us without shouting?" The person may respond, "I'm not shouting!" When someone feels upset or excited, they may not notice their rising vocal volume. They sincerely may not realize it. There's no need to say "Yes, you are." Calling attention to the yelling is usually enough to stop it.

If a team member continues to blame or yell after your intervention, call a break. Breaks provide an all-purpose remedy to many meeting ills. They give you time to think and everyone else time to reset. Talk to the person privately. Let them know how the behavior affects the group. Ask for their agreement to express emotion in a nonthreatening way. If the person is unwilling, ask (don't tell) them to leave. Offer them the option to return when they have more self-control.

Stomping Out

When a team member stomps out or leaves the virtual team room abruptly, let him or her go. Ask the team, "What just happened?" They will have an idea. Ask whether it's possible to continue without the person who left. Most of the time, they'll say they can continue, though they may need to talk about the departure.

If this happens more than once, another issue is at play. Talk to the individual outside the retrospective.

Inappropriate Laughter and Clowning

It's great to have fun in a retrospective and enjoy the team's time for learning together. Yet, people also may use laughter and humor to deflect from a sensitive topic. Notice when the laughter has an edge or when your team has developed a pattern of avoiding a topic. It's time to step in. Make an observation and ask a question: "I've noticed that every time we get near this topic, someone tells a joke. What's happening?" They'll tell you and potentially engage in the topic.

For more on how to handle "elephants in the room," see our approach on page 178.

Silence

Outbursts aren't the only emotional cues to manage. Uncharacteristic silence can be a problem, too. When a team that has been voluble goes quiet, something is going on. Again, step in with an observation and a question: "It seems to me that the group is being awfully quiet. There was a lot of energy and conversation earlier. What's going on now?"

Team members may simply feel tired and need a break. Or they may be unsure how to approach an uncomfortable issue. Once you ask the question and wait, someone will figure out how to broach the topic. Then the proverbial dam will burst. In cases like this, your ability to stay comfortable with extended silence will serve you well.

The fact that a team goes quiet may not mean anything. They may be thinking, tired, or merely a quiet group. When the silence is sudden or out of character, it's a clue worth following. You may discover a topic that's trying to emerge.

Remember Your Own Oxygen Mask

Whew! After thinking through all those potential challenging group dynamics, you may need a break. Remember that taking care of yourself and your own emotional balance is important too. Put on your proverbial oxygen mask before agreeing to facilitate, particularly if you sense challenges lurking in your upcoming retrospective. With any luck, you won't encounter all of these in one retrospective!

Look for opportunities to lead retrospectives in routine circumstances first. Consider volunteering to help the nonprofits or religious organizations you care about. They could probably inspect and adapt their ways of working to gain improvements. Some of us have held occasional retrospectives in our families.

The next few chapters provide lists and instructions for activities that you can choose for each step of the flexible framework. Use them along with the early chapters to design and facilitate an effective retrospective for your team. They'll add to your toolbox. We offer a useful set of activities, and others have offered many more. As you facilitate more retrospectives and experience different situations, you will gain skill and confidence. Good luck!

Part II

Selecting Activities

Chapters 5 through 9 offer a selection of example activities for each of the five phases of a retrospective. For each activity, you will find step-by-step guidance about when and how to use the activity.

Chapter 10 provides examples of how we might combine those activities into a full retrospective in response to common scenarios teams tend to face.

CHAPTER 5

Activities to Set the Stage

Setting the stage prepares the team for the work they'll do in the retrospective. This can be as brief as reviewing the focus and agenda and then checking in. Other times, you will want to go into more detail, such as reviewing retrospective working agreements and other activities.

Usually, team members are switching from a different sort of work when they arrive at their retrospective. They may have been heads-down involved in their latest story or task. They may have attended an all-hands meeting with company announcements. Perhaps there's a distraction at home. In any of these cases, you'll need to help the group shift gears and get ready to participate well in the retrospective. If the group topic is weighty or there's potential for conflict, spend extra time setting the tone and creating safety.

Whatever amount of time you have set aside for the whole retrospective, plan to use 5 to 10 percent of it on setting the stage. Time invested in setting the stage will save time later on.

For example, for a five-minute micro-retrospective in an ensemble programming team, thirty seconds might be enough to remind the team of their focus. For a three-day end-of-project retrospective with a large group, plan to spend the first hour or two getting everyone ready to work together.

Many of the activities from the first edition have become familiar favorites for retrospective facilitators around the world. We're including those again. In Chapter 11, Retrospectives When the Team Isn't Colocated, on page 183, we've added recommendations for how to adapt them when you're working with a remote team or group.

Avoid Icebreakers, Games, and Energizers

As we mentioned in Chapter 2, A Retrospective Custom-Fit to Your Team, on page 23, avoid generic icebreakers, games, and energizers that participants can't easily connect to the work at hand.

That genre of activities has its place in other kinds of events where the purpose is to help people get to know each other better or simply have fun together. Unless you've chosen "getting to know you" or "having fun" as your retrospective focus, look for another activity that will contribute to the focus you have.

Get to Know the Activities

There's one setting the stage activity you should almost always include: introducing the focus topic and agenda. Beyond that, activities in this phase fall into three categories: check-ins, activities that support effective participation, and activities that build or reinforce safety.

The Essential Activity

If you only do one activity to set the stage, do this one:

• Introduce the Focus Topic and Agenda, on page 81

Check-Ins

Check-ins help people shift gears, and acknowledge what's on their minds. A check-in can give you a sense of the group's mood.

• Check-In Question (Includes One-Word Check-In), on page 82
• ESVP, on page 84

Activities That Support Effective Participation

These activities help create social contracts about how people will treat each other during the retrospective.

• Focus On/Focus Off, on page 87
• Retrospective Working Agreements, on page 89
• Variation: Team Working Agreements as Meeting Ground Rules, on page 91

Activities That Build or Reinforce Safety

When there's conflict, controversy, or general hesitation around participating, consider an activity to build safety. Psychological safety has always been a concern for facilitators. We celebrate that in the last few years, there's been much more awareness about the role of safety in collaboration, creativity, and team development across our industry.

- Variation: Meeting Ground Rules for Conflicts or Controversy, on page 92
- Retrospective Prime Directive, on page 92
- Fill-in-the-Blanks, on page 95
- Temperature Reading, on page 97
- Temperature Reading Alternatives, on page 100

The rest of this chapter explains these exercises in detail.

Introduce the Focus Topic and Agenda

Description and Rationale

In every retrospective, participants will need time and a reason for collaboration. Start each retrospective with a statement of purpose (see Shape the Focus on page 25) and a description of how you'll guide their time and effort.

Time Needed

3–10 minutes, depending on the group's familiarity with retrospectives. As the group becomes more experienced, the time needed to cover the agenda will become shorter.

Facilitator Guide

Commenting on the focus topic and the planned agenda at the beginning lets participants know you respect their time. You've thought about the session in advance and have a plan. Bringing these two artifacts together with an activity to follow gives everyone time to adjust to a new center of attention.

For instance, for some agile teams, it might mean changing from thinking about their product demo or work review. For others, it could be production work. They may need a moment to mentally, emotionally, and physically let go of whatever engaged them just before this meeting. Have the focus topic and agenda written for viewing or distributed ahead of the retrospective.

Steps

1. Welcome everyone to the session and the location (physical space or remote tool space).

2. Display the agenda (even if you sent it out in advance).

3. Point out the various parts of the agenda. Share the duration you expect for the meeting and your intention to stick to the timebox commitments.

4. Share the focus topic and how you arrived at it.

5. Share the flow of activities described on the agenda. Note that what you're doing now is included in getting started.

6. Ask for questions or comments. If there are none, segue smoothly into the next activity.

Materials and Preparation

After preparing your own facilitator's guide notes, prepare an agenda document. For an example, see Chapter 2, A Retrospective Custom-Fit to Your Team, on page 23.

Notes

Introducing the focus topic and agenda gives you, the facilitator, a chance to show that you will not waste the group's time. Move quickly through it, check for understanding, and move on to the next activity for the Set the Stage phase, which will begin interactive participation and engagement with team members.

Check-In Question (Includes One-Word Check-In)

Description and Rationale

Shift to engaging team members. Help people put aside other concerns and focus on the retrospective. Help people articulate what they want from the retrospective.

Time Needed

5–10 minutes, depending on the size of the group and the depth of the question

Facilitator Guide

After welcoming the participants and reviewing the focus and agenda, the retrospective leader asks one brief question. Each person answers in round-robin fashion. Suitable for in-person or remote retrospectives.

Steps

1. Ask one question that each person can answer with a word or short phrase. Here are some sample questions to choose from:

    a. What is one word that describes what you need for yourself from this session? (Note: Some teams use a list of human needs. You can also create a shorter subset of needs descriptions for team members to choose from—for example, "connection, understanding, physical comfort, purpose, growth, challenge, trust.")[1]

    b. What is one word that expresses how you're feeling coming into this session? (Note: Some teams identify a set of four to five emotion descriptions to use—for example, "happy, angry, apprehensive, sad, hopeful." Each team member checks in by reporting their emotional state using one of these words.)

    c. Combining the previous two questions: What is one feeling and one need that describe your current state?

    d. In one or two words, what is happening for you right now? Or, what is one thing that's on your mind? (Note: If you use one of these questions, also ask what each person needs to do to set their distraction or concern aside. Sometimes writing it down and putting it in a notebook or pocket— literally, physically setting it aside—helps people mentally set their distraction or concern aside. Using this type of check-in is helpful when team members have joys or challenges in their personal lives—because it makes it OK to experience the effect of strong feelings unrelated to work.)

    e. In a word or two, what are your hopes for the retrospective?

2. Go around the group listening to each person's answer. You may thank each person (be sure to thank every person if you do). Refrain from offering evaluative comments such as "good," "wonderful," or "that's stupid."

3. Alternative: For remote teams, ask team members to add their words to their thumbnail names. Then ask each one of them to offer their answer.

Allow People to Pass

 It's OK for people to say "I pass" on any question. Even saying "I pass" will make sure their voice is heard in the room.

---

1. https://www.cnvc.org/sites/default/files/needs_inventory_0.pdf

Materials and Preparation

Prepare and choose a question ahead of time.

Ben's Story

Ben Ziskoven, Scrum Master at Post/NL, offered a variation on the check-in. He wanted to help his team reduce distractions by identifying any undiscussed, big issues right at the start of the retrospective. In this way, he and the team could decide whether something would need attention right away or could be saved for discussion later.

In his experience, "it gives attention to important points and impediments that might be too big for the daily scrum." Yet it will still leave time for the planned retrospective focus activities. He describes it, "I asked before we start the retrospective if anyone needs to get something off their chest. Team members liked this. It took 10–15 minutes away from the retrospective 'agenda' I had prepared, but was always great to have discussed."

ESVP

Description and Rationale

ESVP (short for Explorer, Shopper, Vacationer, or Prisoner) helps the retrospective leader understand people's attitudes toward the retrospective. It's particularly useful if you're not a regular team member in the facilitator role. Use it when you suspect some participants haven't attended willingly. Since the responses are collected anonymously, it encourages honest responses and leads to collaboratively creating working agreements for the retrospective.

Time Needed

10–20 minutes, depending on the size of the group and whether the setting is in-person or remote.

Facilitator Guide

Each participant anonymously reports their attitude toward the retrospective as an Explorer, Shopper, Vacationer, or Prisoner. The retrospective leader collects the results, creates a histogram to show the data, and then guides a discussion about what the results may mean for the group. For additional tips, see the following "Notes" section.

Steps

1. Explain that you're taking a poll to learn about how people view their participation in the retrospective.

    a. Show the flip chart and define the terms:

        i.   Explorers are eager to discover new ideas and insights. They want to learn everything they can about the iteration/release/project.

        ii. Shoppers will look over all the available information and will be happy to go home with one useful new idea.

        iii. Vacationers aren't interested in the work of the retrospective but are happy to be away from the daily grind. They may pay attention some of the time, but they are mostly glad to be out of the workspace.

        iv. Prisoners feel that they've been forced to attend and would rather be doing something else.

2. Distribute slips of paper or small index cards for people to record their attitude toward learning in the retrospective. Instruct people to fold their paper in half for privacy. For remote retrospectives, ask participants to use the private chat with the facilitator or another method to maintain each person's anonymity. Some retrospective platforms support this natively.

3. Collect the responses. Mix the order you've received them.

4. Ask one of the participants to make tick marks on a physical or virtual histogram as you read the responses.

    a. When in-person with the group, put the responses in your pocket after you read each one. When you've read all the slips, tear them up and throw them away. Be conspicuous about this so people know that no one will try to identify who responded with what from the handwriting.

    b. When leading a remote retrospective, tell the group when you delete the responses.

5. Refer to the histogram and ask the group, "What do you make of this data?" Then lead a brief discussion about how the attitudes in the room will affect the retrospective. Comment to the group that every response reflects a valid stance. People have good reasons for their response.

6. Debrief by asking, "How are these categories like our attitudes toward daily work?"

7. If there are several "prisoner" responses, ask the group for suggestions on how to make the retrospective more valuable for everyone. Propose adopting as agreements any suggestions that gain positive reactions from the group.

8. In some cases, you can invite any remaining "prisoners" to skip the session, with the caveat that the remaining participants will make decisions that will affect the whole group.

Materials and Preparation

For colocated groups, prepare voting slips or index cards, pencils or pens, and a flipchart or whiteboard for the histogram.

For remote teams, decide how to collect responses while maintaining anonymity. Some retrospective platforms support this natively.

Prepare a virtual histogram template for adding responses. Instead of virtual sticky notes, you can also use an online anonymous polling tool to gather responses.

Notes

Check in with your group about the impact of the four words. The word "Prisoner" can have a particular impact. As the facilitator, it's helpful to know if you're in an organization rife with coercion and mandates. This activity can assist in understanding the presence or absence of psychological safety and a learning culture.

If the majority of the people in the room are Vacationers, that's interesting information about how people feel about their work environment. You may want to turn on a dime and make that the major focus of discussion for the retrospective.

In the following ESVP activity example, one person feels like a Prisoner. If you do have Prisoners in the room, suggest that they can choose how they will spend their time—they can engage or not. If they don't engage, the group will be the poorer for it.

If you plan to take a break in a longer retrospective with a large group, suggest that if people choose to return after the break, they are choosing to attend the retrospective—they aren't Prisoners anymore.

If you've done your research, chances are you won't be surprised by finding a room full of Prisoners. As in the situation with many Vacationers, if the majority of the group feels they are Prisoners, that's what you need to deal with; you won't get anywhere in the retrospective if you don't.

The following figure shows an example of a completed ESVP graphic chart for a team of eighteen people. Most of the team is interested in learning from the retrospective (Explorers and Shoppers). There's one Prisoner and three Vacationers—and that's OK.

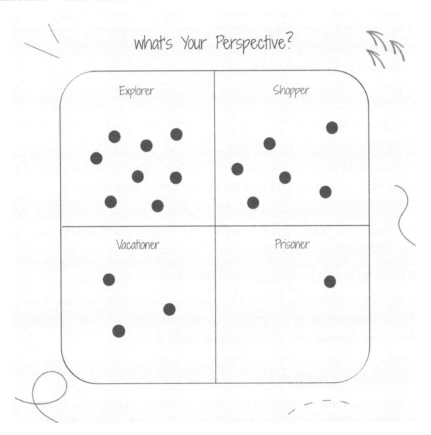

Focus On/Focus Off

Description and Rationale

Focus On/Focus Off brings attention to participant behaviors and how they affect team members. It establishes a mindset for productive communication and builds psychological safety. It encourages participants to set aside blaming and judgment—and fear of blaming and judgment. As with the pre-vious activity, you can use this activity as a lead-in to establish working agreements for the retrospective.

Time Needed

8–12 minutes, depending on the size of the group.

Facilitator Guide

After welcoming the participants and reviewing the goal and agenda, the ret-rospective leader describes productive and unproductive communication patterns. After describing those patterns, the participants discuss what they could mean for the retrospective.

Steps

1. Draw attention to the Focus On/Focus Off poster and briefly read through it.

2. Form small breakout groups, with no more than four people per group. Assign each group one pair of words to define and describe.

3. Ask each group to discuss what their two terms mean and what behaviors they represent. Have them describe the impact each would have on the team and the retrospective.

4. Each group reports on their discussion to the whole team.

5. Ask people whether they are willing to stay in the left column, that is, the Focus On behavior descriptions. In virtual settings, ask participants to show their agreements with icons or hand signals.

Materials and Preparation

Present the contrasts using a physical or online method. The image on page 89 represents a flipchart of the Focus On/Focus Off contrasts.

Notes

These are the "classic" pairs. It's possible to adapt this activity by using other comparisons related to communication. For example, "Effective over Efficient," "Curious over Blaming," or "Understanding over Explaining." Team members will find it easiest to work with if you keep the list to no more than five pairs.

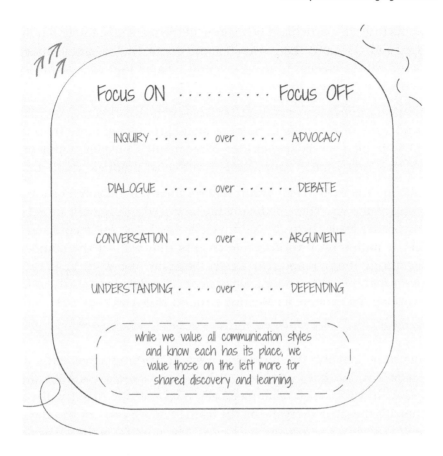

Focus ON · · · · · · · · · Focus OFF

INQUIRY · · · · · · over · · · · · ADVOCACY

DIALOGUE · · · · · over · · · · · · DEBATE

CONVERSATION · · · · over · · · · · ARGUMENT

UNDERSTANDING · · · · over · · · · · DEFENDING

while we value all communication styles and know each has its place, we value those on the left more for shared discovery and learning.

Retrospective Working Agreements

Description and Rationale

Establish a set of behaviors that will support the team in having productive discussions. Encourage team members to take responsibility for monitoring team interactions. Provide candidates for day-to-day working agreements if the team doesn't already have them.

Time Needed

5 minutes to review and affirm preexisting working agreements. Up to 30 minutes to create new ones, depending on the size of the group.

Facilitator Guide

Team members work together to generate ideas for effective behaviors in the retrospective (and in other team meetings) and then choose three to five agreements to guide participant behaviors. (If the team absolutely wants more than five, add no more than two. Remind them that a small number of agreements will be easiest to keep in mind. Teams find that eight or more agreements become easy to ignore.)

After the retrospective leader welcomes the participants and reviews the focus and agenda, the team works in pairs or small groups (no more than four in a group) to develop candidate working agreements. Consider completing the sentence that begins with, "Our meetings are most productive when..."

Going around the room, each group reports their most favored or impactful proposed agreements. When all the unique proposed agreements are collected, the retrospective leader helps the group make needed amendments and select five (plus or minus two) working agreements that will set the standard for behavior during the retrospective. Later, they may also want to adapt these agreements for their daily working agreements (see the next activity, Adapting Team Working Agreements as Meeting Ground Rules on page 91).

Steps

1. Explain the activity: "We'll develop a set of working agreements for the retrospective so that everyone will know our expectations for working together. It will be each team member's responsibility to follow the agreements. It's the job of everyone on the team to notice and bring to the team's attention when an agreement is violated. The purpose of the agreements is to support the discussions we need to have during the retrospective."

2. Form pairs or small groups, no more than four per group.

3. Ask each group to develop three to five working agreements that, if followed, would help the team have productive discussions during the retrospective. Invite the small groups to finish the sentence, "Our meetings are most productive when..." Remind the group that these don't include things they already do as routine. These agreements call out new behaviors or ones that aren't yet habits for the group—ones they aspire to make routine, but haven't yet.

4. In round-robin fashion, ask someone from each group to report that group's most preferred agreement and write it on a shared, viewable document (flip chart, online whiteboard, or other collaboration space). Continue asking for another proposal one at a time until you've captured all the unique proposed agreements.

5. Explain that for the retrospective, the group should choose three to seven agreements. Five is the sweet spot—enough to have an impact and not too many to track. Having more than seven is too hard to remember and follow.

6. Affirming agreements

   a. If there are five or fewer proposed agreements in total, ask if everyone fully understands the proposals. If they don't, ask for their questions. When everyone understands the proposals, use a consensus "thumb vote" to accept or reject each one. Thumb up means I agree. Thumb sideways means I'll support the will of the group. Thumb down means I veto. Any proposal with no vetoes is accepted.

   b. If there are more than five unique proposed agreements, use dot voting to prioritize. Give each team member three dots to vote with. Each person can put one dot on three separate items or all dots on one. Use a consensus thumb vote to ratify the top five (or so) vote-getters.

Materials and Preparation

Flip chart, markers, sticky notes and dots, or their virtual equivalents.

Notes

We're frequently asked for examples of typical meeting agreements. Teams often have agreements on participation, use of time, attendance, decision-making, idea generation, listening, and many others. Each team develops ground rules that reflect their unique concerns. They tend to arise in response to past experiences in team meetings. Team members bring memorable instances and create agreements that might amplify positive outcomes or dampen problematic situations or concerns.

In addition, teams may use working agreements to fit different situations. See the following variations for ideas.

Variation: Team Working Agreements as Meeting Ground Rules

Description and Rationale

When the team has previously developed a set of working agreements for their daily work, examine them to determine how each would apply in a retrospective.

When the team has previously developed a set of agreements for their retrospectives, examine them to determine how each would appear and apply in their daily work.

Facilitator Guide

Adapt the previous activity by framing the scope of the agreements for this meeting, this time.

Variation: Meeting Ground Rules for Conflicts or Controversy

Description and Rationale

The team has previously developed a set of working agreements, but it needs additional specific agreements for a meeting about existing or potential team conflict.

Facilitator Guide

Given the emotions surrounding the issue, it's important to establish agreed-upon ground rules that can be used as guardrails on process and group norms. Consider completing the sentence that begins with, "As a team, we handle conflict most effectively when…"

You might consider ground rules that prevent blaming and shaming, for example, or ground rules that maintain mutual respect by avoiding personal attacks or loaded language.

Steps

Use a similar process as described in the working agreements activity on page 89.

Retrospective Prime Directive

Description and Rationale

Bring this activity when you need to encourage your retrospective participants to take a more systemic view of their team collaboration and processes. Some retrospective leaders begin with it routinely as a reminder and general meeting ground rule.

Norm Kerth's "Retrospective Prime Directive" (see the facilitator guide below) emphasizes the importance of understanding behavior in context and as a system effect. The Retrospective Prime Directive encourages greater psychological safety, trust, and dignity for all members of the group—even when the team effort doesn't turn out as planned or expected, as will certainly occur sooner or later. By giving others the benefit of the doubt, team members give themselves it as well.

Time Needed

It depends on the size and mood of the group. Allow at least the equivalent of five minutes times the number of participants or more if you know there will be those who are inclined toward critical thinking and discussion. Then add five minutes for introducing the activity.

Facilitator Guide

Display a visual representation of the Prime Directive where everyone can view it. Invite the participants to use this statement to guide their discussions.

> "Regardless of what we discover, we understand and truly believe that everyone did the best job they could, given what they knew at the time, their skills and abilities, the resources available, and the situation at hand." Norman L. Kerth, *Project Retrospectives: A Handbook for Team Review [Ker01]* (Dorset House, 2001)

When participants see this statement for the first time, they often have questions. People are more used to being criticized, blamed, or "held accountable" than being offered another explanation for things that go wrong. See more explanation in the "Notes" section.

Steps

1. Introduce the Prime Directive. You may want to point out that the originator, Norm Kerth, coined the term "retrospective" as a useful concept and practice for improving software development, products, and services.

2. Ask each participant for one brief comment on what stands out for them in the statement. Make sure to let them know they can also say, "Pass," if they have no comment. Let them know there will be time for questions after this first round.

3. Give time for questions and brief answers.

4. Invite the group to adopt this perspective as they proceed through the rest of the session. Ask, "Who will adopt this mindset?" and request a show of hands (or another simple, visible means of voting).

5. If the group agrees, keep the Prime Directive visible throughout the session. Refer to the group's agreement on it, as needed.

6. If the group cannot agree, continue with the retrospective and the group's usual ground rules. Let it go, and try again another time.

Materials and Preparation

Create a representation of the Prime Directive quote to fit your group: whiteboard, online whiteboard, flip chart/pinwall, or another easily accessible version. Your preparation will center around getting ready to discuss what may become a contentious topic.

Notes

The Prime Directive serves as a guide to the retrospective way of working. It's also particularly effective in retrospectives that include a large number of participants. If one or more participants object on the basis that "It isn't so! Some folks are just slackers." ask whether they can agree to adopt this perspective, if only for the duration of the session.

If you have had experiences that put your own understanding at odds with the Prime Directive, don't use it. Whoever facilitates using the Prime Directive must have a sincere belief in its virtue.

It can help to translate the sections of the quote:

"We understand and truly believe that everyone did the best job they could…"—We're willing to hold this point of view for the time of the retrospective. (Some of us have learned through hard experience that it actually *is* true.)

Given "what they knew at the time…"—Did everyone have access to the information, data, alternative explanations, and so on that they would have needed to do a better job? How can we make those available in the future? What prevented it this time?

Given "their skills and abilities…"—Was the person or group a good match for the job to be done? Did they need additional support for learning? Did they have the background?

Given "the resources available…"—Were the equipment, tools, access to experts, and so forth available in a timely way? Were there handoffs in place as they were needed?

Given "the situation at hand"—Was the person or group in tip-top shape that day? Were they or their families stressed by illness or other concerns? Was the purpose of the work clear to everyone? Was the workplace conducive to the kind of output required? People experience so many possible variations on this context question.

For another useful explanation of this activity, see *Retrospective Antipatterns [Von21]* by Aino Vonge Corry (Pearson, 2021).

Consider another use for the Retrospective Prime Directive–a very personal use. After a difficult experience of leading a retrospective (or any other work for that matter) say to yourself, "Whatever I discovered, I understand and truly believe, I did the best job I could, given what I knew in the moment, my skills and abilities, the resources available to me, and the situation at hand." Feel the relief, then get busy learning how to overcome that kind of difficulty next time.

Fill-in-the-Blanks

Description and Rationale

In this activity, team members explore psychological safety by characterizing how they respond to safe and unsafe environments. These questions get the team out of the abstract and into people's actual lived experience. They make the contrast very clear.

Facilitator Guide

Each participant completes the blanks in two sentences, using single words or phrases. Ensure the group's responses are confidential and anonymous. In a colocated space, use index cards or sticky notes. In a remote space, you might use a word cloud app.

Steps

1. Introduce the activity as a way to understand how safety affects behavior. Hand out two different colors of index cards or sticky notes, so that everyone has one of each. (See the "Remote Adaptations" section.)

2. Share sentence number one: "When I feel unsafe, I ____." Ask participants to complete the sentence.

3. Share sentence number two: "When I feel safe, I ____."

4. If you're using physical cards, collect the answers to both sentences, keeping them in separate stacks. Then shuffle each stack. This helps create anonymity.

5. Whether you've used physical cards or a word cloud, share the responses. Read out the sentence endings for Sentence #1, "When I feel unsafe...." Let the words wash over the group. Allow some time for the responses to sink in. Then read the responses to sentence #2, "When I feel safe..." The contrast is usually dramatic and illuminating.

6. Ask how people would prefer to work. After a brief discussion, ask whether working agreements would help (see the activity for working agreements on page 89).

Remote Adaptations

Use an online app that creates word clouds. Set up one cloud to represent "When I feel unsafe, I..." responses. Set up a second cloud to collect "When I feel safe, I..." responses.

Materials and Preparation

The important part of this exercise is that people experience the impact of the responses. That can happen aurally or visually.

Notes

Variations on the theme of safety have given rise to a large number of activities. See the following story for one. Use your own understanding of the team to decide the degree of anonymity versus transparency that will best fit your team.

Wim's Story

For teams that have become used to the transparency that a public declaration requires, Wim Van Nieuwenhoeven, application developer at Liantis, contributed another form of "safety check."

He shared, "I started with a little check, a safety gauge if you like, to see if everyone was OK with doing the hard work that had to be done. 'Do you feel safe entering this retrospective, knowing we have some frustrations and tensions to tackle?' A simple yes or no.

We heard one minor hesitation, mentioning confrontation isn't something easy to deal with, but everyone was giving me the go. Body language was betraying a little nervousness, or at least that was how I read it, but I guess that was normal considering the circumstances."

If you notice hesitance, ask, "What would make you feel safer?" Then follow up with making a handful of agreements that address concerns.

Temperature Reading

Description and Rationale

A Temperature Reading offers a chance to check on "where we are" in this present moment. It's useful when you'd like to discover a focus topic that fits the moment. Adapted from the work of Virginia Satir, this activity offers a practical way to process what is happening for the group (*A Resource Handbook for Satir Concepts [Sch90]*). A Temperature Reading allows people to include aspects of group life that are usually ignored: appreciations, puzzles, and hopes and wishes.

Time Needed

10–30 minutes, depending on the size of the group and their experience with this activity.

Facilitator Guide

Team members have the opportunity to report on what's happening for them individually as well as what they want for themselves, for the team, and for their work product. The Temperature Reading format serves many purposes. Use it to discover a timely focus for your retrospective when you haven't found one yet. Use it to set the stage or to close the retrospective. See the following "Notes" section.

Steps

1. Introduce the activity by saying, "Let's look at what's happening in our group. You can contribute in any of the sections, but participation is voluntary. The aim is to hear from others, so no one may comment on another's contribution. While we need to hear your responses, the biggest opportunity is to hear what others have to say."

2. Point to the poster "The Elements of Temperature Reading" as you describe the parts of the activity. Comment briefly on each of the five sections and then allow plenty of time for people to contribute.

   a. Appreciations provide an opportunity to notice how others have contributed and what they bring to the team. The facilitator demonstrates the form by offering a sincere appreciation to someone in the group. The form is "(Name of person), I appreciate you for...." Add a brief statement of the impact on you.

b. New Information offers a time to share information that may be relevant to the group that is not yet widely shared or known.

c. Puzzles describe things we don't understand, but we're curious about. Puzzles, by definition, don't have answers yet—so don't try.

d. Opportunities for improvement allow people to point out what they'd like to be different and options for improving them.

e. Hopes and wishes let us say what we hope either for the retrospective or for going forward after the retrospective.

3. Wait between each section. Record puzzles and opportunities on a shared document immediately visible to the entire group.

Materials and Preparation

Prepare by writing the sections of the Temperature Reading on a shared document to help everyone follow along, see the example on page 99.

Notes

We've learned a trick for leading the Temperature Reading activity. Learn to count silently to yourself. This format is unfamiliar to most people. It can take them a while to become comfortable with it. Silent counting gives the facilitator something to do while waiting and ensures that people have time to gather their thoughts.

After demonstrating how to give an appreciation, start counting slowly to yourself. Look around the group with an inviting expression as you count. Stay with appreciations until you've counted to 75. Well before then, someone will step forward. Stop counting when someone speaks up. One person giving an appreciation usually gets the group going. When the number of appreciations offered slows down, count to 20 after the last one. If no one speaks up, then move on to Step 2b, New Information. Describe the next element, and start counting to 20. Afterward, use a count of 20 to help wait through each pause. Once a team has become used to Temperature Readings, they jump right in. You won't get to count.

Temperature Reading

Appreciations

What can we
appreciate?

Puzzles

What things are we
curious about?

Opportunities for
Improvement

What would we like to change?
(with suggestions)

New Information

Is there any
new info that
the team should know?

Hopes and Wishes

What are we hoping for?

More on Facilitating the Temperature Reading

When Temperature Reading is new to the team, people may not know how to respond. To help team members feel more comfortable, try these techniques. Emphasize that each section is an invitation. No one is obligated to respond. Point out that it's not necessary to have an appreciation for every team member every time or from every team member every time. Appreciations have an impact only when they are meant sincerely. Also, mention that receiving an appreciation only requires a simple acknowledgment. A brief "thank you" or "I'm happy to help" can be enough.

Because appreciations are often the most unfamiliar, consider demonstrating an appreciation using the exact language, for example, "David, I appreciate you for pairing with me." The most effective appreciations are very direct. Every extra word that creeps in diminishes the impact.

It's also worth noting that as long as your Temperature Reading starts with Appreciations and ends with Hopes and Wishes, the other three elements can work in any order that fits your situation. Our example shows an order that's worked for us, but we've also tried it in other sequences.

This is one of the few activities that can also serve as the basis for an entire retrospective. In that case, you'll spend more time in each part, which provides an opportunity to dive deeply into the dynamics of team life.

We've used Temperature Reading to initiate and inform status meetings for teams in a variety of situations. One team met monthly for project planning. The team members stayed energized and focused throughout the year of meetings. They ended the year with strong working relationships.

Temperature Reading Alternatives

The power of the Temperature Reading activity is how flexible it is. You can use it all or segment by segment, according to your needs. The following are two stories of how facilitators have used this activity.

Acknowledgments and Apologies

Anthony Bonfante, Enterprise Agile Coach at MaxAgililty Corp, shared a variation on Temperature Readings from his experience.

Anthony's Story

"I read the *Agile Retrospectives* book voraciously when I first became a Scrum Master. I was nervous about working with technical people since my background was pretty far from that. I decided that I should run my retro by the book, your book, and keep my fingers crossed. I was timid and anxious about (setting the stage) with this group, thinking they'd kick me out the door for wasting their time with something so 'silly' but I stuck to the book. I trusted that there is a right way to get people engaged and that I should do it.

I opened with 'Acknowledgments and Apologies' and held my breath waiting for their reaction. The first person to 'take the bait' was an IT manager who publicly apologized for failing to properly onboard the new tester, leaving him without proper equipment and application access for over a week. Whew! It worked! The rest of the retro was a breeze after that major sheet of ice was broken.

It acknowledged the humanity of the group. I mean, they were just doing work. It allowed us to bring the human to the retrospective. They had never experienced that before. So it was their first experience of making it OK. To make mistakes and recognizing (the impact on) other people. [It] reminded us that we're people and fundamentally friends. If we only think of work, we lose those stronger bonds."

Opportunities for Improvement (or Get Something off Your Chest)

Ben Ziskoven, Scrum Master at PostNL, shared a way to approach Temperature Reading, which worked well for him.

Ben's Story

"It's important that people aren't distracted during the retrospective by some big elephant in the room. If there are any, I want to address them right away.

I asked first if, before we can start the retrospective, anyone needs to get something off their chest. Team members liked this. It took 10–15 minutes away from the retrospective 'agenda' I had prepared but was always great to have discussed.

Ben's Story

Giving attention to important points got some team impediments too big for the daily scrum, on the table, and out of the way. It gave people more psychological safety, by giving them an explicit space for sharing. And usually takes less than 10 minutes after which there is more focus and engagement in the retrospective."

The Stage Is Set

The best activities to set the stage quickly create an initial introduction and focus attention.

In addition, they encourage the kind of interaction you'll need for success in the rest of the meeting. Always include a focus topic and agenda for how you'll use the team's time. Always.

Refer to meeting ground rules, if the team has them. Then add something extra to energize interaction, set a collaborative tone, and begin focused work on the topic.

Use the activities to set the stage to prepare your participants for their next task and move smoothly into Chapter 6, "Activities to Gather Data," our next chapter.

Activities to Gather Data

Teams gather data in a retrospective to create a shared picture of what happened during the recent period of work. Without data, the team can only guess what changes and improvements will help them work more effectively.

There are two types of data: objective and subjective. Objective data represents things that you can see, hear, count, measure, or verify in some way. Subjective data is information from a personal perspective, such as feelings, perceptions, and concerns. Both can be useful to bring to your retrospective. See Chapter 1, Help Your Team Inspect and Adapt, on page 3, for a more complete explanation of the difference between objective and subjective data.

Get to Know the Activities

The remainder of the chapter focuses on activities for gathering and presenting data. They're grouped by the type of data the team will be working with: objective, subjective, and a combination of the two.

Activities for Objective Data

When the team is using objective data, consider preparing the data ahead of time. Otherwise the team will have to rely on memory and opinion or spend precious time looking up information.

- Simple Objective Data Discussion, on page 104
- Gathering Data from an Improvement Action, on page 105

Activities for Subjective Data

Subjective data focuses on experiences and qualities that we can observe, but cannot easily measure. It's the data we have when the team is discussing teamwork, relationships, and perceptions. There are ways to measure some subjective factors. However, simple individual responses are often sufficient.

Generally, you can gather point-in-time subjective data (for example, how the team perceives their skill with technical practices) quickly during the retrospective. There are cases when looking at trends in subjective data is useful (for example, perception of autonomy or engagement can change over time).

- Simple Subjective Data Discussion, on page 106
- Satisfaction Histogram, on page 106
- Team Radar, on page 109

Activities for Combined Data

Sometimes it's useful to look at both facts and perceptions about those facts, combining objective and subjective data.

- Timeline, on page 112
- Variation: Timeline with Color-Coded Dots, on page 114

Now we'll describe the activities in detail.

Simple Objective Data Discussion

Description and Rationale

Share data relevant to the focus to ground the discussion. A visual presentation helps people absorb information and make sense of it.

Time Needed

It varies. Preparation time will vary depending on how much research you have to do and whether the data is in a form you can easily work with. If there's a lot of data, send it ahead of time. Reviewing charts and graphs in the retrospective may take 5–20 minutes.

Facilitator Guide

Different people absorb data at different rates. If there is a lot of data, make it available for both group and individual viewing in such a way that people can progress independently, that is, they control scrolling if the data is available electronically. Provide any URLs with the agenda/meeting invitation.

Steps

1. State how the data relates to the focus.
2. Invite people to review the data. Invite initial comments or questions, then segue into the Generate Insights phase.

Materials and Preparation

Materials can range from simple charts on flip chart paper to graphs generated by a spreadsheet program. In most cases, prepare the data ahead of time. An exception might be when team members tallied some sort of data during the iteration (for example, number of interruptions, code check-ins, time spent refactoring, and so on), which you can collect quickly.

Gathering Data from an Improvement Action

Description and Rationale

Provide tangible evidence related to an experiment or action.

Time Needed

15–20 minutes

Facilitator Guide

This would be a follow-up on an improvement action from a previous retrospective. For example, if the team had decided to experiment with holding office hours to reduce interruptions, show the data both from before and after the experiment.

Steps

1. Remind the team of the agreement to follow up on an improvement action or experiment from a previous retrospective.

2. Collect data from each team member, one by one, so that the whole team can see the aggregate and any emerging patterns.

3. Ask team members for their initial impressions. Document them.

Materials and Preparation

Review the ways to present objective data mentioned earlier in this section. Choose a way of graphing that best fits the kind of data you're collecting.

Simple Subjective Data Discussion

Description and Rationale

This activity helps the team process perceptions.

Time Needed

It varies. Preparation time will vary depending on what data you want to collect and from whom. Often, you can gather team members' perceptions in the retrospective in 5 to 15 minutes. However, if you want to look at customer perception data or how other groups perceive the work of your team, you'll need to gather that data ahead of time.

Facilitator Guide

If you're sharing data that's been gathered prior to the retrospectives, allow time for people to read the data. Different people absorb data at different rates. Make it available in such a way that people can progress independently. For data that's available electronically, allow individuals to control scrolling, rather than projecting or screen sharing. Provide any URLs with the agenda/ meeting invitation.

Steps

1. State how the data relates to the focus.
2. Invite people to review the data. Invite initial comments or questions, then segue into generating insights.

Materials and Preparation

Materials can range from simple charts on flip chart paper or a virtual white-board to graphs generated by a spreadsheet program.

Satisfaction Histogram

Description and Rationale

Team members use a histogram to gauge individual and group satisfaction with practices and processes. This is a point-in-time measure but may become a baseline for assessing change over time.

Alternative Use

 This activity also works great as a setting the stage activity!

Time Needed

5–10 minutes

Facilitator Guide

This activity highlights how satisfied team members are with a focus area. It provides a visual of the team's current status in a particular area to help the team have deeper discussions and analysis. It shows differences in perspective among team members.

The goal is to keep individual responses anonymous and produce a summarized picture of the satisfaction level of the team as a whole. In person, the retrospective leader can collect responses and shuffle them before posting. When using a tool, use anonymous mode if available.

Steps

1. Introduce the activity by commenting that the team will create a baseline measure that they can reexamine in future retrospectives to track progress.

2. Review the histogram definitions and distribute physical or digital blank notes, one to each team member. Ask each team member to write a number from 1 to 5 on their notes to indicate their satisfaction level.

3. Keeping the responses anonymous, collect the notes and ask for a volunteer to mark the graph as you read them. Read the number on each card. Wait for the tally before going on to the next.

4. Read the results from the graph. Ask for comments.

You may comment on the data yourself, for example, "It seems we have three people who are very satisfied on this team and two who aren't, and the rest of us are somewhere in the middle. As we continue with our retrospective, we can keep these results in mind as we choose experiments for the next iteration. We'll check back to remeasure in a few iterations."

Materials and Preparation

Prepare two graphics. One will define the scale. The next example shows a scale from 1 to 5 with the accompanying definitions. Feel free to make your own definitions.

The graphic on page 109 lists only the numbers for the scale, with room to tally and display the results. You can use a visual like the following one or simply use tally marks.

How Satisfied Are We?
Teamwork

5 = I think we are the best team on the planet! We work great together.

4 = I am glad I'm a part of the team and satisfied with how our team works together.

3 = I'm fairly satisfied. We work well together most of the time.

2 = I have some moments of satisfaction, but not enough.

1 = I'm unhappy and dissatisfied with our level of teamwork.

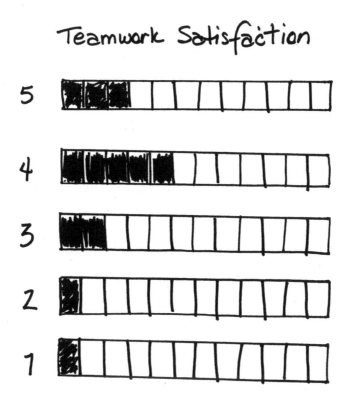

Notes

"Teamwork" is just one possibility for a satisfaction histogram. Some other possibilities are quality of the product, process, interactions outside the team, or engineering practices.

Team Radar

Description and Rationale

Help the team gauge how well they are doing on a variety of measures, such as engineering practices, team values, or other processes. Team members have communicated the factors about process or development practices that they want to examine. This activity aggregates and presents individual team member data for team review.

Time Needed

15–20 minutes

Facilitator Guide

Pay attention to clusters of ratings and ranges of ratings; each view offers useful information about the team's status.

The following image is an artistic representation of a virtual team radar on Retrium. In this image, the average is prominent and gives an overall sense of where the team feels they are. You may also find that the distribution of the ratings is helpful to inspect as it indicates the level of agreement and disagreement on the team about each topic. The richest discussion may come not from the average or distribution, but from exploring why people rated a particular factor differently.

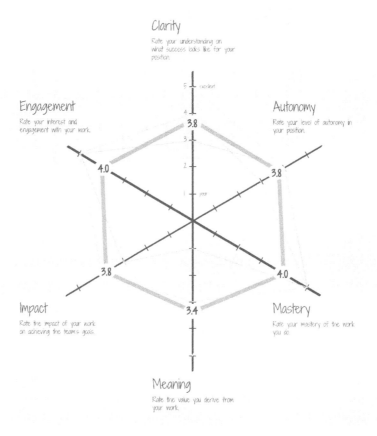

Steps

1. Introduce the activity by saying, "This is a set of factors that are important to our work. Let's assess how well we think we are doing, using a scale of 0 to 10. Zero means not at all, and 10 means as much as possible."

2. Display a blank radar graph with labeled spokes. Ask each team member to place a dot or some other mark on the chart that shows their rating for each factor.

3. Lead a short discussion about how the factors affect the work of the team. Consider asking questions such as the following:
   a. Where do you see us in strong agreement on these?
   b. Where do you see us diverging on these?
   c. What other patterns do you observe here?
   d. What's behind the ratings?

4. Save the completed graph. Run the activity again later, if the team hopes to see movement for this factor.

Materials and Preparation

If you know ahead of time what the team will measure using the radar chart, draw the spokes and label them ahead of time. If the team will brainstorm the measures during the retrospective, draw the radar chart during the retrospective.

Team Radar Story

The Team Radar enables you to gather subjective data that's intended to generate discussion. This is especially useful when you suspect there's no common definition or criteria to measure against.

For example, one team used a radar to examine how team members perceived their use of a number of engineering practices, including refactoring. One team member rated their refactoring at 8; another rated it at 3. During the discussion that followed, it became clear that each had different ideas on when to refactor. Further, the team member who rated her refactoring low was upset with the team member who rated his refactoring high because he was "slacking off by not refactoring enough."

Fortunately, the team was able to have a productive conversation about their differences. By the end of the retrospective, the team arrived at a common definition. Over the next few iterations, the team was more consistent when they refactored, and resentment faded.

Timeline

Description and Rationale

Use the Timeline activity to gather data about what's happened over a period of time and how people perceive those events.

Even when a team is in the same workspace, they may see and experience different events. A timeline allows people to see a bigger picture of what happened and includes multiple perspectives. In addition, a timeline can help stimulate memories and counteract recency bias—the tendency to give more weight to recent events. The following image shows the timeline from one team's retrospective. The events are objective—they actually happened. The energy line is subjective—it shows how people felt about events.

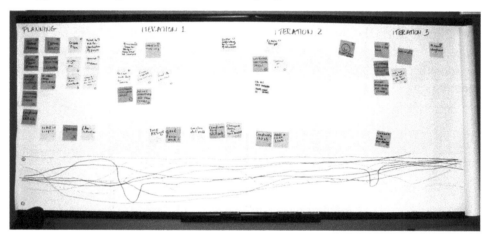

Time Needed

20–90 minutes, depending on the size of the group and the length of the increment of work.

Facilitator Guide

Group members write cards to represent memorable, personally meaningful, or otherwise significant events during the increment of work. Then, they post them in (roughly) chronological order.

Keep people who worked closely with each other together (affinity groups). It's better to have two small groups representing one affinity than one big group.

The retrospective leader supports the team in discussing the events, and the relationship between events, to understand facts and feelings that occurred.

Steps

1. Set up the activity by saying, "We'll fill in a timeline to create a fuller picture of the work we did during (fill in the period of work or interval). We want to see it from many perspectives."

2. If the team has more than five members, divide the team into pairs or groups no larger than five people.

3. Hand out markers and index cards or sticky notes, if in person. Refer to the stickies if using a virtual board.

4. Describe the process. Ask people to think back on all the memorable, personally meaningful, or significant events of the work interval. Ask them to write those down, one per card or virtual sticky notes. Remind the group that the point is to see many perspectives—so they don't arrive at a consensus about which events go on the timeline.

5. Time box the writing down activity. If you're color coding (see the next activity, *Variation: Timeline with Color-Coded Dots*), explain what the colors mean and post a legend.

6. Monitor the level of activity as people start talking about events and writing cards. If people haven't started writing cards after five minutes, remind them to start writing.

7. When the groups have a stack of cards, invite people to start posting them.

8. When all the cards are posted, invite the team to walk by the timeline and see what others have posted. It's OK for people to add new cards as they remember more events.

9. Take a break before analyzing the timeline.

Materials and Preparation

You can use an electronic or physical whiteboard, a series of flip chart pages, or a wall covered with paper to draw the timeline template. Which one you choose depends on how long a period of time you want to depict, how many people are involved, and your degree of comfort with the tools and/or materials.

Variation: Timeline with Color-Coded Dots

To provide additional subjective data on the team's timeline, ask the team to make one more pass at looking at the events and indicate another aspect of their experience during the increment of work.

For example, give each team member five dots of two different colors. Use one color for high points and the other for low points. Ask them to distribute their dots on the timeline event items.

Choose how you will contrast the highs and lows. Some options are "Proud"/ "Sorry," "Energized"/"Drained," or "High Impact"/"Low Impact." Pick the aspects most useful for the focus.

To debrief, look for items that have the most dots of a single color and ones that have a close to 50/50 mix, or any other intriguing pattern. Then invite the team to discuss what they see in the patterns.

Shared Data Provides the Foundation for Improvement

Very often, people skip this stage, assume everyone is on the same page, and jump straight into analysis.

Gathering data for a retrospective creates a shared understanding of data, events, and recent experiences. Individuals may feel differently about the importance of facts, but they can't argue about the facts that they've all witnessed together.

Once we have data, we can now discover the implications behind the data and the possibilities for actions, as we move to Chapter 7, "Activities to Generate Insights."

Activities to Generate Insights

Business culture often values taking action *fast*. Generate Insights helps the group slow down, think, and learn together. The benefit is gaining a deeper understanding of the issue(s) and avoiding surface level solutions. In Generating Insights, teams analyze data from the previous stage.

Get to Know the Activities

The following activities are grouped by the three different mental activities involved: interpreting data, seeking insights, and exploring options.

Activities to Interpret Data

These activities enable you to interpret the data we just gathered in the previous phase of the retrospective. It may seem obvious, but it's almost always worthwhile to explore more than one possibility.

- Pattern Spotter Questions, on page 116
- Fishbone Diagram, on page 117

Activities to Seek Insights

These activities help the team explore the data in fresh ways to uncover new ways of thinking.

- Circles and Soup, on page 120
- Force Field, on page 123

Activities to Explore Options

These activities prompt the team to develop and explore options—before choosing a course of action.

- Brainstorming/Filtering, on page 126
- Prioritize Issues, on page 128

The rest of this chapter explains these exercises in detail.

Pattern Spotter Questions

Description and Rationale

Viewing the data with a disciplined set of questions, the team will find insights, especially in complex situations (see *Adaptive Action: Leveraging Uncertainty in Your Organization [EH13]*, pages 39 through 43).

Time Needed

20–30 minutes, depending on the size of the team and the intricacies of the data.

Facilitator Guide

This is a fill-in-the-blank activity, in which team members complete four different sentences (see the following "Steps" sections). No endings are right or wrong. Ensure team members have enough time to offer multiple responses. Capture the answers on real or virtual sticky notes.

Steps

1. Introduce the activity as a way to learn from the data. The team will have a couple of minutes to consider how they might finish the sentences. Mention that each incomplete sentence builds on the ones before.

2. Introduce the first sentence, "In general I noticed..." Encourage participants to look broadly across the data to identify values, themes, or patterns that recur throughout the data. Write each ending on a separate sticky. Team members may read their answers aloud as they post them one by one. Or they may post them, and then someone in the group reads all the responses.

3. Ask about similarities and differences among the responses. Stay curious about why those might arise.

4. Continue the same pattern with the other four incomplete sentences:

   a. "In general I noticed..., *but...*" Look for exceptions to the commonalities.

   b. "On one hand I noticed..., and on the other hand..." Look for contradictions or something that seems to expose a tension in the team or system. Look for differences that may provide leverage points for improvements.

    c. "I was surprised that..." Look for the unexpected and emergent. Surprises hint at new insights.

    d. "I wonder..." When team members begin to wonder together, they begin to learn in the direction of their questions and ask, "What if?"

5. Carry the endings into the next activity as a base for further exploration.

Materials and Preparation

Display each incomplete sentence and choose a way to collect the team's responses. We usually use real or virtual sticky notes.

Notes

Reveal the incomplete sentences in order. The order guides the collective, collaborative thinking process.

If this activity clicks with the team, they may want more time to delve into the responses and the wonders. Allow for that if you can, or let their curiosity lead into another activity for insights or decisions that build on this one.

Fishbone Diagram

Description and Rationale

Also known as an Ishikawa Diagram or a Cause-and-Effect Diagram, Fishbone helps teams look for potential causes of the effects they are seeing. It provides a simplified system's view of interdependent areas and helps to identify possible places to look for quality improvement potential.

Time Needed

30–60 minutes, depending on team size and focus of the problem complexity.

Facilitator Guide

In this activity, the team seeks factors that may cause, contribute to, or affect a problem or situation. They use the diagram to organize their ideas and theories about causes.

After they've made an informed guess about which may be the likely causes, they can look for ways they can make small changes or influence those factors.

(Note: More than likely it's not one root cause but several contributing factors working together to create an emergent situation.)

Steps

1. Introduce the activity and explain how it will build on the prior data gathered.

2. Ask individual team members to remember the data they just considered and then write the first clues (ideas or theories) they perceive on sticky notes or lists.

3. If they have trouble getting started, ask prompting questions. For example, start with a single category and ask, "What are the [fill in a category name here] issues that may contribute to [fill in the problem here]?", "Who may be involved with [category name]?", "When does this most often occur in [category name]?", and so forth. Repeat for each category.

4. Transfer ideas directly onto the lines of the Fishbone diagram (which looks like a fish's skeleton). Discuss which of the proposed ideas may describe primary bones and which are secondary or third-level contributors.

5. Ask for more ideas, now that the discussion has started. Continue asking "Why is this happening?" As new ideas are added to the skeleton, adjust as needed to reflect new insights. Stop when the causes, ideas, and theories are outside the team's control or influence.

6. Discuss which items are actual causes. If the relationship between contributors and causes needs clarifying, that may indicate a possible action toward improvement the team can take.

7. Look for items that appear in more than one category. These may be the most likely causes.

8. Engage the group in looking for areas where they can make a difference. Use the results in the next phase, Decide What to Do.

Materials and Preparation

In advance, draw a blank Fishbone diagram (see the following image as an example). If you are on a remote team, find a retrospective platform that supports this activity. Write the observed effect, situation, or issue in a box at the fish's head. Label the bones of the fish with categories that are best fit for your focus. Typical categories are as follows:

• Methods, Machines, Materials, Staffing

- Place, Procedure, People, Policies
- Surroundings, Suppliers, Systems, Skills

You can use these in any combination, or the team can identify their own categories. Choose a set of categories that relates well to your retrospective focus. Add categories as needed.

The Fishbone diagram will end up looking like the following image.

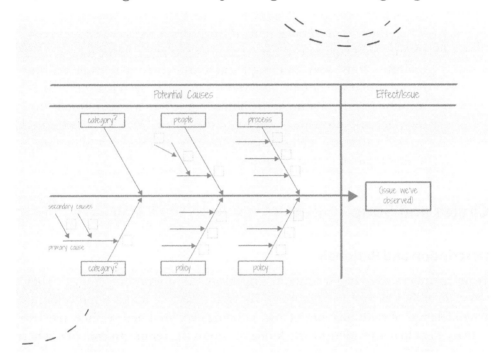

Notes

Use a Fishbone activity to dig into what contributes to the problem, but don't stop there. Fishbone looks at the problem space. Pair it with another activity to look at the solutions space.

If you suspect that a lot of what will come up in the retrospective may be due to issues outside the team's control, digging into all the problem sources may drain the team's energy. Choose a different method.

When the issues are more local to the team and under their direct control or potentially susceptible to influencing actions, the team may be energized by tackling the bones.

Fishbone Story

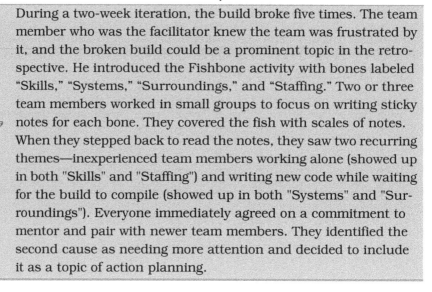

During a two-week iteration, the build broke five times. The team member who was the facilitator knew the team was frustrated by it, and the broken build could be a prominent topic in the retrospective. He introduced the Fishbone activity with bones labeled "Skills," "Systems," "Surroundings," and "Staffing." Two or three team members worked in small groups to focus on writing sticky notes for each bone. They covered the fish with scales of notes. When they stepped back to read the notes, they saw two recurring themes—inexperienced team members working alone (showed up in both "Skills" and "Staffing") and writing new code while waiting for the build to compile (showed up in both "Systems" and "Surroundings"). Everyone immediately agreed on a commitment to mentor and pair with newer team members. They identified the second cause as needing more attention and decided to include it as a topic of action planning.

Circles and Soup

Description and Rationale

Team members may begin to point fingers at the ubiquitous "they." "They" must do things before the team can move forward or make improvements. When feelings of victimization, blame, or being overwhelmed surface, use this activity to help teams identify the kinds of action the team can consider when they decide what to do.

Time Needed

About 30 minutes

Facilitator Guide

Blame kills retrospectives and the perception of persecution stalls any hope of forward motion. When this comes up, shift this conversation fast!

Team members may also perceive so much room for improvement they become paralyzed and can't decide where to start. Use "Circles and Soup" to help the team visualize their issues and clarify where they can take direct action.

Steps

1. Invite team members to contribute concerns that they've spotted in their data gathering and write each separately.

2. Display the foundation diagram for Circles and Soup. Describe the three circles. "Team Controls" is for concerns the team can improve on their own. "Team Influences" is for concerns that others control, but the team might influence. "Soup" is for policy, procedure, and environmental or organizational, system-wide concerns beyond the team's control or influence. Note that everything that affects the team will fall into one of these areas.

3. Ask team members to work individually or in pairs to decide where each concern belongs in the diagram. Give five to fifteen minutes, depending on the number of items the team has generated.

4. After all the items have been placed, ask the team members to reflect. What do they notice about the distribution of items? What do they notice about the concerns they surfaced? If these are redundant or closely associated, group them closer together.

5. Describe the different kinds of actions (direct, persuading, or responding) available to the team in each circle of the diagram. Which are more or less relevant to the focus of the retrospective?

6. Ask team members to work in pairs to address one or two items with the retrospective's focus theme in mind. Their task is to develop one or two ideas for improvement actions for each item.

7. Take those ideas for improvement actions into the next phase, Decide What to Do. Preserve the whole populated diagram to use for considering focus themes for future retrospectives.

Materials and Preparation

Prepare the template in advance, or quickly sketch it out in response to the team's need (see the Circles and Soup illustration on page 122). Make sure you draw the circles large enough to accommodate a lot of items.

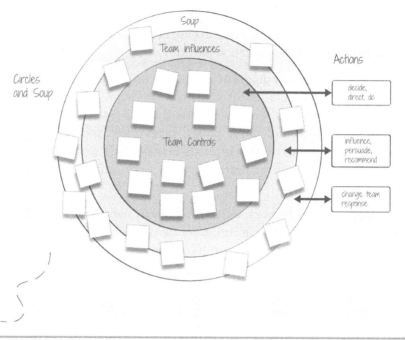

Mark's Story

Mark Kilby, Distributed Agile Guide and founder of K5 Labs, turns to Circles and Soup in a variety of retrospective situations, particularly those that span organizational boundaries. He shared a few typical times when he added it to his retrospective design.

"So let's say the team is having a little bit of a head-butting competition with another team. Their retrospective could become a blame game. I would suggest that we invite the other team." He expects the teams to react cautiously at the idea and is ready to say, "I know that makes you uncomfortable, but what would make you comfortable? What would make it safe for you to really engage in some open dialogue around the issue?" When the teams come together, he said, "We set some ground rules and we split up and do something like a Circles and Soup exercise."

Circles and Soup "is really good for when the team struggles with multiple issues and they don't feel like they have control." He added a practical analogy, "For those of us here in good old Florida, we have hurricanes. We can't control or influence those hurricanes, but we know how to react and prepare for them. And I've certainly been through my share of organizational hurricanes."

Force Field

Description and Rationale

Use Force Field to examine what factors in the organization will support a proposed change and which will inhibit the change. This activity is best in a single team-sized group at any level of the organization, from senior leadership to delivery teams. Use Force Field as a planning exercise to create viable ideas to take into the next phase—Decide What to Do.[1]

Time Needed

45 to 60 minutes, depending on the complexity of the desired change under discussion. More complexity will take longer.

Facilitator Guide

The team defines a desired state they want to achieve. Work in groups no larger than five to identify the factors that could either constrain or enable the change they want. Examine the linkages between factors. For example, the desire for a better-trained staff might lead to a factor of employee development. On the other hand, the costs of such development might lead to a factor of budgetary constraints or time away from work.

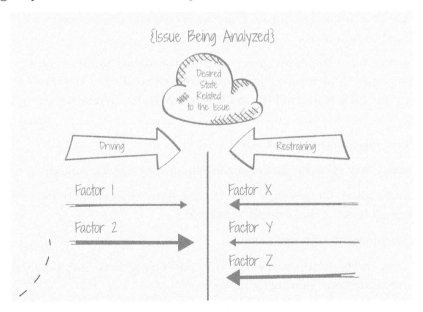

---

1.   https://doi.org/10.1080/14697017.2013.788052

Steps

1. Describe the following process overview, then break the group into smaller groups of three or four people.

   a. "Each group works for __ minutes to identify factors that will enable or support the change."

   b. "We'll do a round-robin report of what you discover and post the results. Then we'll repeat the process for restraining or inhibiting factors."

   c. "We'll also look at which factors stand alone and which are linked."

   d. "After we've listed all the factors and links, we'll assess their relative strength and discuss what course of action would be most helpful for implementing the change we want."

   e. Monitor time and activity level.

2. While the groups are working, prepare a blank diagram similar to the one shown in the previous Force Field analysis figure. Don't fill in the factors yet.

3. When the group is finished with the first task (identifying enabling or driving factors), collect factors in a round-robin fashion, asking for one factor at a time. There's no need to repeat duplicates; collect only the unique factors.

4. If you've used breakout groups, bring the whole group back together. Examine each factor and gauge its strength relative to the other factors. Place the factors around the central line to indicate relative strength. Do this first for unlinked enabling factors.

5. Repeat for constraining factors.

6. Discuss how constraining and enabling forces may be linked.

7. Identify which factors may produce the most effective actions, or where the team has the most direct influence.

8. Move the group into discussion:

   a. Ask the team members how they can strengthen enabling factors or mitigate constraining factors.

b. Ask the team members whether enhancing enabling factors or reducing constraining factors is more likely to achieve the desired state.

9. Wrap up the activity by asking the group which ideas they will choose for deciding on possible improvement actions. Document the ideas.

Materials and Preparation

Identify an issue to analyze, perhaps from a list of proposed improvements or another generating insights activity.

Notes

Force Field Analysis is another tool that ensures that the changes your team identifies in their retrospective actually happen. Combine creating the Force Field Analysis graph with a discussion of influence and control. What can the team directly control to make a change? What can't they control, and where are their points of influence in the situation? Most teams have more ability to influence conditions than they realize. However, a team needs to think about the most effective ways and times to use their influence.

Influence the VP—a Story

A team came into their retrospective wanting to change the way they interacted with the product owner. They felt dissatisfied with the limited contact and communication that occurred during their recent work. The product owner considered their questions, but only provided answers after several days had passed. The team was frustrated with the wait.

 Before they analyzed the situation by drawing a Force Field Analysis poster, they understood that the product owner's travel schedule and the times of availability were outside their control. After their Force Field discussion, they also saw they could exert influence best by explaining their concerns (enabling factor) to the VP of Marketing, another person with a crazy travel schedule (constraining factor).

The Force Field also showed that tracking down the VP would take more team effort than they felt they could afford. Instead, they made plans to get the most out of the few product owner contacts available to them.

Brainstorming/Filtering

Description and Rationale

When there's a long list of possibilities, whittling the list down to a reasonable few can take a lot of time. This activity helps the team members identify the most viable ideas and create criteria for what constitutes a "reasonable" number of ideas that have a high potential for follow-through.

Time Needed

25–45 minutes

Facilitator Guide

This activity helps a team brainstorm and filter their ideas against a defined set of criteria. Team members can generate ideas using the brainstorming method that fits them best (Method 1, 2, or 3) and then test whether each idea applies to the current situation. Choose a method while planning your retrospective.

Steps

1. Introduce the activity. To move beyond their usual thinking, the team will spend the next chunk of time brainstorming. Once they've generated new approaches, they'll filter the ideas to find the ones that fit best for their situation.

2. Describe the guidelines for brainstorming:

   a. Strive for quantity. The best ideas are rarely the first ideas offered.

   b. Offer all ideas, no matter how silly. Don't edit; throw ideas into the mix and filter them later.

   c. Be outrageous, humorous, and wild. (You never know what crazy idea will stimulate another team member's creativity.)

   d. Build on the ideas of others.

   e. Withhold judging, evaluating, or criticizing. Filtering comes later.

   f. Build a visible record of all the ideas.

3. Challenge the group to come up with fifty ideas, but set a time limit that adds to the challenge, usually ten to twelve minutes. Few teams can find fifty ideas in this amount of time, but the challenge usually gets them past habitual thinking.

4. Describe which brainstorming method you will use. Brainstorm using one of three methods:

    a. *Brainstorming Method 1: Free-for-all.* People call out ideas at random. (This tends to favor the extroverts and loquacious team members.)

    b. *Brainstorming Method 2: Round-robin.* Pass a "talking token" around the circle. Only the person holding the token can talk. It's OK to pass when your turn comes. Encourage folks to pass the token quickly to get to fifty ideas within the time block. Encourage listening to each other's ideas as the token moves around the circle.

    c. *Brainstorming Method 3: Individual lists.* Give people five to seven minutes to silently and individually generate and write down as many ideas as they can. When the time is up, use Brainstorming Method 1 or 2 for ten to fifteen minutes.

5. Monitor time, and call when the time has run out. If you haven't reached fifty ideas, ask the group if they'd like more time. If they do, ask them how much time they estimate they'll need to get to fifty ideas.

6. Ask the group what filters they should apply to the ideas. Accept four to eight suggestions and briefly discuss the merits of each. Then vote using a show of hands to determine the top four. Make the four selected filters visible to everyone on the team.

7. Apply the filters one at a time to the ideas on the brainstorm lists. Eliminate items that don't pass the filters. Highlight ideas that pass each filter.

8. Look for ideas that pass all four filters.

9. Ask for comments on the ideas. Ask the group which ideas they *want* to carry forward. Which will have the greatest beneficial impact? Which do team members feel the most energy and enthusiasm about to pursue?

10. Ask whether anyone feels strongly about taking responsibility for any of the ideas. If someone does, it's a good bet that it will carry forward. Otherwise, use the simple majority vote.

11. Carry the selected ideas into the next phase, Decide What to Do.

Materials and Preparation

Choose ahead of time which method of brainstorming will work best with your team. Make brainstorming guidelines that will remain visible to the group.

Create a list of examples of possible filters. Some possibilities are:

- It can be done by our team.
- It fits within our budget.
- It doesn't affect a release date.

Notes

Brainstorming has been around for years, and many people have heard of it. The problem with traditional brainstorming (Brainstorming Method 1) is that it favors people who are comfortable thinking aloud. It also favors people who are comfortable shouting out their thoughts in a group. That leaves out many smart, creative people.

Brainstorming Method 2 helps people participate who otherwise aren't comfortable shouting out in a group. It also leaves an escape (by saying "pass") for people who haven't thought of anything…yet. It can help to encourage fast movement around the circle. Provide a way for team members to capture key words for ideas that come to them when it's someone else's turn to talk.

Brainstorming Method 3 helps people who need time to gather their thoughts. Then they're ready to participate in Brainstorming Method 1 or 2.

Prioritize Issues

Description and Rationale

When team members need an easy way to select among several good ideas to find a viable improvement action, prioritizing can help. Prioritizing with dots helps a group narrow down a long list of items.

Time Needed

5–20 minutes, depending on the number of options and the size of the group.

Facilitator Guide

The facilitator can gauge how the group prioritizes a long list of candidate changes, proposals, and so forth, for future retrospectives. Introduce the activity by saying, "We have a great list; we can't pursue all of the items, so let's see what the group views as the top priorities."

Steps

1. Give each team member ten dot votes. Post a legend allocating the dots.
   a. #1 priority receives four dots
   b. #2 priority receives three dots
   c. #3 priority receives two dots
   d. #4 priority receives one dot

2. Read the dot allocation scheme. Review the items under consideration. Ask for clarifying questions about any of the items.

3. Allow a few minutes for people to place their dots next to the items under consideration.

4. Count the number of dots on each item. Write the number next to the item.

5. When it's clear which items have received the most dots, ask the group whether they want to proceed with these items.

6. When there's a tie at the top (four or more items receive the same number of dots) and it's not feasible to pursue all the top issues, ask the group to discuss why they see each one as a top priority, and then revote (preferably with a different color of dots).

Materials and Preparation

Choose a method of voting with dots.

You can have people put check marks next to the items, but dots are more fun and easier to count.

Notes

1. We've found that we get significantly different results depending on how we phrase a question. Here are some variations to consider:
   a. Which is the most important to work on?
   b. Which will have the greatest impact?
   c. Which do you want to work on most?

2. Keep in mind, you want action and decisions the group will support. The best choice is the one the team will do something about.

With Insights It's Time to Decide What to Do

The best activities to generate insights provide the team with opportunities to build on their data and gain more understanding of its impact and implications for the team. We look for ways to stimulate "aha" moments. Very often this phase appeals to knowledge workers, like software developers, because they prefer analytical thinking techniques.

Now that your team has insights about the problems it faces and potential actions, it's time to transition into deciding what to do.

CHAPTER 8

Activities to Decide What to Do

You're almost at the end of your retrospective, but not quite. The team needs to decide what to do.

In the Generate Insights phase, the team examined the issue and started to develop their ideas on how to address the situation.

The Decide What to Do phase moves the team's focus to the next time period. Usually, the team decides on some sort of action or experiment. They may also choose a learning goal, a plan to influence someone (to address an issue outside their control), or simply realize that they need to change their own response. There are also times when there is no "action," but reflection, or internal commitment. We discuss each of these in more detail in Chapter 12, Catalyzing and Sustaining Change, on page 201.

Even when one course of action seems in some way superior to others, if people don't have the will to do it, it won't get done. We prefer forward motion over "optimal" or "most important" actions.

Get to Know the Activities

The method you use to decide what to do depends on whether the team is evaluating options on the merits or expressing a preference. We have activities for both.

Sometimes a discussion gets stuck in details or takes on the tone of arguing back and forth. Then it's time to test for agreement. This isn't necessarily a binding vote, but a way to see where people stand. Often there's more agreement that might be suggested by the tone of the conversation.

We've included activities that gauge preference, test for agreement, and evaluate options. Sometimes, there's not a clear path. Then the path forward may be an experiment to learn and gather more information.

Not the Whole Retrospective

 Teams have an unfortunate tendency to choose one of these activities as the only activity in their retrospectives. These activities, by themselves, don't constitute an entire retrospective!

Instead, their purpose is to help you decide what to do.

Gauging Preference

These activities are for determining what the team wants to work on without applying specific criteria. They can also be useful when time is short.

- Short Subjects, on page 133
- Express Preference/Dot Voting, on page 134

Testing for Agreement

Testing for agreement gets information about where people currently stand. It's not a vote or a binding choice. This activity gives a sense of how much support an option has prior to making a choice. After testing for agreement, the team may want to adjust options to address concerns.

- Gradient of Agreement, on page 136

Evaluate Options

When there are multiple viable options, testing them against criteria or comparing them can help the team decide.

- Compare Options, on page 137
- Impact and Energy Decision Criteria, on page 139

Design Experiments

Experiments are about learning more about a situation or testing assumptions.

- Design Experiments, on page 142

These activities are covered in detail in the rest of the chapter.

Voting vs. Testing for Agreement

 You may notice we don't have an activity for an up or down vote. That's in part because most people know how to do a vote, either by show of hands or anonymous tally.

A vote is a choice. It doesn't reveal anything about the strength of the voter's support—or lack thereof. People often vote for things they aren't crazy about because they view the alternative as even less appealing.

Voting is fine when you need to make a decision and move on, or when the stakes are low. When buy-in matters, testing for agreement before taking a vote can result in an improved option and better follow-through.

Short Subjects

Description and Rationale

Based on insights, develop ideas on what to do. Then choose what improvement action the team will undertake in the next period. Help to discover differing perspectives on actions related to the focus area, the data the teams looked at, and insights regarding the situation.

Categories may include the following:

- What Worked Well/Do Differently Next Time
- Keep/Drop/Add
- Stop/Start/Continue
- Prouds/Sorries
- Plus/Delta (related to focus topic)

Time Needed

10–20 minutes

Facilitator Guide

The team brainstorms lists of ideas for action in response to prompts.

Steps

1. Display the category to the team. Give team members 3 to 5 minutes to reflect privately and write notes.

2. Capture ideas using real or virtual sticky notes. Consider grouping the responses if you have a large number of them.

3. Ask the team to identify the top 20% of the items—those items they believe have the potential for the greatest benefit. Lead a short open discussion and then vote with dots. (See the next activity, *Express Preference/Dot Voting*.)

4. If there are more than two or three high-priority items, reduce the remaining number of issues to a manageable few.

5. Keep the brainstormed lists for a historical review at subsequent retrospectives to help identify areas of persistent issues.

Materials and Preparation

Choose a way to display categories in columns and a way to capture each individual idea. Ensure you can move the ideas to the appropriate column.

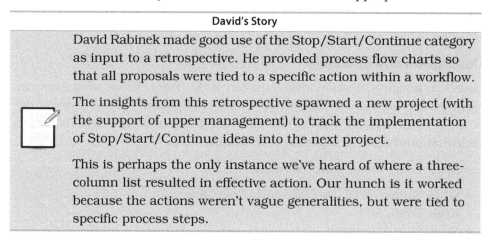

David's Story

David Rabinek made good use of the Stop/Start/Continue category as input to a retrospective. He provided process flow charts so that all proposals were tied to a specific action within a workflow.

The insights from this retrospective spawned a new project (with the support of upper management) to track the implementation of Stop/Start/Continue ideas into the next project.

This is perhaps the only instance we've heard of where a three-column list resulted in effective action. Our hunch is it worked because the actions weren't vague generalities, but were tied to specific process steps.

Express Preference/Dot Voting

Description and Rationale

Dot voting can be used to narrow a list of items or to select a final option. Dot voting expresses *preference* for items. It doesn't judge the merit of items. This is a relatively quick and familiar way to make choices.

Time Needed

5–7 minutes

Facilitator Guide

Options with more dot votes can be refined, or you can choose the one with the most dots and be done.

A general rule of thumb is to reduce the number of items by 3 and then add 1. So for a list of 6 items, the formula is 6/3 = 2 + 1 = 3. In this example, that would be three dots per person.

To narrow a long list to a specific number of top ideas, choose the number of ideas you want to end up with and add 1. Say you want to identify the top 5 ideas from a list of 20. The formula is 5 + 1 = 6 (or 6 dots per person). Be sure the result, X + 1, is less than the total number of ideas in the list. Specify that people can't use more than one of their dots per item (no one can throw all or most of their weight behind one option).

You can use physical dots, virtual dots, or have people make tick marks on the flip chart page.

Steps

1. Give each participant a fixed number of dot votes. Each participant places their dots next to the options they prefer. Eliminate the options with few or no dots.

2. Ask the group to identify the top ideas or the most preferred idea, depending on the goal.

Materials and Preparation

Create a way to display the list of items to choose from that will be easy for participants to assign their votes individually.

Choose your preferred way to calculate the number of votes per person, as described in the previous "Facilitator Guide" section.

Notes

The downside of dot voting is that it can be easy to game. All someone has to do is hang back, see where the dots are, and use all their votes to swing the result. There are ways around this, but they make it not so quick and easy.

One method that decreases the likelihood of gaming uses containers that resemble an old-fashioned ballot box—a covered container with a slot on the top. Create a container for each option, and identify it by option. Provide a number of tokens using this method. Participants drop tokens into the container associated with their preferred options.

Alternatively, collect responses written on cards, and tally them.

While these options reduce gaming, they add time and complexity. If the stakes aren't high, it's probably not worth it.

If you have a remote team, find an online tool that doesn't reveal the votes until everyone is done. This eliminates most gaming.

Gradient of Agreement

Description and Rationale

A Gradient of Agreement provides a more nuanced view of the degree to which people support or oppose a proposal. For example, if a team member is only mildly opposed to a proposal, it might mean that a small revision or adjustment would be enough.

A gradient also reveals when there's only tepid support. It's helpful to surface that rather than demanding a binary response.

Time Needed

5–20 minutes. If everyone in the group agrees, this may go quickly. If there's disagreement, allow time to modify options and address concerns.

Facilitator Guide

If responses are mostly high or mostly low, there is energy and passion around the proposal. You can work with that by hearing objections and soliciting revisions.

Ironically, when most of the support is mid-range, this is the clearest indicator to abandon the proposal and choose something else because no one cares one way or the other.

Steps

1. Display the gradient to the group. Ask the participants to place a mark on the line that represents their level of support for the proposal.

2. If everyone is at the top end of the scale, you know you have strong support. Ask the group to confirm.

3. When all the marks fall at the low end of the scale, ask, "What is the smallest change that would increase your support?" Consider options, adjust the proposal if possible, and test again.

4. If most of the marks are in the middle, the likelihood that team members will follow through is lower. Ask if anyone has a different proposal.

Materials and Preparation

Create a gradient that resembles the following illustration, with a scale of one to five (one being "veto" and five being "endorse").

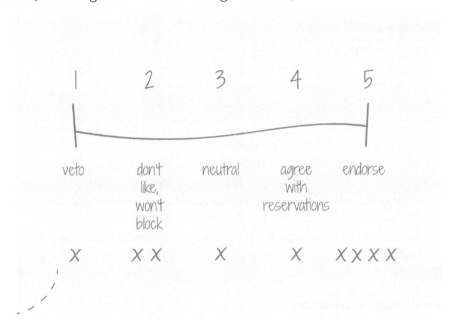

Notes

This is similar to the Fist of Five activity, familiar to many facilitators. In Fist of Five, people hold up the number of fingers that corresponds with the scale. Hopefully, they won't use the middle finger to indicate "one"!

Compare Options

Description and Rationale

This is a method for looking at two or more candidate approaches to address an issue. While you can use this approach for any type of issue, it's particularly useful for technical and process issues.

Unlike Gradient of Agreement or Dot Voting, Compare Options helps a group consider the *merits* of different alternatives. We've observed people often get tangled up in these discussions because 1) they aren't entirely clear on what's included in each proposal and 2) they talk about them all at the same time.

This process eliminates both those issues.

Time Needed

20–40 minutes depending on the number and complexity of the candidate approaches.

Facilitator Guide

Chances are good that some options will be obviously less suitable than others. But, if all would work reasonably well and none has undesirable downsides, make the final choice based on preferences. Or flip a coin.

Steps

1. Display the charts of the alternatives.
2. Invite the group to fill in the three columns of the first alternative.
3. Encourage the group to analyze the responses to the first alternative.
4. Move on to the second alternative proposal and repeat steps 2 and 3 for it.
5. If there's a third alternative, repeat steps 2 and 3 for it.
6. Restate the overall issue or problem the team is addressing with these proposals.
7. Now review each option, comparing, contrasting, and testing against the problem.

Materials and Preparation

Once the team has two to three proposals, provide a three-column template (see the following figure) for each proposal. In the title area labeled "Alternative" in the figure, briefly summarize the proposal. Label the three columns Plus (+), Minus (-), and Interesting (!).

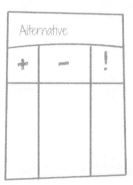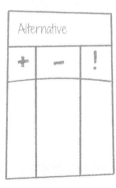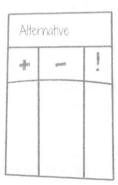

Impact and Energy Decision Criteria

Description and Rationale

We've heard many teams complain about the do-nothing retrospective. Team members generally have little difficulty identifying many things they wish were different in their work environments. They may make a choice based on what seems most important or most effective but fail to follow through. This activity helps to stimulate team members to follow through on action plans by following the energy.

For more on encouraging follow-through after the retrospective is over, see Chapter 12, Catalyzing and Sustaining Change, on page 201.

Time Needed

15-20 minutes

Facilitator Guide

Please don't be intimidated by the granularity of the following steps for this activity. It actually moves much more swiftly than this would suggest, and it provides a lot of benefits.

The purpose of this activity is to help the team converge quickly on a single improvement action that has the team's sincere commitment. The team makes action planning decisions based on three filtering criteria, and things get done.

In this activity the filters are the following:

1. How much team capacity will an action require?
2. What is the likely benefit the team will capture?
3. Most importantly, what does the team have energy for? What does the team really want to make happen?

Before facilitating Impact and Energy, you will build on ideas brought forward from your previous Generate Insights activity or proposals from the Design Experiments activity.

Steps

1. Introduce the activity as a way to evaluate the options for actions based on Effort, Impact, and Energy.

2. Review ideas for action from the Generate Insights activity, proposals from Design Experiments, or other sources that you're bringing forward from earlier in the retrospective.

3. If many options are available, winnow them down by a process of "first cut" selection. Depending on the size of the group, you may want the group to work individually or in pairs, and pick one or two ideas for actions they'd most like to explore. If an idea isn't selected, it's a good indication no one is interested in pursuing it at this time.

4. Add the selected ideas to the first column of the chart labeled "Option." Ask for any clarifying questions so that every team member understands all the proposed options.

5. Now, apply the filters Effort and Energy.

6. The second column, labeled "Effort," represents a rough estimate of how much work the option would take. Ask participants to use T-shirt sizes (S, M, L, or XL) to rate team effort. Use a judgment call for the collective effort estimate. Move quickly.

7. Use dot voting in the next column, labeled "Impact." Team members can use all their dots on one idea or distribute them across up to five ideas. Give each team member five votes (dots) to use for the ideas they think will have the greatest beneficial impact once implemented. Avoid asking for the "most important." It's an abstract concept and won't give the team the practical results they need.

8. Once everyone has distributed their votes, review the pattern of impact votes and write the total votes for each item on the list. Ask the group about the patterns they see between "Effort" and "Impact," if any.

9. Ask team members to vote one more time in the column labeled "Energy." This time each person has only two votes. Each team member checks in on their own levels of interest and enthusiasm for implementing every specific idea. They vote for up to two ideas that energize them the most. Use the questions "What do you really want to make happen for our team? Which ideas give you energy?" to stimulate the team. They can vote twice for the same idea if their energy for that one is particularly high or vote once each for two ideas.

10. Whatever the outcome from the "Effort" and "Impact" columns, suggest to the team that going with the idea that gains the most energy makes the most sense. It's the one they are most likely to follow through with.

11. You may want to add an additional column on the chart to record who will take the lead on the chosen action. Alternatively, just make a note. Then ask for one or two additional volunteers to support the lead person in case they need help or something gets in the way. Public commitment reinforces follow-through.

Materials and Preparation

Display the columns "Option," "Effort," "Impact," and "Energy" on a flip chart or online whiteboard. The following image shows what a chart might look like. Leave the columns visible, or consider covering the column titles until you're ready for the team to add their votes to that column. We've found this can add curiosity, playfulness, and interest to teams new to this activity.

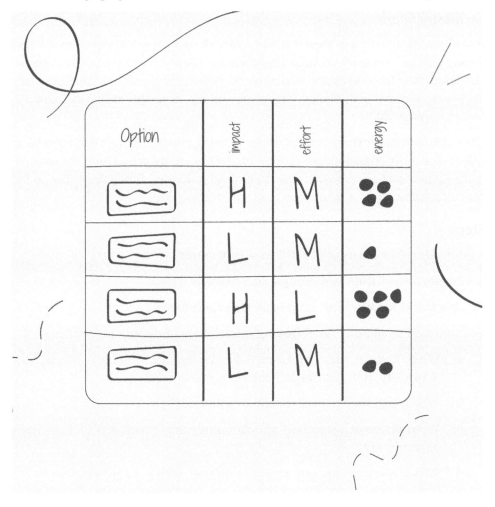

Design Experiments

Description and Rationale

When your analysis doesn't yield a clear action, it may be time for an experiment. Experiments are small actions designed to increase team understanding. Sometimes they reveal a path forward. But sometimes they show that the system didn't respond the way you thought it would—and it's time to try a different approach.

Time Needed

15–30 minutes

Facilitator Guide

Introduce the concept of experiments. Offer the group questions (see the following "Steps" section) to help them shape their experiment. The biggest challenge may be to keep the experiments FINE (Fast feedback, Inexpensive, No permission needed, Easy). For more, see the description of FINE experiments on page 203.

If the group is larger than four, consider forming smaller groups each of which will design a proposal for an experiment. Follow up by presenting the experiments. You don't necessarily have to choose only one. Since they should be very small, the team may choose to do more than one.

Steps

1. Introduce the concept of FINE as a mnemonic.

2. Divide into at least two groups, like pairs or triads.

3. Ask the groups to draft proposals for experiments.

4. Share all or some of the following questions as prompts for drafting:

    a. What factors may contribute to the current problem situation? (Curiosity and observation will help you here!)

    b. Which factors can you control or influence?

    c. What is your Description and Rationale for choosing this particular experiment?

    d. Which question are you trying to answer with your experiment?

    e. What can you observe about the situation as it is now?

f. How might you detect that your experiment is moving the situation in the desired direction?

g. How might you detect that your experiment is moving the situation in an undesirable direction or notice undesirable side effects?

h. What is the natural time scale of the experiment? When might you expect to see results?

i. If things get worse, how will you recover?

j. If things improve, how will you amplify or spread the experiment?

k. What is your hypothesis for the experiment?

5. Ask the groups to share briefly (in two minutes or less) their proposals for experiments. As part of the presentation, allow a minute or two for clarifying questions from the others.

6. If the choice seems obvious, simply have a confirming vote on which experiment to carry forward. Otherwise, consider using the activity Impact and Energy Decision Criteria, on page 139, to pick an experiment to implement. Express Preference/Dot Voting, on page 134, or Gradient of Agreement, on page 136, also can work well.

Materials and Preparation

Familiarize yourself with the list of questions in the "Steps" section before the retrospective. You can add your own questions or otherwise adjust the list.

Notes

In our experience, questions f and g are often the most difficult to answer. Most of us have been trained to think about Measurement with a capital *M*. So we look for big things to count, related to the big problem. That's not what is needed with experiments. With an experiment, look for indicators that the experiment is having an effect, even if it's a subtle one. For more on this, see Steering Signals, on page 215.

First Steps Toward Action

Some teams decide by argument. Then the best at arguing wins, not necessarily the best argument. Structured methods for choosing ensure that everyone has a voice in the choice. The best decision is the one that addresses the issue and that people will support.

By this point in the retrospective, the team has done a lot of work together. They've shared and considered data. They've developed insights and considered how to approach their focus issue.

Now, it's time to wrap up the retrospective—summarize, acknowledge contributions, and put a bow on it. We'll share ideas on how to do that in Chapter 9, "Activities to Close the Retrospective."

Activities to Close the Retrospective

The Close the Retrospective phase allows for reflection on what happened during the retrospective and gives team members the time and space to mentally and emotionally transition into other work.

We recommend that you routinely include an expression of gratitude during this phase. Gratitude adds a valuable tone and leaves the group predisposed to appreciate the facilitator's future efforts.

Get to Know the Activities

The Close the Retrospective phase includes activities that stimulate improvement action, reflect on participation, and reflect on the retrospective.

Activities to Stimulate Improvement Action

Create energy for improvement before the retrospective ends. Momentum will assist with follow-through. It can be as simple as creating a story card describing the improvement action and asking a team volunteer to carry it into the planning meeting.

Activities to Reflect on Participation

The success of every retrospective depends on the team members' willingness to participate. In the following activities, the team has the chance to hold up a mirror to itself to check how both the team as a whole and individual team members are interacting and maintaining a collaborative attitude.

Activities to Reflect on the Retrospective

Reflection brings benefits. A facilitator benefits from feedback on their work. The whole team benefits when even one person shows them the good that can come from seeking feedback. Use the following activities to help you improve your retrospective design and facilitation skills.

- Helped/Hindered/Hypothesis (HHH), on page 155
- Return on Time Invested (ROTI), on page 156

The rest of this chapter explains these exercises in detail.

Hopes and Wishes

Description and Rationale

Spending time to uncover each team member's hopes and wishes gives insight into ideas they may not usually speak about. Yet, our hopes and wishes motivate us and pull us into the future. In addition, once these become public and an explicit part of the team's context, members can aid each other in achieving their dreams for team success.

Time Needed

5–15 minutes

Facilitator Guide

Introducing a discussion of team members' hopes and wishes may strike team members as too "touchy-feely." Having aspirations is an integral part of human life, but people don't have much opportunity to share them, especially at work. When you first use Hopes and Wishes, introduce it as a team- and work-focused activity. Over time, team members may share more personal aspirations as they become familiar with the idea and gain benefit from it.

Steps

1. Use a script similar to: "We'll close this retrospective with one round of hopes and wishes. Each person may express what they hope will lead to greater team success. You'll have time to consider what you'd like to share. When it comes to your turn, you may also pass." Feel free to put this in your own words.

2. Give team members 1–2 minutes to consider their hopes and wishes for the team and its product. Explain that these won't be written responses and you don't plan to keep a record of who said what.

3. Ask each member in turn to contribute one hope or wish. The only rule is that no one comments on another person's response. Start with the first person and continue until each person who wants to state a hope or wish has done so.

4. Thank everyone for sharing their hope or wish.

Materials and Preparation

Choose the pattern for collecting responses: popcorn, alphabetical order, each one picks the next, or another process you like. Use a method that's fit for your team and that's fast.

Notes

Sharing "Hopes and Wishes" works best with twelve or fewer participants. More than that takes a lot of time, and people may become anxious. If you have a large group, break out into small groups of four to eight people.

Ola's Story

After a retrospective built around an Appreciative Inquiry themed retrospective,[1] Ola Ellnestam, CEO of Agical, closed with Hopes and Wishes. He wrote:

"We had planned on running a full 'Temperature Reading' as a closing activity. However, we ran out of time and opted for 'Hopes and Wishes.' By this time the group was steaming with positive energy and really going. Despite the fact that we had been going for pretty much 90 minutes straight.

"Hopes and wishes are stuff that the participants would like to see, or have happen, in the future. Like, 'I would really like to pair program more' or 'I wish I could visit our customer more often.' This closed the retrospective and kept that positive note right to the end. I will definitely do this again."

---

1. https://ellnestam.wordpress.com/2009/11/12/an-ai-retrospective/

One "Now" Thing

Description and Rationale

This activity encourages the team to start immediately with one tiny step in the direction they want to continue before they leave the retrospective.[2]

Action overcomes inertia and tends to create further action. By beginning their improvement action during the retrospective, team members build momentum.

Time Needed

5–15 minutes

Facilitator Guide

Use this as an ad hoc activity when you want to move the team from deciding what to do to beginning to *do* it. Before choosing this activity, assess whether the improvement action they selected seems amenable to an initial tiny step. You can't know until you're already at this point whether this is a good fit for closing the retrospective.

Steps

1. Thank the team for identifying their improvement action (and reiterate what it is). Invite them to get started with action now.

2. If you have one, tell a short(!) story about a small change that had a bigger than expected impact. Comment that every bigger action contains small steps within it.

3. Ask team members to take a moment (30–120 seconds) to consider possible tiny steps with the following prompting questions:

   a. What is one tiny step we can take now to move us toward our improvement action goal?

   b. Where can we act without needing permission from others?

   c. What can we do using only the resources and authority we have right now?

4. Initiate a short (five-minute) discussion on possible tiny steps.

---

2. https://www.liberatingstructures.com/7-15-solutions/

5. Use a simple voting process to choose one step and *do* it right then.

6. Congratulate the team on getting started toward their improvement goal.

Notes

You'll need to make the decision on leading this activity in the moment.

Have another possible activity you can use, if this one seems inappropriate. Consider leaving the determination of whether this is possible up to the team. They may see possibilities that you don't.

If they can't find an immediate tiny step, congratulate the team on getting their thinking started in the right direction. Then continue to close the retrospective.

Learning Matrix

Description and Rationale

In this activity, team members examine the retrospective from four perspectives. They get fast feedback on how the retrospective served them, in a short amount of time. The activity focuses on the types of learning available, including both content and team collaboration during the meeting. Team members can pull the most significant aspects, pro and con, from their interactions.

Time Needed

15–25 minutes

Facilitator Guide

Lead the group through examining their experience of the retrospective from four perspectives. The group gives themselves feedback so they can continue to improve their retrospectives. As shown in the figure on page 150, Learning Matrix is a quick way to capture feedback on the retrospective.

The lines demarcating the four quadrants of the poster tend to serve as natural "brakes" on the discussion for each section. People fill up all the quadrants and stop offering ideas when they get to the lines at the edges of each quadrant. Then ask, "What one additional idea about this quadrant should we include?" and write it around the title area. This ensures that the best ideas aren't lost and you can stick to the timebox.

Steps

1. After a brief discussion to reinforce the improvement action they will implement, encourage team members to take a meta-view of their retrospective experience.

2. Display the Learning Matrix template. Describe the four quarters:

   a. Top left, items they feel sorry or disappointed about: "What would we like to change?"

   b. Top right, items they feel pleased or proud of: "What would we like to remember to continue?"

   c. Bottom left, items that capture new ideas for future retrospective: "What new ideas would improve our retrospectives?

   d. Bottom right, items to express appreciation for teammates' contributions or quotes: "Who do we want to appreciate?"

3. Tell team members they can fill out the quarters in any order as thoughts come to them. Provide a five to seven-minute timebox for this part of the activity.

4. Add items to the chart in the corresponding section.

5. When the flow of ideas slows down, review the comments on the chart. Ask the group, "Is there anything you notice that's missing from these

items? What haven't we documented that will be important to going forward?" Lead a brief discussion, and make additions, if needed.

6. Give each team member five dot votes. Ask them to vote for the items that you believe have the highest priority to get attention for planning the next retrospective.

7. Acknowledge the prioritized list. Later on, you can use that as feedback for designing the next retrospective. Next time, you can also mention this feedback during the Set the Stage phase.

Materials and Preparation

Prepare a template in quarters with icons for the four sections: a "smiley face" for "What did we do well that we want to continue?"; a "frowny face" for "What would we like to change?"; a "light bulb" for "What new ideas have come up?"; and a "bouquet" for "Who do we want to appreciate?"

Notes

Ensure team members add their own comments, rather than you acting as a scribe.

Variation: Give every team member a stack of sticky notes (real or virtual) to write their ideas, one per sticky note. Each team member puts his or her notes in the appropriate quarter of the chart.

When You Need Fast Feedback for Your Retrospective

We introduce the Learning Matrix whenever we are pressed for time to close the retrospective. This can happen in sixty to ninety-minute retrospectives where the previous phases turn into longer discussions than we expected. We still want a rich feedback discussion, but we have to get it as efficiently as possible.

Offer Appreciations

Description and Rationale

Offer Appreciations is a versatile activity. You can use it to Set the Stage for appreciating how team members worked together. You can use it to Close the Retrospective to appreciate another team member's contribution to the meeting. You can use it as a refreshing pause in the middle of the retrospective if the team needs a break.

Time Needed

Officially, 15-30 minutes, depending on the size of the group. In reality, allow two to three minutes per the number of people present. Some will need less time, others will need more. Prepare for flexibility.

Facilitator Guide

This activity fits well for many different retrospective focus themes. Used in the Close the Retrospective phase, this activity makes for timely, encouraging feedback on participative, collaborative behavior in the meeting. Keep in mind that offering appreciation is always optional. Everyone doesn't need to offer or receive an appreciation every time.

Use this activity to end the retrospective on a positive note. For more details see *The Satir Model: Family Therapy and Beyond [Sat91]*.

Steps

1. Introduce the activity by saying something like, "As we think back on our collaboration, let's take this opportunity to notice and appreciate how others have contributed during the retrospective."

2. Demonstrate the form of appreciation with a team member. Even though it's a demonstration, choose a person that you can speak to sincerely.

3. Say the name of the person, then, "I appreciate you for____." Fill in the blank with something they do or did. You can also add a brief description of the impact on you. As an example, "Jody, I appreciate you for helping me understand the customers' need for the X feature. You really helped me rethink my comments."

4. Remind everyone that offering appreciation is optional.

5. Sit down. Wait. Someone will offer an appreciation. Then someone else, and then the ball will get rolling. Someone may ask if they can offer more than one. When the appreciative comments slow down, wait. Allow silence. Count to twenty (or more) in your head if the silence feels uncomfortable. You may feel like you aren't doing anything, but you are. You are allowing a generative silence for the group.

6. When a minute or so has passed with no one speaking up, appreciate the group and then close. Alternatively, if the group is on a roll, point out that it's possible to appreciate others outside the retrospective and bring the meeting to a close.

Materials and Preparation

Write up the form so that it's visible to everyone and no one has to rely on their memory.

"*Person's name*, I appreciate you for..." (option: add the impact they had on you).

Decide in advance how you will invite the participants to offer their appreciations. One at a time works best in smaller groups or highly cohesive teams.

In larger groups, you can let everyone go at once in an "appreciations melée." It saves time and generates energy as people get out of their chairs and scramble around to get to all the folks they want to appreciate.

The "everyone at once" can also be more comfortable for team members who shy away from being called out in public in the spotlight.

Notes

Used in the Set the Stage phase, the Offer Appreciations activity is a closing for the previous work chunk and a chance to start off the upcoming work on a good footing. With it, you make a space for team members to notice and appreciate each other and the value they bring to the team. Appreciations may pop up for helping one person, contributing to collaboration, solving a problem, and many other interactions.

When the team is working remotely, Offer Appreciations works with the online gallery, as well. After you demonstrate, invite the team to leave space after each person offers an appreciation. Explain the option to pass. Some teams "pass the ball." One person offers an appreciation, then the receiver becomes a giver to someone else, and so on around the team.

This activity has several tricky parts for new facilitators.

Tricky part 1: New facilitators worry that no one will be willing to share. In reality, we've never seen it go awry. It's fine if the group only generates one appreciation the first time. The person you appreciate in your example demonstration may be the only one who gets appreciated, and that's OK. You're building momentum for the future. Practice brings comfort.

Tricky part 2: People tend to add a lot of extra words that reduce the impact of their appreciation. When someone says, "I'd like to appreciate (Name) for...." while looking around the room, it doesn't carry the same impact as "(Name) I appreciate you..." while looking them in the eye. We often comment, "Well, if you'd *like* to appreciate them, why not just do it?" There may be a cultural component in the way people phrase appreciations. If people persist with saying "I'd like to appreciate," let it go.

Tricky Part 3: People may shy away from this activity. One time, a project manager said, "Our developers will never go for that! They're engineers. Anyway, they know we appreciate them." The project manager never noticed the engineers shaking their heads in disagreement. That felt sad. Every time we've brought this activity to a group, members have made genuine and heartfelt appreciations. And you can see the other team members light up when they receive an appreciation.

The Offer Appreciations activity also works for setting the stage, during a daily standup meeting, or anytime really. It's a great feeling when you notice team members spontaneously appreciating each other throughout their daily work. That happens most often when they've had the chance to get used to the idea in their retrospectives. In our experience, most teams take to "offering appreciations" quickly and enjoy it.

One group told us later that they'd done only one thing as a follow-through from their retrospective: "We started using appreciations at our weekly meeting. It's changed the way we relate to each other. We don't have fights anymore. We still disagree, but now we know that we really do value each other. And that makes the tough times easier."

Irene's Story

Offer Appreciations has become one of the most popular activities from our first edition. When we asked our retrospective facilitator colleagues for stories from their real lives, we received several that reflected its popularity.

Irene Asay, Scrum Master at Titansoft, gave the Offer Appreciations activity a new twist by adding a few prompting questions in setting the stage. She had designed a retrospective for a newly formed team made up of two previously separate teams. She asked the new team members to form pairs and interview their partners. She suggested three topics for the report:

1. What were some interesting things I found out about my partner that I did not know before?

2. What skills/values have I learned from my partner?

3. What do I want to keep learning from my partner?

Helped/Hindered/Hypothesis (HHH)

Description and Rationale

The Helped, Hindered, Hypothesis (HHH) activity highlights team learning and encourages team members to think about how and what they learn best. As teams focus on whole-team learning, they get better at it.

Time Needed

5–10 minutes

Facilitator Guide

Gather feedback from team members to discover what helped the group in three areas. They give feedback on working and learning together during the session. They find out what got in the way of their effectiveness in the retrospective. They offer ideas for the facilitator and participants. about what else to try in future retrospectives.

Steps

1. Show a three-column chart. Ask the group for help to become a better retrospective leader with feedback on this retrospective. Point to the three columns and explain how each represents things about the retrospective:

    a. Helped: Things that helped the team to think as a group and learn about the iteration.

b. Hindered: Things that hindered or got in the way of thinking or learning.

c. Hypothesis: Things (their hypotheses) you could do differently to improve the next retrospective.

2. Ask team members to add responses to the chart with their initials on each note.

3. End by thanking the team. Let them know you will review their notes and use them to help improve your facilitation. Ask whether you may contact team members later if you need clarification or have questions.

Materials and Preparation

Prepare a blank three-column chart, each column titled, "Helped," "Hindered," and "Hypothesis."

Discovering the Split: A Story

When a team ended its retrospective with HHH, they noticed that about half the team wanted more individually focused activities and the other half of the team wanted more paired and small group activities. As team members discussed this split and what it could mean for future retrospectives, they realized these differences had implications for their daily work as well. The discussion alerted facilitators to pay attention to what activities they chose for their designs. The team also changed their midweek, hour-long, free-for-all status meetings to fifteen-minute, focused, daily standup meetings that better suited the needs of both groups.

Return on Time Invested (ROTI)

Description and Rationale

A classic from the first edition, the Return on Time Invested activity generates feedback on the retrospective process and gauges the effectiveness of the session from the team members' perspectives.

Use in the closing phase for any retrospective or at the end of any meeting you'd like to improve. This multi-perspective assessment of how the facilitator and the team used their time provides good subjective data.

Time Needed

10 minutes

Facilitator Guide

At the end of the retrospective, ask team members to give feedback on how well they spent their time. Examining the return on their time invested in retrospectives helps the team make wiser decisions about how they allocate time and effort. The team represented in the following figure finds the retrospectives worthwhile and can still make suggestions for improvement.

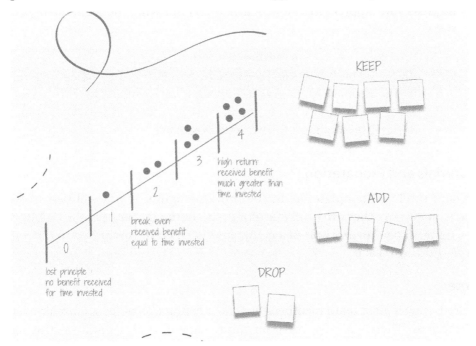

Steps

1. To introduce the activity, discuss the types of benefits that might come out of the group process. Types of benefits include:

   a. *Decision-making*—did the retrospective result in decisions that move the team forward?

   b. *Information-sharing*—did team members receive useful information or answers to questions?

   c. *Problem-solving*—were team members able to state and solve problems, find alternative solutions, and choose actions?

2. Show a blank graphic similar to the one in the previous figure.

3. Give each team member a dot to place near the number that reflects their personal assessment of the team's return on time invested.

4. After everyone has responded, ask those who rated the retrospective 2 or higher to say briefly what benefits they received. Then ask those who rated the retrospective 0 or 1, what they wanted but didn't get.

5. Even if many people rated the meeting at 3 or 4, ask the whole group to tell you what to keep or change about the process.

6. Express your appreciation for their help in improving the team retrospectives.

A Variation (Optional)

 Along the bottom of the ROTI area, create three sections and label them, "Keep," "Drop," and "Add." Ask team members to write sticky notes that reflect their views so you can refer to them when you design and facilitate future retrospectives.

Materials and Preparation

Prepare the ROTI template, as in the previous figure. If you will use sticky notes, make sure they are available along with dark marker pens for visibility. The figure shows an example of a completed ROTI chart, including the "Keep, Drop, Add" variation.

Notes

We're happy if most team members feel the meeting was at least a break-even investment. There's always room for improvement, and it's still worthwhile to ask follow-up questions. One team that gave high ratings to the retrospective found a better meeting room after thinking about what could change.

Don't assume that a rating of 0 means you did a bad job as the retrospective leader. A 0 rating may simply mean the person was distracted by outside circumstances or conditions in the room. Make sure to ask questions to discover the thoughts and feelings behind the ratings (*The Roti Method for Gauging Meeting Effectiveness [Der03a]*). It's so much better than wondering or trying to second guess a team member's intention.

Wrapping Up

Congratulations! The retrospective is over. The best activities for the Close the Retrospective phase provide the team with opportunities to give feedback to the facilitator, reflect on their own participation, and move toward the action they chose in the Decide What to Do phase. We look for ways to wrap up the retrospective and help the team move into their next work.

Chapter 10, "Retrospectives for Common Scenarios," shows how we can string these techniques together to design complete retrospectives based on common scenarios teams tend to face.

Retrospectives for Common Scenarios

We believe strongly that every retrospective should be unique–tailored to fit the people, focus, and context. However, when you're designing a retrospective, it can be hard to start from a blank slate. It can be tempting to rely on the flow and activities that you already feel comfortable with or the ones that have worked for the team before. Sometimes, it may seem easiest to string together whatever activities seem intriguing or fun. None of these habits are the best way to ensure you have an effective retrospective.

In this chapter, you'll learn how we might design a retrospective in response to a variety of common situations teams tend to find themselves in. You'll think about which activities are a good fit and how to fit them together into a coherent flow.

For each scenario, we've laid out one possible retrospective flow. Our examples are by no means the only way to do things and might not fit your context exactly. Still, we hope that the scenarios will get you started, give you some ideas, and help you think about creating a flow of activities that'll best support your team, given the topic they need to deal with.

We've organized the scenarios roughly from the easiest to the hardest, based on which seem to us to be the most challenging to design and orchestrate. What makes a retrospective challenging can be the topic, the team dynamics, or the complexity of facilitating the exercises themselves.

If you haven't yet read Chapter 2, A Retrospective Custom-Fit to Your Team, on page 23, and Chapter 3, Leading Retrospectives, on page 49, we recommend you start there, then come back here when you're done.

Many of the activities referenced in this chapter are described in the five previous activity chapters. However, we've also included a variety of activities that don't appear in those chapters. Some we found while researching retrospective activities online. Others we custom-designed as we considered the specific scenario at hand. As you gain experience with retrospectives, you may want to do the same. See DIY Activities, on page 44, to learn more.

Let's get started.

A New Team Is Forming

Your team is brand-new. Everyone is excited about what they're going to build together. People are looking forward to their collaboration. You're gathering the team together for a specific type of retrospective called a futurespective—one in which you imagine your project/product was already successful and look back on what made it that way.

One approach we recommend:

Set the Stage

Activity: Check-In

Instructions: See this activity on page 82.

Rationale: Allowing people the opportunity to share what's going on for them *right now* brings the team closer together, helps the team put aside concerns, and encourages people to focus on the retrospective.

Gather Data

Activity: What Went Well/What Didn't Go Well

Instructions: Ask everyone on the team to think about the best team that they've ever worked on. What went well with that team? Why was it so effective and enjoyable? Then ask everyone to think about the worst team they ever worked on. What didn't go well with that team? Why was it so ineffective and disagreeable?

Rationale: These questions are designed to help the group think through what they want and what they don't want with this new team.

Generate Insights

Activity: Report Out and Synthesis

Instructions: Share the work from small groups and create a smaller subset of action ideas to consider in the decision phase. This will move a step closer toward converging on the team's shared action.

Rationale: There will likely be a lot of data collected in the previous phase. A good way to make sense of the data is to split into smaller groups, ask each subgroup to look for characteristics of high- and low-performing teams, and report back to the whole group. This also gives the new teammates a chance to work together in a smaller setting.

Decide What to Do

Activity: Working Agreements

Instructions: See this activity on page 89.

Rationale: From the insights gathered in the previous phase, we recommend having the team commit to specific working agreements. In this way, the newly formed team will have agreed upon a way of working together based on their previous experiences on other teams.

Close the Retrospective

Activity: Hopes and Wishes

Instructions: See this activity on page 146.

Rationale: This team is excited to start working together. Ending the retrospective by holding space for hopes and wishes gives everyone the opportunity to share their positivity and excitement with one another.

After a Successful Release

The team just finished a successful release with no major issues. You want to take the opportunity to make conscious choices about how to maintain team cohesion and momentum into the next release.

One approach we recommend:

Set the Stage

Activity: Satisfaction Histogram

Instructions: See this activity on page 106.

Rationale: This activity gives everyone a quick picture of how satisfied people were with the release, both in terms of outcome and process. It'll help you understand the level of agreement (or disagreement) on the team about both the product they created and how they went about it.

Gather Data

Activity: Proud and Sorry

Instructions: Ask the team to write down and share what they are proud of and what they are sorry about with regard to the release.

Rationale: This goes deeper into the general sentiment of the Satisfaction Histogram, revealing more specifics about what the team might want to build on or shore up in the way they're working.

Generate Insights

In this case, we'd recommend two activities to generate insights. Start with the first before moving on to the second.

Activity: Pattern Spotter Questions

Instructions: See this activity on page 116.

Rationale: These questions help people make sense of data collected from Proud and Sorry, highlighting common threads and outliers.

Then move on to the second activity.

Activity: Drop/Add/Keep/Improve (DAKI)

Instructions: Ask everyone on the team what they would drop, add, keep, or improve going forward.

Rationale: Based on what comes up with the Pattern Spotter Questions, this will help the team hone in on more specific actions.

Decide What to Do

Activity: Dot Voting

Instructions: See this activity on page 134.

Rationale: The previous activity likely resulted in a large number of potential actions. This activity helps the team choose the ones it can truly commit to. If the chosen actions require more detail or planning, create a card to carry into the next release.

Close the Retrospective

Activity: My Team Is Amazing

Instructions: Ask each team member to complete the sentence: *My team is amazing because* _____, *and that makes me feel* _____.

Rationale: Taking the time to acknowledge and reinforce what makes the team special, along with how that makes each individual feel, can help encourage continuing team cohesion going forward into the next release.

Poor Feedback from Customers After Delivering a New Feature

Customers are unhappy with the latest feature release. The team is frustrated that it appears all their efforts went to waste. The product team and the development team are getting together to debrief.

One approach we recommend:

Set the Stage

Activity: Focus On/Focus Off

Instructions: See this activity on page 87.

Rationale: There's a potential for finger-pointing here, so cut that off from the start by focusing the team on positive problem-solving behaviors.

Gather Data

Activity: Present Objective Data About Customer Response

Instructions: See this activity on page 104.

Rationale: Having actual customer responses will help focus on the deficiencies in the feature, not the deficiencies in the people. Knowing what users like and dislike may reveal opportunities related to customer knowledge and design. Different companies will have different sorts of data available.

Generate Insights

Activity: Pattern Spotter Questions

Instructions: See this activity on page 116.

Rationale: These questions help people make sense of data collected in the previous activity, highlighting common threads and outliers.

Decide What to Do

In this case, we'd recommend two activities to decide what to do. Start with the first before moving on to the second.

Activity: Dot Voting

Instructions: See this activity on page 134.

Rationale: Pattern Spotter Questions may reveal one compelling area for action, but often several issues emerge. If so, you need to narrow down the areas for further investigation or action. However, if there is only one obvious issue to work on, skip the dot voting.

Then move on to the second activity.

Activity: Design Experiments

Instructions: See this activity on page 142.

Rationale: Look for small experiments to run that the team hypothesizes will improve one or more factors that emerged from the Pattern Spotter Questions.

Close the Retrospective

Activity: Offer Appreciations for the Team

Instructions: See this activity on page 151.

Rationale: Rather than offering individual appreciations, appreciate the qualities that this group of people brought to the table to work on this problem.

After an Outage or Issue

Whether it's a server going down, a security issue, a data leak, or something else entirely, nearly every team working on production-grade systems will eventually have to respond to unexpected and, at times, critical issues. Priority number one, of course, is putting out the fire. But beyond that, it's important to gather everyone who was involved in the incident together to discuss what happened, discover root causes, and look for opportunities to learn together.

One approach we recommend:

Set the Stage

Activity: Retrospective Prime Directive

Instructions: See this activity on page 92.

Rationale: When an unexpected issue occurs, team members may act on an impulse to start blaming others. By reaffirming the Prime Directive, we ensure our team is instead focused on curiosity and learning.

Gather Data

Activity: Timeline

Instructions: See this activity on page 112.

Rationale: Responding to critical incidents can be a chaotic experience for the team. In many cases, the nature of the incident demands immediate action that cannot wait for consensus building or information sharing. As a result, it becomes easy for the people on your team to experience the incident in widely disparate ways, at different times, or in different orders due to information delays. That's why constructing a shared timeline of events makes sense—it allows everyone to build a shared understanding of what happened.

Generate Insights

Activity: Simple Questions

Instructions: Use questions like "What can we learn from this?" and "What surprises you?" to prompt further conversation.

Rationale: Once the group has a shared understanding of the timeline of events, you have a choice to make as a facilitator. If the team is having a productive conversation organically, it might be best not to interrupt the flow.

Alternative Activity: Fishbone Diagram

Instructions: See this activity on page 117.

Rationale: Alternatively, there are situations in which it makes sense to do a deeper dive using a structured activity like Fishbone (especially when the problem spans multiple areas of concern). In this case, you should take a particularly complex or sticky issue from the Timeline and translate it into a problem statement that sets the context for Fishbone (for example: "It took excessively long to discover the data breach").

Decide What to Do

Activity: SMART Action

Instructions: See our description on page 202.

Rationale: Sometimes the conversation will lead to specific remediations or actions, in which case we recommend writing them down in a SMART way.

Alternative Activity: Simple Questions

Instructions: Ask the team "What have we learned?"

Rationale: Many times, simply gathering the team together, building a timeline of events, and building a shared mental model is enough. Learning is the primary goal, not action.

Close the Retrospective

Activity: Aha!

Instructions: Go around the room and instruct the team to complete the sentence: *"One thing I learned/was surprised by was..."*

Rationale: Your epiphanies from the retrospective may be different from your colleagues'. This activity gives everyone the opportunity to share with the group their own "aha!" moment to make sure what's obvious to one person is shared with everyone.

Time to Deliver Features Is Increasing

Both customers and management have noticed that the team's cycle time—the time from first commit to release—is increasing. The department director has asked the team to look into what might be behind the issue. (Note: Typically, the team chooses the focus for their retrospective. In this case, the director has instructed the team to make the increasing cycle time the focus of their retrospective.)

One approach we recommend:

Set the Stage

Activity: Check-In

Instructions: See this activity on page 82.

Rationale: This doesn't seem like a sensitive or contentious issue, so there's probably no need for specific working agreements around safety. A quick check-in will suffice.

Gather Data

In this case, we have presented two mutually exclusive flows. In Flow 1, you'll use data prepared ahead of time to examine a value stream map. In Flow 2, you'll gather data in the retrospective to find factors that influenced the situation.

Flow 1: Prepare Data Ahead of Time, Review During the Retrospective

Activity: Simplified Value Stream Map

Instructions: Create a diagram that shows the steps and handoffs in your process from feature prioritization through the point the feature is in use.

Rationale: Visualizing your process reveals inefficiencies.

Flow 2: Gather Subjective Data During the Retrospective

Activity: Finding Factors

Instructions: Brainstorm a list of factors that might influence the issue. Afterwards, ensure that all factors are neutral or positive and potentially measurable.

Rationale: Finding factors also points to system influencers that are potentially measurable. Rather than arriving at them through research, the team arrives at them by using their current knowledge of the system.

Generate Insights

Flow 1 continued

Activity: Examine the Value Stream

Instructions: Examine the value stream map by identifying areas that are obvious places for improvement, and areas that need more research.

Rationale: A value stream map lets you see where things get hung up, and where things take much longer than expected. They point to tangible starting points, based on data.

Flow 2 continued

Activity: Circle of Factors

Instructions: Choose ten factors that seem most relevant. Place them in a circle and draw one-way arrows to indicate which factors affect others.

Rationale: Get a sense of how the factors identified in the Gather Data phase interact and which ones seem to have the biggest influence on the overall situation. This is often sufficient for finding a starting point, especially when many factors contribute to the situation. You don't need to find the *perfect* place to start. You simply need a place to start.

Decide What to Do

In this case, we'd recommend two activities to decide what to do. Start with the first before moving on to the second.

Activity: Impact/Energy

Instructions: See this activity on page 139.

Rationale: The team may not have the influence, energy, or bandwidth to work on many of the areas they discovered. It almost always makes most sense to go with the energy.

Then move on to the second activity.

Activity: Create a Modified SMART Goal

Instructions: See our description on page 202.

Rationale: Since you're looking for something(s) to change in the system, you probably have a good idea of whether you want more or less of it. Figure out what to measure or observe. Keep in mind that the goal isn't a target, but rather an indicator that you hope to move either up or down.

Close the Retrospective

Activity: ROTI

Instructions: See this activity on page 156.

Rationale: While you won't have solved the problem in the retrospective itself, you should've gotten some concrete direction on how to unravel it. That in of itself can feel rewarding and hopeful. So, see how people felt about using their time in this way.

An Experienced Team That Doesn't Feel the Need to Run Retrospectives Anymore

Your team has been together for a long time and everyone seems to get along just fine. The product you're working on is successful. Recently a few of your colleagues said, "I'm not sure we need to run retrospectives anymore given how productive and happy our team is!" As a result, the mindset of many people on your team is that the upcoming retrospective will be a waste of time.

One approach we recommend:

Set the Stage

Activity: Constellations (on Topics Unrelated to Work)

Instructions: Make a nonwork related statement like "Star Wars is better than Star Trek" or "mountain vacations are better than beach vacations" and instruct the team to move closer to you if they agree and farther away from you if they disagree. Continue with additional questions until the energy in the room runs out or time is up.

Rationale: This activity isn't only fun and energizing, it also helps you learn more about your teammates. Even for groups that have been working together for a long time, this activity can help bring people even closer together.

Gather Data

Activity: WRAP (Wishes/Risks/Appreciations/Puzzles)

Instructions: Ask everyone on the team what they wish for, what risks they see, who or what they appreciate, and what they are puzzled by.

Rationale: Given the team's belief that this retrospective is going to be a waste of time, the goal of this activity is to uncover hidden information that helps the group learn about itself in a way that would have been unlikely otherwise. Does everyone wish for the same thing? Maybe, maybe not…

Generate Insights

Activity: Simple Questions

Instructions: Spur the conversation by asking questions. Choose questions like, "What surprises you?", "What does this tell us about our work going forward?", and "What patterns do you see?"

Rationale: Open-ended questions that prompt thoughtful discussions will help your team gain more than a surface-level understanding.

Decide What to Do

Activity: More to Explore?

Instructions: Review the answers from the previous phase and ask for insights or areas that need more exploration.

Rationale: In a retrospective like this, it's possible that the team won't arrive at a specific action but instead will have simply learned more about one another. That's perfectly OK! If the team started the retrospective thinking it would be a waste of time, yet ended the retrospective with the realization that it learned something—or that there's something deeper to explore in the next retrospective—that's a huge win.

Close the Retrospective

Activity: ROTI

Instructions: See this activity on page 156.

Rationale: This activity reveals the perceived value of the retrospective to its participants. Remember, this team came into the retrospective expecting it to be a waste of time. Was that still the case after the retrospective was over? This is how you find out.

The Remaining Scenarios Are Challenging

A caution is in order for the remaining scenarios—they are best suited for experienced facilitators ready to tackle more complicated and charged team scenarios.

To address a challenging team scenario in a retrospective, focus on safety first. Cautiously build the strongest possible context for difficult conversations. Sometimes you'll "stack the deck" with activities focused on creating the safest possible container for discussion and decision.

For example, in the next scenario, you'll notice that we have front-loaded the Set the Stage phase with three activities and used ESVP (normally employed to set the stage) for the Gather Data phase.

New Team Forming, Issues Loom

You sense that some people aren't thrilled to be on the team—whether they were assigned without consultation or for other reasons unknown to you. You've decided to address the issue head on. You hope to shift the energy, so that people feel just enough interest and affinity to become a team.

One approach we recommend:

Set the Stage

For this phase, we recommend the following three activities.

Activity: Introduce the Focus Topic and Agenda

Instructions: See this activity on page 81.

Rationale: Given that this isn't a team yet and trust hasn't yet been established, we recommend spending extra time setting the stage. If people aren't willing to open up at least a little, you won't be able to accomplish what you need to in this retrospective.

Set the focus topic as "How Do We Work Together?" Share the product vision and team mission stated as either the problem the team will solve or the benefit the team will create for which group of people.

This group isn't a team yet. If people aren't thrilled to be there, they might be skeptical or suspicious of the meeting. Our reasoning for sharing the team goal is that if it's compelling, that might be enough to spark some interest and energy. It is the context for this team.

Then move on to the second activity.

Activity: Retrospective Prime Directive

Instructions: See this activity on page 92.

Rationale: People may feel resentful or guarded. The Prime Directive can reduce judgment, which can lessen defensiveness.

Then move on to the third activity.

Activity: Working Agreements

Instructions: See this activity on page 89.

Rationale: This activity is a small way for people to create something together, as a team. They're agreeing on how they'll work and interact during the meeting.

Gather Data

Activity: ESVP

Instructions: See this activity on page 84.

Rationale: This activity puts it all out there—whether people want to be there or not. That can feel risky! However, dealing with the reality of the situation is the best chance of changing it.

Generate Insights

Activity: ESVP Continued

Instructions: Process the information from the ESVP exercise. Brainstorm and affinity sort using questions such as:

1. Looking at this information, what are the implications for this group if nothing changes?
2. No matter what your response is, what is one thing you might learn or get out of working on this team?
3. What ideas do you have that would make this a more energizing situation for you and others in the group?

Rationale: These questions assume that this situation is not inevitable, and the group can—at least to some extent—shape it.

Decide What to Do

Activity: Control/Impact Matrix

Instructions: Create a 2x2 matrix that compares Control and Impact. Control includes In/Out of Team Control, and Impact includes High/Low Beneficial Impact. Ask the group to place ideas from the previous phase in the quadrants.

Rationale: This is another opportunity for the group to do something together and to feel some agency.

Close the Retrospective

Activity: What Has Shifted?

Instructions: Check for movement. Ask who feels even slightly more positive about being assigned to this group.

Rationale: This offers the possibility that perspectives can change. If no one has shifted, acknowledge that and promise to check back once the agreed upon action is done.

Activity: Offer Appreciations

Instructions: See this activity on page 151.

Rationale: End on a positive note, and acknowledge the risk people took to share how they truly felt about being in this group.

A Team with Low Psychological Safety

You've started working with a team that has been together for a while. You've observed interactions where people bring up other's past mistakes. You've also noticed that the team seems to avoid talking about critical problems. Based on this, you have a sense that the team suffers from low psychological safety.

One approach we recommend:

Set the Stage

Activity: Fill-in-the-Blank (Safe/Unsafe)

Instructions: See this activity on page 95.

Rationale: When you ask if people feel safe or unsafe, these questions take us out of theory and into people's lived experience. They make the contrast clear in a visceral way.

Gather Data

Activity: Team Radar (Using Amy Edmonson's Seven Questions)

Instructions: See this activity on page 109. Use Professor Amy Edmonson's seven questions to assess the perception of psychological safety on the team. *The Fearless Organization: Creating Psychological Safety in the Workplace for Learning, Innovation, and Growth* [Edm18]

Rationale: Creating an anonymized radar using the seven questions from Amy Edmondson's survey asks people to reflect on their experience with the team. Because they focus on the team, they are less likely to focus on individuals.

Generate Insights

Activity: Use 1-2-4-All to Discover "What Would Increase Your Rating by One?"

Instructions: Begin by asking each individual to think to themselves, then move to pairs of two, then groups of four, before reporting out to the entire team.

Rationale: Focusing on what would make things better is likely to keep things positive rather than delving into past events. Keep in mind, 1-2-4-All naturally converges on a consensus view. If this occurs for your group, they've already decided what to do and you can move to the Close the Retrospective phase.

Decide What to Do

Activity: Dot Voting

Instructions: See this activity on page 134.

Rationale: If the team did not converge during the Generate Insights phase, help the team choose one action. The awareness they gained through learning about psychological safety and looking at their own team will probably result in additional spontaneous changes in individual behavior.

Close the Retrospective

Activity: Helped/Hindered/Hypothesis (HHH)

Instructions: See this activity on page 155.

Rationale: This activity invites people to offer ideas about what might improve the next retrospective.

A Conflict on the Team

There's a big conflict on your team, one that threatens to divide people. People have different interpretations of the facts of the situation. They're telling themselves—and reacting to—those different stories. Your plan for the retrospective is to make people aware of their different stories and with luck bring the temperature down.

One approach we recommend:

Set the Stage

Clarify that in this case, the desired outcome of the retrospective isn't necessarily action, but understanding. It's critical that the team comes into this retrospective with a growth mindset. The goal isn't to convince others about your perspective, but rather to learn from them.

Activity: Working Agreements

Instructions: See this activity on page 89.

Rationale: Given the emotions surrounding the issue, it's important to establish working agreements that can be used as guardrails on process and group norms. You might consider working agreements that prevent blaming and shaming, for example, or working agreements that maintain mutual respect by avoiding personal attacks or loaded language.

Gather Data

Activity: Facts, Stories, and Emotions (FSE)

Instructions: Ask everyone to share what unarguable facts exist about the situation. Remind the group that these must be indisputable. Then have everyone share what stories they hold about those facts. Explain to the group that a story is anything in your head that isn't a provable fact, and so could be open to interpretation. Finally, ask the group to share how those facts and stories are making them feel.

Rationale: Many contentious issues aren't the result of disagreements about the facts; they are the result of unsaid stories and unshared emotions built upon those facts. This activity has two benefits. First, it helps each person think through what parts of their story are unarguably true and what parts are actually just stories. And second, it enables the group to ensure everyone agrees to the same set of facts. If the group doesn't even agree on what is true, how can it possibly have a conversation about the stories people have?

Generate Insights

Activity: What I Hear You Saying Is

Instructions: Have individuals who disagree with one another paraphrase each other's stories.

Rationale: The goal of this retrospective is not to convince one another of your "side of the story." Rather, the goal is to better understand each other. Paraphrasing others' stories helps to increase understanding—*even if you don't agree with the story being told.*

Decide What to Do

Activity: Personal Insights and Resolves

Instructions: Ask everyone to write down at least three insights from the conversation.

Rationale: This activity encourages the team to think hard about what's come to light during the retrospective.

Close the Retrospective

Activity: Pleased and Surprised

Instructions: Ask everyone to share one thing that pleased or surprised them about the experience.

Rationale: By the end of the retrospective, the goal is to have a new appreciation for others' perspectives and stories and perhaps to loosen your grip on your own. Some of what was learned might even be surprising or even pleasant! Closing the retrospective by reflecting on this helps give the group an appreciation for their shared experience.

Elephant in the Room

Working on this team can feel like walking on eggshells. One issue in particular, the "elephant in the room," causes emotions to run especially high. People would do almost anything to avoid discussing it. Enough is enough. You decide to focus the next retrospective on the one thing that people won't discuss.

Not for Individual Issues

 If you sense that the issue to be discussed relates to an individual's performance or behavior (rather than to the group as a whole), stop. The retrospective isn't the appropriate space for having this conversation. Rather, handle these issues privately and directly. If that's not possible, or if it makes you feel unsafe, involve management and/or HR.

One approach we recommend:

Set the Stage

Activity: Ground Rules

Instructions: See this activity on page 92.

Rationale: Given the emotions surrounding the issue, it's important to establish agreed-upon ground rules that can be used as guardrails on process and group norms. You might consider ground rules that prevent blaming and shaming, for example, or ground rules that maintain mutual respect by avoiding personal attacks or loaded language.

Gather Data

Activity: Art Gallery

Instructions: Ask participants to draw a picture that depicts the situation.

Rationale: By definition, an elephant in the room means the group isn't *talking* about something important. But they might be willing to *draw* it! Drawing is a vastly different form of expression. Plus, it has the potential to inject some humor into the room at a time when everything otherwise feels serious.

Generate Insights

Activity: Simple Questions

Instructions: Ask the team open-ended questions like "What themes emerge from the pictures?" and "What patterns do you see?"

Rationale: Spur the conversation by asking questions. For some groups acknowledging the elephant is enough for now. Other groups may be ready to tackle the now-named elephant. So, the following are two potential paths forward.

Flow 1: Awareness Is Enough for Now	Flow 2: Ready to Tackle the Issue
Nothing. Proceed to the Decide What to Do Phase	Activity: Circles and Soup
	Instructions: See this activity on page 120.
	Rationale: This activity helps people see where they have control and influence, which might point people to ways they can respond differently to the elephant.

Decide What To Do

Flow 1 continued	Flow 2 continued
Ask whether there is energy to have another retrospective about this topic. If you get a yes, recognize that's a big step forward. If not, accept the team for where they are.	Activity: Dot Voting
	Instructions: See this activity on page 134.
	Rationale: Since the team seems ready to tackle the issue, this activity helps the team select one action within its control or influence.

Close the Retrospective

Activity: Offer Appreciations

Instructions: See this activity on page 151.

Rationale: Talking about the elephant in the room isn't easy. It takes significant effort and vulnerability. Give the team the opportunity to appreciate each other for their willingness to take this important step.

Flows, Not Plans

In this chapter, you have seen examples of different situations that a team and a facilitator might encounter and how an entire retrospective might flow from activity to activity to form a cohesive design. This idea of flow and of how the group's energy, enthusiasm, and curiosity drive inquiry and decision-making is critical to an effective retrospective.

The impact of an effective retrospective naturally flows forward into the future. Dropped actions and short-circuited learning are crucial signs that your retrospectives don't have this flow.

If you face any scenarios similar to the previous ones, use this chapter as a guide and a stepping stone to improvisation.

Part III

Considerations

The final section of the book goes over a variety of special circumstances and challenges that can be critical to retrospective success. These include how to facilitate retrospectives on remote and distributed teams, how to keep the improvement momentum going after the retrospective is over, how to handle issues beyond the team's control, and how to overcome objections to retrospectives.

CHAPTER 11

Retrospectives When the Team
Isn't Colocated

When we wrote the first edition, colocation was considered an absolute requirement for successful teams. Agile emphasized frequent and direct communication—with the assumption that meant in-person, ideally in the same room. In fact, having a colocated team is one of the Principles of Agile Software Development: "The most efficient and effective method of conveying information to and within a development team is face-to-face conversation."[1]

There's a lot to be said for colocated teams. There's ample opportunity for casual conversations that build camaraderie. Shared space makes shared learning via task walls and information radiators easier. Nothing gets in the way of pulling out a pack of sticky notes and Sharpies to generate ideas.

The figure on page 184 represents a colocated team. Everyone is in the same place.

Our Covid-induced "two year, 50-million-person experiment"—to steal the headline from a NYT article[2]—proved that remote teamwork still works. Working sessions happen over video conference. Frequent communication happens over chat. In fact, some teams work just as well remotely, and some work even better. Remote work doesn't mean the end of effective teamwork any more than it means the end of effective retrospectives.

But, as with colocated retrospectives, effective remote retrospectives require intention and planning. Fortunately, we've seen enormous improvement in tools that support remote work over the last decade.

---

1. http://agilemanifesto.org/principles.html
2. https://www.nytimes.com/2022/03/10/business/remote-work-office-life.html

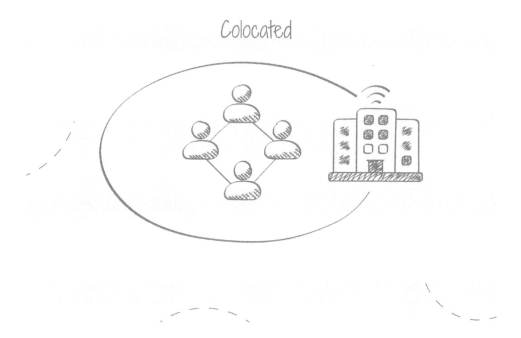

Video conferencing software is more widely accessible and easier to use than ever before. Online whiteboards more closely mimic the in-person whiteboards that inspired them. There's even been a blossoming of tools built specifically to support remote retrospectives, including Retrium (the product David and his team have created) and others.

In addition, knowledge and practices for creating collaborative virtual spaces keep expanding. We are big fans of *The Remote Facilitator's Pocket Guide* [CM20], for example.

In Chapter 2, A Retrospective Custom-Fit to Your Team, on page 23, we talked about considering the team's context, deciding on logistics, and selecting exercises. In this chapter, we'll focus on challenges unique to remote retrospectives and offer ideas on how to have a good remote retrospective—even a great one. To do so, you'll need to pay more attention to some aspects and tweak others.

Two Principles for Remote Retrospectives

Two principles can guide how you adapt to facilitating retrospectives on non-colocated teams:

- Equalize participation
- Increase certainty and clarity

Equalize Participation

In any retrospective, it's important to have a plan that enables all participants to have a relatively equal opportunity to participate. That's because equal participation is one of the most important predictors of a high-performing team.[3] The opposite—unequal participation—depresses collaboration.

With remote retrospectives, it's easier to disengage. Whether due to distractions like checking email, video conference fatigue (we'll talk about this later), or not being able to see everyone's faces, it takes more planning to keep everyone involved.

You will want to spend extra time finding a structure that supports (roughly) equal participation.

Increase Certainty and Clarity

Sometimes we learn by actively listening to others speak to us. Other times we learn by subconsciously listening to the "background noise" around us. This is called osmotic communication.

Esther gives this nonwork example, "I once surprised the heck out of myself when I recognized the call of a particular sort of tree toad. I hadn't made any effort to learn frog and toad calls, but someone in my household had. I didn't pay any attention, I learned as if by osmosis."

This sort of osmotic communication happens all the time for people on colocated teams (assuming team members aren't wearing headphones or otherwise blocking out background noise). Working remotely makes it more difficult. Open chat channels can help, but they don't replace it. Be aware of that, and increase attention to creating shared meaning.

---

3. https://rework.withgoogle.com/print/guides/5721312655835136/

A lightweight structure helps in almost all meetings. In remote or hybrid meetings, structure matters even more. Structure helps people anticipate and participate. Knowing what's coming and what's expected helps put people at ease. Plus, structure can make up for some of the social cues we notice more easily when we're face-to-face.

Putting the Principles into Practice

Many practices that increase clarity and certainty make it easier for people to participate. Conversely, many practices that foster greater participation increase certainty and clarity.

We've found the following practices greatly bolster the likelihood of an effective retrospective when the team isn't face-to-face.

Send the Focus and Agenda Ahead of Time

Include any URLs needed (for example, if you're using a retrospective tool, or if you're referring to data in an internal system) with the agenda. Make them available in a way that people don't have to search for them during the session.

Kirsten Clacey and Jay-Allen Morris, co-authors of the aforementioned *The Remote Facilitator's Pocket Guide [CM20]*, use a slide deck to keep the agenda, URLs, and instructions in front of the group. They don't use it as a slide show, though. They display it in editing mode with all the slide thumbnails visible on the left side of the screen. This way, people can always orient themselves to the agenda.

Let People Know Expectations for Camera Use

In most cases, unless your team has a working agreement that cameras will be turned on, we advise making camera use optional. That's because many people have valid reasons for turning off the camera. They may have family stuff going on in the room, the room may be a mess, or their hair may be a mess. When contexts collapse—work is at home and home is the workplace—strict separation isn't reasonable. Plus, allowing people to choose whether or not to turn on the camera supports autonomy and safety.

Regardless of whether the expectation is camera on or camera off, let people know ahead of time what to expect. As Irene Asay, Scrum Master at Titansoft, points out, when people know ahead of time, they can be prepared and thus more comfortable.

Indicate When You Finish One Agenda Item and Move On to Another

In remote meetings, it's easy to get distracted or lose the thread of the conversation (we've been guilty of this many times ourselves!). This is one area in which the best retrospective tools shine: they make it clear which topic is currently being discussed.

If you're using a slide deck as Jay-Allen and Kirsten recommend, refer the team to the appropriate slide number in their slide deck. Some slide software offers the ability to show who is looking at a slide. This is helpful because it tells you if someone has missed a beat and can offer the information again.

Find a Digital Replacement for the Physical Arrangement of People

In a colocated retrospective, people are often seated around a table or in a semi-circle. That physical arrangement makes all sorts of things easy. It's easy to go around the table for a check-in or report-out. It's easy to form small groups by moving chairs around. It's easy to pass sheets of paper to each other or get up and post a sticky note on the board.

In a remote retrospective, you can't count on constant positions on a screen. Instead, you will have to get creative. One way to do this is by passing a virtual ball as you might in an in-person meeting. This gives the individuals in the group control over speaking order. Ask for a volunteer to start. Ask that individual to pass the virtual ball by choosing the next person and then that person chooses the next, and so on. Your job as a convener is to track that everyone has had a chance to speak. This method has the advantage of giving a bit of autonomy to the participants.

There are cases in which, as the convener, you want to influence the speaking order—for example, if there are individuals who are always the first to speak up, or when someone's opinion is likely to sway the group. To manage the order as the leader, create a visual talking circle with everyone's name.

Pick a person to start and then proceed around the circle. Feel free to shake things up by creating new circles with different orders. Or try starting at different places in the circle, or even going in the opposite order. Regardless, these methods have the advantage that everyone but the first person knows when their turn is. When people are dialed in, it's all too easy to tune out—especially when the retrospective is the fifth or sixth hour of video calls for the day.

Video Conference Fatigue

After two years of mostly online meetings, most of us have experienced fatigue from nonstop video conference calls. It happens whether you're on Zoom, Microsoft Teams, Google Meet, Blue Jeans, or some other online video meeting platform. A study by Jeremy Bailenson of Stanford University gives some clues as to why that is.[4]

It's not normal to see yourself in the course of meetings and interactions. But with video conferencing, there you're on the screen along with everyone else. This makes people hyperaware of how they look—the expression, gestures, or how their hair looks. This isn't only distracting, it's exhausting. Consider hiding self-view.

 In many cultures. it's neither normal nor considered appropriate to stare directly into someone's face and have prolonged eye contact. Yet this is the effect on screen. Plus, because we mostly see headshots, there's the illusion that we are close to others—uncomfortably close. Even though people obviously aren't two feet away from each other, the visual cues create the effect that they are. Both are uncomfortable for many people. Try to adjust your camera or your seated position so that more than your head shows up.

Finally, video calls limit our mobility. To stay in frame, people move less. You don't even have to move to "go" to a breakout room. When people are in several hours of meetings a day, this gets to be a lot. Sitting that much isn't just bad for health, it's bad for productivity. Most people think better and get less tired when they can move around more.

Use Nonverbal Cues

When you're with other people in a room, nonverbal cues naturally abound. Someone leans back and looks up—possibly signaling that they are turning over an idea in their mind. Another furrows a brow, and tilts their head, perhaps signaling puzzlement. A hand cupped around an ear may be a request to speak up. A slight lean forward and a hand part way up telegraphs "I have something to say."

---

4.   https://news.stanford.edu/2021/02/23/four-causes-zoom-fatigue-solutions/

Some remote teams use cue cards to replace these signals. We've seen cards such as these:

- *You're on mute*
- *Slow down*
- *Got something to say* (both with a period and a question mark)
- *BRB (be right back)*
- *Logging back in*
- *Agree*
- *Disagree*
- *I didn't hear that. Please repeat.*
- *I have a question*
- *Your video is frozen*
- And many more!

Some groups have color-coded cards to signal whether they are *ready to move on* or *need more time*. Color cards can support decision-making, too. For example, green can signal strong support for a proposal, yellow for lukewarm support, and red for an objection.

Establish a Protocol for Interjecting

Some people are very comfortable interjecting, and others aren't. Establish a protocol, so that people don't struggle to find an opening. It could be raising a hand, a color card, or simply saying "I wish to speak." The key is to make it agreed upon and ritualized.

For example, Helen Garcia, an Agile Coach at Maykit, uses a camera on/camera off protocol for certain activities. Everyone turns their cameras off and only turns the camera on when they want to speak. This protocol has some advantages. It makes it easy to focus on the person who is speaking and reduces the chance of talking over others. It also makes it more obvious when certain people speak a lot or not much at all. That can be interesting information for the group, and the retrospective leader.

Increase the Frequency of Process Checks

In any retrospective, it's useful to check in with the group from time to time to see how everyone is doing. In remote retrospectives, this becomes even more critical, so increase the frequency of these "process checks."

Ask whether people have questions. Ensure everyone is following along. Ask whether the pace is too fast or too slow. Check with the group before moving on to the next stage.

If you have no visual cues—perhaps you're communicating on the phone or without video due to bandwidth issues—help people key into who is there with a check-in that includes names. It's not always easy to identify people only by voice, even when you've known them for a while. If the team is new to each other, try having people say their names before they speak. Yes, it's awkward. And yes, it helps.

These adaptations help ensure that people aren't left out or left behind because of missed cues. Furthermore, time zones and bandwidth can disadvantage some participants, even when the retrospective design and facilitation don't. Connection quality can vary, and there may be little to no overlap of "normal business" hours. In these cases, an asynchronous retrospective may be the best option.

Asynchronous Retrospectives

We may be able to overcome distance with technology, but we can't bend time. We've worked with many teams that had little to no overlap in normal working hours, or even normal waking hours. The best of these teams figure out how to make the most of together-time when or if they have it. They learn how to communicate and collaborate without constant face-to-face interaction.

These teams have a choice to make: whether to hold their retrospectives synchronously or asynchronously.

If the team chooses to meet synchronously, someone will be inconvenienced no matter what time the team meets. Someone will be up early or late. Someone will miss out on family time. Sometimes, it makes sense to accept the inconvenience of having some team members on a video call in the middle of the night. But this should be rare and the pain should be shared.

When the inconvenience isn't (roughly) evenly shared, it sends a message: some members of the team are privileged and others aren't. This isn't great for the individuals who bear the burden, and it's not great for team cohesion, either. You can't have two classes of people and expect full and open communication. *So share the burden.* Don't assume it will always be the same person or sub-group getting up early or in the middle of the night or disrupting off-work time.

Alternatively, the team can choose to meet asynchronously. The goal of an asynchronous retrospective isn't to save time. The goal is to make the retrospective available on an individual's time. There's a start and an end, and timeboxes for each phase, just like any other retrospective. Unlike a typical synchronous retrospective, an asynchronous retrospective can span several days. Timeboxes need to respect the span of time zones. Exchanges happen in threaded messages or comments. Because of time zones and work rhythms, people dip in and out of a conversation.

The Set the Stage phase may be open for a day, the Gather Data phase for a day or two, and the Generate Insights phase may happen over a week. Selecting something to take forward in the Decide What to Do phase may take a day or two.

This may seem like it contradicts the advice we've given so far in this book. However, asynchronous retrospectives do create a space for teams to discuss how they are working, to learn together, and decide on improvements. It just looks different and happens at a different pace. In some ways, this mirrors how discussions unfold in online forums. A topic starts, and a few people contribute initially. Others respond to what's been posted or add to the discussion. We've participated in several of these forums, and in the best ones, conversations can be deep and meaningful when people care about the topic and follow ground rules for respectful interaction. The same can happen in an asynchronous retrospective.

Kirsten Clacey, who is also a coach at Automattic, a globally distributed company with thousands of employees, has been experimenting with asynchronous retrospectives. One of her observations is that these spaces are great for divergence (the generating insights part of a retrospective) but convergence is more challenging. What does she do as a result? She does the things good facilitators of synchronous retrospectives would do: she summarizes, brings the conversation back to the topic, draws people out, restates, and nudges people toward convergence. As Kirsten points out, "We know how to do it, it's just doing it in text."

Use Standups to Maintain Convergence

Because convergence can be tough in asynchronous spaces, agile coach Mark Kilby uses the daily standup to check in on how the retrospective is going. This gives the team the option to surface questions, ideas, or decisions in a synchronous fashion (assuming your team has synchronous standups!).

If your team uses a Change Ambassador, as we describe later in Chapter 12, Catalyzing and Sustaining Change, on page 201, encourage that person to bring up the retrospective in the standup.

Hybrid Retrospectives

Esther's mother used to tell her that having two kids was more than twice as challenging as having a single child. When adding children to a family, the challenges aren't additive, they are multiplicative. The same is true for retrospectives on hybrid teams, in which some people are in one physical location while others are elsewhere (whether those individuals are in single or multiple additional locations).

In hybrid retrospectives, you have all the challenges of a face-to-face retrospective. You also have all the challenges of a remote retrospective. On top of that, you have the challenge of creating roughly equal participation between the face-to-face people and the remote people, and getting them talking.

The following figure represents a hybrid team. Some people are together and other people in different locations.

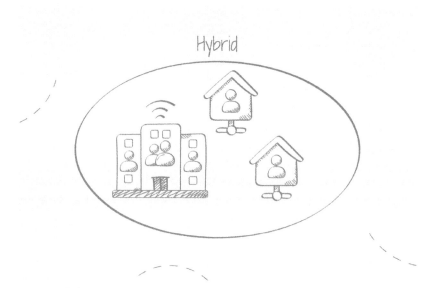

When most of the team is in one location with only one or two working from elsewhere, the "easy way out" is to plan your retrospective as if everyone was colocated. But they're not!

In fact, we hesitate to call *any* of the team members "remote" unless *all* of the team members are called "remote." Why? Do a simple thought experiment with us: imagine 8 team members are in location Alpha and 2 team members are in location Beta. Now ask yourself: which group is colocated and which is remote? You will quickly see that it depends on your perspective.

Holding your hybrid team's retrospective as if it were colocated puts some team members at a disadvantage. These individuals already tend to face hurdles fully integrating into the team. They can't just drop into their manager's office, run into teammates at the coffee bar, or join the team for a lunch outing. Don't add retrospectives to the list of situations where these team members feel left out or left behind.

The alternative approach is to hold your retrospective as if the entire team was fully remote. Ask everyone to call in to a video conference. Use an online whiteboard or retrospective tool to help facilitate the conversation. This approach levels the playing field—assuming bandwidth is relatively consistent across the team—by ensuring all team members share the advantages, disadvantages, challenges, and satisfactions of a remote meeting.

After you've tried this approach, gather some data from the team about what was different, what was surprising, what didn't work, and what worked *better* with a fully remote retrospective. You may be surprised.

Jenny Tarwater, an agile coach and consultant, described this hybrid retrospective she observed (she was *not* the convener!). The majority of the participants were physically together—in the same room, around the same conference table. The rest of the team—each in a different location—dialed in on a conference line, their voices emerging from a gray device in the middle of the conference room table.

The meeting started with a whole group discussion, during which the people who were face-to-face had a lively exchange, and occasionally paused to ask the remote people what they thought. Then, the meeting leader announced, "We're going to do an activity now. It won't work for you folks on the phone."

Whether she intended it or not, the message was clear: *If you aren't in the room, your participation is an afterthought.* This is exactly what you don't want with a hybrid retrospective.

Most of the time the exclusion isn't that blatant. It's not intentional but rather "out of sight, out of mind." The tendency for people to engage with those who can see and forget the people they can't is real. Reduced physical presence results in reduced participation. (*Suddenly Hybrid: Managing the Modern Meeting [RA22]*)

On the other hand, the people who aren't in the room may engage in a robust conversation via chat. If they're using the back channel (see Two Final Tips, on page 198) set up for the retrospective, as the leader you can see, respond, and bring their voices into the conversation. But when they're using some other channel that you can't see and don't know about, you've got a real problem. Whether they're complaining or contributing great ideas that only a subset of the team sees, the retrospective (and the team) suffers.

These breakdowns tend to occur based on different modes of communication: face-to-face, video, or phone only.

As a retrospective leader, you need to design for and encourage participation between the people who are face-to-face and the people who aren't. Ensure that communication doesn't fracture. Get the people in the room talking to people who are remote, not just to each other!

As a leader, you can support participation by monitoring who has spoken, and actively engaging the remote participants.

In face-to-face retrospectives, we urge people to leave their laptops behind and turn off their phones. But in hybrid retrospectives, these devices can help equalize participation and support communication with those in the room and those who aren't.

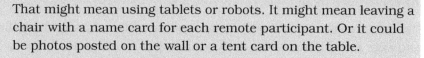

Make People Visible to Each Other

To counteract the tendency to forget the people who aren't in the room, make everyone visible to each other. Find a way to bring the remote people into the physical room.

That might mean using tablets or robots. It might mean leaving a chair with a name card for each remote participant. Or it could be photos posted on the wall or a tent card on the table.

For the people not in the room, create a photo gallery or avatar gallery. Use a virtual talking circle. If your video conferencing supports it, show image tiles for each remote participant.

All of these adaptations are particularly helpful for larger teams, or when the cast of characters in the retrospective changes.

Judy Rees suggests inviting remote people to speak first.[5] In general, we don't like to call on people by name, because people often feel put on the spot. But in the case of a hybrid retrospective, using names highlights that there are participants who aren't in the room. (This is something you might want to include in the agenda packet, so people aren't surprised.)

---

5. https://reesmccann.com/2019/09/11/hot-tips-for-less-horrid-hybrid-meetings/

In a fully face-to-face meeting, we'd discourage using chat. But in hybrid (and remote) retrospectives, chat can be your friend. Use chat to:

- Stack who wants to speak
- Capture responses to questions
- Summarize report outs
- Provide easy access to URLs
- Give written instructions to supplement verbal ones

If the only option you have for group conversation is a speakerphone, use it for what it's good for—one person speaking at a time. Use the speakerphone when the whole group needs to listen or for single-threaded conversations, such as a report out. Mute the speaker phone and pick up mobiles to facilitate conversations among two to three people. Partner in-room participants with remote participants. Assign pairs/triads ahead of time so you aren't wasting precious retrospective time figuring out who talks to whom. Make sure you have everyone's phone number available.

General Guides for Adapting Exercises

It used to be that you could recognize a facilitator, agile coach, or Scrum Master by the case of markers, sticky notes, and rolls of flip chart paper they toted everywhere. These are great tools that support idea generation, clustering ideas, voting, and prioritizing.

Many of the exercises that appeared in the first edition relied on these kinds of tools. The good news is that almost all of these exercises can be replicated using a retrospective tool or virtual whiteboard.

Many tools replicate sticky notes, but you don't have to have something fancy. At the 2018 Regional Scrum Gathering in South Africa, two facilitators demonstrated that about anything you can do with virtual sticky notes you can also do with only Google Slides. Many online tools, ranging in price from free and basic to expensive and fancy, allow you to create canvases ahead of time, just like you might prepare a flip chart.

Interestingly, there are ways to use traditional sticky notes even for remote retrospectives! We learned the idea of having people place colored sticky notes over their cameras to express preferences, moods, or experiences from Oana Junco, Agile Leadership D.J. at Reacteev. This creates a striking—if brief—visual effect indicating group sentiment. As a side note, this is a great way to collect subjective data.

Some tools, particularly ones built for retrospectives, have voting capabilities built in. The best ones make dot voting even more effective than it is in person! They do this by hiding the results of the voting until after everyone has finished, which makes it difficult for participants to "game" the vote by holding back until they see which way things are leaning.

Both passing the virtual ball and using a virtual talking circle (described in the section Putting the Principles into Practice, on page 186) help in report outs and check-ins. Use them to replace going around the table or passing a talking stick. These substitutes help manage the flow of conversation.

For exercises that require people to hand a piece of paper to the person next to them or physically move to another flip chart, recreate the paper or flip chart on a virtual whiteboard. People can still "pass" or "move" to the left or right. If the activity involves groups, establish those before you start. Sorting out how many people are at a virtual board takes more time than doing so in person.

Keep in mind that transitions often take longer in virtual space. This seems paradoxical since no one is actually moving, but experience bears it out. Instructions need to be more explicit and offered in smaller chunks. Give a high-level overview explaining the purpose and steps of the activity. Then give detailed instructions before each step. We usually write down the instructions in the agenda slides. That enables people to follow along or to refer back. This is especially helpful when using electronic breakout rooms.

As a rule of thumb, double the amount of time you'd allocate for an activity in physical space.

Whiteboards or Retrospective Tools?

Online whiteboards and retrospective-specific online platforms are two kinds of tools that can assist your design. Each has a role to play.

For experienced facilitators who have the time, energy, know-how, and interest in designing new remote activities or digital versions of old favorites, open-ended whiteboards offer an exciting blank canvas. These individuals tend to enjoy spending time applying their experience to create the artifacts and plot the flow of a retrospective design. With that said, we've found that the open-ended nature of whiteboards comes at a cost: they tend to be less intuitive for the participants than the best-designed retrospective tools. Be aware that more instruction and guidance on how to use them effectively will be needed.

For a newcomer to retrospectives, a novice facilitator, or someone with little time to invest, retrospective-specific tools are often a better choice. These tools make certain activities "click and go," which is great for those who need or want the time savings, or for those who simply don't have the expertise to build these activities from scratch on virtual whiteboards. The best retrospective tools include a variety of activities, including ones that go well beyond sticky notes. These tools have the advantage that they are purpose-built for retrospectives, and as such many of their features will be particularly helpful to you and your team. For example, some tools save your retrospective history and help you maintain an action plan. Be aware that these tools will be limiting for more experienced facilitators who wish to design and customize to their heart's content.

We suggest newcomers experiment with the retrospective-specific tools first. The best of these tools make facilitating a retrospective much easier than a blank canvas. Then as you gain experience, check to ensure the retrospective-specific tool is growing with you. Does it offer you enough customization? Are the activities you want to run supported by the tool? If so, continue using the tool. If not, you might want to experiment with moving on to an online whiteboard.

Picking a Retrospective Tool

We are heartened by the increasing number of retrospective-specific tools on the market. With so many options out there, it's important to pick the tool that best serves you. Ask yourself these questions:

- Does the tool support the activities you want to use?

- Does the tool make it easier to use those activities for a remote or hybrid team?

- Is the tool designed to protect psychological safety?

- What is the participant's experience like? (Some tools are great for the retrospective leader but subpar for the team!)

- Does the tool encourage your teams to actively participate in the retrospective?

- Does the tool support synchronous and collaborative interactions?

- How high is the learning curve for both the leader and the participants?

Two Final Tips

One of the iconic images of excessive worry is a person who wears both suspenders and a belt to keep their trousers up. When you're working with remote collaboration tools, suspenders and a belt aren't a sign of excessive worry, they're prudent planning.

Technology is great when it works, and annoying when it doesn't. Tools fail. Connections go down. Thus, it pays to have a backup plan.

If your main channel fails, how will people let you know?

A back channel is simply a secondary means of communication for people to reach you should they lose connection, can't hear the facilitator, or can't get a word in edgewise. We've used Slack, WhatsApp, SMS, IM channels, *and* phone numbers. You may have other options. It doesn't much matter as long as people have a secondary communication channel when there's a blip with the primary channel.

Mention the back channel as part of Setting the Stage, and list it along with any URLs relevant to the retrospective. Outline the backup plan when you send out the notice for the retrospective. Many companies have somewhat redundant platforms for video or voice connection. In one particularly glitchy meeting that started on Skype, the team fell back to Zoom, Facebook video, and then FaceTime. It did take several minutes to cycle through these options. (Most companies are far more locked down!) Yet, the team had a good—though shorter than planned—conversation and agreed on an action.

But what if a glitch affects your entire group, not just one person? If no one can connect to anything, you may need to reschedule. But there's a lot you can do to keep going if you have a fallback plan. Just make sure to communicate what the plan is when you send out the agenda. Then, people won't be scrambling when something goes wrong. Because eventually, something will.

Most Importantly, Don't Be Ruled by Your Tools

Tooling can make a big difference in remote, hybrid, and asynchronous retrospectives. It's true, but it doesn't work well when they begin to dictate the meeting design or assert that one activity can become a whole retrospective. Choose tools that support your retrospective design. Avoid defaulting your design to what the tool offers.

Bumbling around getting the technology to work isn't a good look for a retrospective leader. That can turn off the participants. When you plan to add a new tool or use a new feature, practice ahead of time. Also, give the participants time and means to practice ahead of time.

Many meetings derail when participants aren't familiar with a tool. They may struggle and not be able to fully participate. At worst, they will disengage completely.

Switching between tools introduces friction and takes time. There's a trade-off between the efficiency provided by the perfect tool and the cognitive load of jumping from one interface to another. Sometimes it's more efficient to stick with a tool that's second best for some particular task than switch to one that's perfect.

It may be helpful to have a "producer"—someone whose role is to focus on the tools—so that the retrospective leader can focus on the process and participation.

Finally, use online tools for what they are good for, but *never* let them dictate how you design your retrospective. Even when a tool has a template set up to categorize virtual sticky notes in three columns, it doesn't mean you are limited to that. Use the capabilities of the tool to *support* your design—not *to be* your retrospective design.

CHAPTER 12

Catalyzing and Sustaining Change

Productive teams judge retrospectives by their results. Yet results don't just magically happen.

Instead, results happen only after changing something meaningful, habitual, or impactful. And if you've ever tried stopping a nail-biting habit or starting a daily exercise routine, you know how difficult that can be.

The same is true for changing teams' and organizations' behavior.

In fact, we've consistently found that a lack of follow-through *after* the retrospective is over is one of the most common reasons that retrospectives don't produce real results. At a high level that's because not changing is, by definition, easier than changing. While there's no way of guaranteeing that you will be successful in catalyzing and sustaining change, there *are* clear, simple steps you can take to increase the odds.

That's what this chapter is all about.

We'll provide advice on how to best approach each of the five retrospective outcomes—action items, experiments, influencing others, changing our own response, and learning—to turn intentions into reality.

Action Items

Let's start with action items. Action items are concrete next steps the team believes will solve the problem at hand. While action items seem straightforward (just write down what you're going to do!), in reality, how you write your action items has a big impact on the odds of them being successful.

Here's an example. Imagine your team has discovered that it tends to over-commit at the beginning of an iteration, which has resulted in everyone feeling overwhelmed, tired, and even a bit embarrassed at its inability to accomplish its goals. As a result, the team decides to commit to the following action item:

Take on less work each iteration

The way the action item is written makes it difficult to judge its impact. Why?

Imagine at the end of the next iteration, the team looks back to see how the action item turned out. How will the team know if it made the change? What does "less work" actually mean? Is it fewer story points? Fewer user stories? Or something else entirely?

And even if the team agrees on a definition of "less work," *how much* less are we talking about? One person might imagine a slight reduction in work while another might imagine a significant reduction.

And even then: what do the words "slight" and "significant" mean?

That's why it's critical to write down action items in a deliberate fashion that makes observing their impact possible.

SMART Criteria

One of the most effective ways to do this is to write action items using the SMART criteria.

SMART stands for:

- Specific—what is it that you want, exactly?
- Measurable—how will you know if you accomplished it?
- Achievable—is it possible to accomplish?
- Relevant—is it related to your goals?
- Time-bound—when will it be done by?

Now, let's rewrite "take on less work each iteration" using the SMART criteria:

In our next planning meeting, we'll accept a maximum of three backlog items into our iteration backlog.

This is significantly improved! It's *specific* as it's about backlog items, not "work" more broadly. It's *measurable* as it includes a number—three backlog items. It's *achievable* as the team has control over how many backlog items it commits to. It's *relevant* as it's connected to the original problem. And it's *time-bound* as it's due at the next planning meeting.

An additional benefit of writing action items using SMART criteria is that the conversation involved will help build a shared mental model across all team members. How many times at a meeting has your team committed to work on something only to realize later that different people had different under-standings of what that thing actually was? SMART helps solve that problem.

Reserve Extra Time

It can take a meaningful amount of time to write action items using SMART criteria (especially when you first adopt them). That's because there will likely be extra debate on what *exactly* the team is agreeing to, how to measure it, and when it will be done.

The extra time is a worthwhile investment, as the additional clarity will greatly increase the odds your action will lead to real results.

Experiments

When confidence in any particular course of action is low, teams can turn to experiments. Whereas action items are clear paths forward, experiments are like dipping your toes in the water to see if it's too hot or too cold and adjusting course based on what you find.

What do we mean by *experiment*, exactly? In our lingo, experiments are *not* scientific! Your grade school science teacher might object, but our type of experiments don't have isolated variables and controls. They aren't falsifiable. They don't even have to be repeatable!

Instead, the experiments we are referring to are tiny interventions intended to help you and your team learn about how a system responds. Our experiments are *FINE: fast feedback*, *inexpensive*, require *no permission*, and *easy*.

Fast Feedback

Slow changes tend to activate organizational inertia. Slow changes lead to long feedback loops, and long feedback loops make it difficult to assess the effectiveness of the change. With that said, it's also important to ensure you allow *enough* time for your experiment. We've seen teams try out difficult new practices for just a few days, struggle, and declare the experiment a failure. These teams never even had a chance.

Inexpensive

It's easy to rationalize not working on expensive experiments. You'll hear people say, "Oh that would cost too much money, so let's skip it for now." Or, "It would take a lot of time and effort to test that idea, so let's try something else." Pick an inexpensive experiment, and those objections go away.

No Permission

Experiments shouldn't need external permission because the change is, well, experimental. If the change doesn't work, you can always reverse course.

Easy

When a change is easy, why not give it a try? The easier the experiment, the higher the odds the team will actually give it a shot.

Experiments are particularly helpful when the team disagrees on what to do next. Of course, healthy disagreements are encouraged and productive. But we've also observed disagreements that become personal, involve blaming and shaming, and lead to a lack of action.

Experiments can help overcome this problem. They make it easier to "get to yes." Rather than debating the *right* action, commit to trying something that's "good enough for now and safe enough to try."

You can say to the team, "It looks like we can't agree on the best next step. That's OK. Instead, let's simply agree to give this experiment a chance without agreeing on whether it will work or not. If it works, great—we're all better off! And if it doesn't, we'll simply try the next experiment."

In this way, people become less attached to "getting their way" and become more willing to try others' ideas.

How to Think About Experiments

As your team brainstorms experiments, here are ten questions to consider:

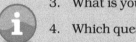

1. What factors may contribute to the current problem situation? (Curiosity and observation will help you here!)

2. Which factors can you control or influence?

3. What is your rationale for choosing this particular experiment?

4. Which question are you trying to answer with your experiment?

5. What can you observe about the situation as it is now?

6. How might you detect that your experiment is moving the situation in the desired direction?

7. How might you detect that your experiment is moving the situation in an undesirable direction or notice undesirable side effects?

How to Think About Experiments

8. What is the natural time scale of the experiment? When might you expect to see results?

9. If things get worse, how will you recover from the situation?

10. If things improve, how will you amplify or spread the experiment?

11. What is your hypothesis for the experiment?

Picking a Next Step

Many teams rush to commit to the first action or experiment that's brought up. We recommend aiming for at least three options before committing. In addition to giving the team choices, finding alternatives gives the team a chance to think with fresh perspectives.

Once your team has brainstormed at least three potential next steps, now it's time to decide what to do (we share a variety of activities to help in this regard in Chapter 8, Activities to Decide What to Do, on page 131).

You might wonder: Why does it matter which action or experiment we choose when we can't possibly know the right approach ahead of time? Couldn't we just pick one at random and see how it goes?

The answer, of course, is yes you could. But just because you can't know the right solution ahead of time doesn't mean each of the options has equal potential. Some actions *do* have a better shot at working than others. And so when you're faced with a list of candidate actions or experiments, you'll need to narrow it down.

When thinking through which option to pick, consider:

- Your *confidence* that it will work
- How much *impact* you believe it will have
- The level of *control* your team has over its outcome
- The amount of *effort* it will take

In other words, all else being equal, an action or experiment that you're *confident* will work, has high *impact*, is under your *control*, and has low *effort*, is significantly better than one you rate lower on one or more of these factors.

Follow the Energy

The overriding principle in deciding what to do is "follow with the energy." Following the energy is important because when an action or experiment truly energizes your team, the likelihood it will *actually* get worked on increases tremendously. In fact, we've found that one of the most common reasons teams don't follow through on their retrospectives is that they weren't truly committed to the change in the first place.

Practically speaking, the best way to follow the energy is to...ask! Instruct each team member to vote for one or two ideas that energize them the most. You can ask questions like, "What do you really want to make happen? Which idea(s) gives you energy?" You can see this approach in action in the following picture:

In this example, you will notice that the idea with the most energy is the third one. It has five votes in the Energy column.

We discuss this approach in more detail on page 139.

The Change Ambassador

At this point, you're off to a great start: you've followed the energy. You have a whole-team commitment. And yet, in our experience, change rarely happens without clearly identifying a single person who is responsible for shepherding the change through. We call this person the Change Ambassador.

The Change Ambassador helps your team avoid the tragedy of the commons in which "individual users, acting independently according to their own self-interest, behave contrary to the common good of all users."

In other words, while "the team" might have the energy to do the work, "the team" isn't actually capable of acting. Only individuals can take action. When actions and experiments are the responsibility of the team, too often everyone on the team assumes someone *else* will step up and get it done.

That's where the Change Ambassador comes in. The Ambassador should ensure the action or experiment is on track by:

- Reminding the team of its commitment
- Visualizing progress
- Aiding the team in removing impediments that are preventing progress

Importantly, the Ambassador is *not* individually responsible for implementing the change itself (that's the team as a whole). Nor should the Ambassador be judged on, or accountable for, the success or failure of the change. Rather, the Ambassador acts as a servant leader who guides, encourages, and enables the team to see the change through.

The Ambassador is a volunteer position. This should *not* be an assigned position. If you Follow the Energy, this will likely be easy: someone should be eager to be the Ambassador! In fact, if you find that no one is volunteering for this role, it's likely a sign that there wasn't real energy in the room in the first place. From that perspective, you've lucked out! It's better to determine the lack of energy upfront than it is to waste cycles hoping progress will be made.

As the Ambassador, you will want to bring up the action or experiment on a regular basis. This doesn't mean additional meetings! Instead, the Ambassador can use previously scheduled check-ins (like the daily standup) to remind your team of its commitment. Keep the questions and answers short: "In a word or two, how is the experiment going?" or "What blockers are slowing down progress on the action item?" and use the responses as a gauge of how the change is going.

Share Responsibility for Making Changes

One issue we've repeatedly seen is teams in which a single person tends to regularly grab responsibility for the change. This leads to three problems:

1. Your team may come to look upon one team member as a heroic rescuer. The rescuer may rely on the heroic role for emotional reasons—to the detriment of the team. Whether the team relies on a rescuer or a rescuer seeks the role, the dynamic kills collaboration and shared ownership.

2. When a formal or informal leader consistently takes responsibility (except for system problems outside the team), that person teaches the team to be helpless victims. Collaborating to make improvements strengthens the team. Taking away that responsibility cripples them.

3. When a team consistently assigns responsibility for problem resolution to a subgroup within the team, it creates a perception that the subgroup is the source of all problems. Scapegoating breaks the team. Share responsibility, and rotate leadership.

Influence Others

When the solution to a problem lies outside the team's control, in many cases the best course of action is to attempt to influence those who *can* make a difference. The goal of influencing others is to educate and persuade that person or group to provide more resources or help enable the change.

When It's Clear Whom to Influence

In some cases, it's clear whom you will need to influence. You might know, for example, that your boss has the ability to move some meetings to provide your team with additional focus time. Or, you might realize that there are too many dependencies between your team and another with whom you have a close relationship.

In these situations, we recommend building out a Role Empathy Map (see the figure on page 209) that helps you build empathy for the person you will be speaking with. A Role Empathy Map answers key questions like:

- What situation are they in?
- What is their role?

- What are the expectations of their role?
- What does success look like for them?
- What are they rewarded for?
- What do they do today?
- What can you imagine them doing?
- What do they value?
- What are their goals?
- What are their frustrations, fears, and anxieties?
- What are their wants, needs, hopes, and wishes?

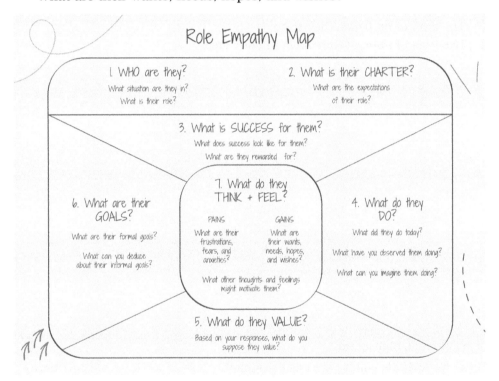

Role Empathy Map

Taking the time to better understand the individual will help you find common ground and a mutual purpose.

When It's Less Clear Whom to Influence

In other cases, whom to influence is more nebulous. This is especially true when the issue at hand is well outside your circle of influence (for example, large organizational initiatives or change programs with backing from the top of the organization chart).

In these situations, we have found stakeholder analysis, an approach developed by organizational development expert Peter Block, to be highly effective.

Stakeholder analysis "identifies those who have influence in a system. It provides a framework to help understand the needs that they have and how to respond to those needs."[1]

Stakeholder analysis will help you recruit and mobilize the right people in your organization to aid in the change you're after.

To do stakeholder analysis, you'll build out an Influence/Interest grid (others use the word "power" instead of "influence," but we prefer the latter).

An Influence/Interest grid helps you bucket the stakeholders according to:

1. The level of *influence* they have
2. The level of *interest* they have in your idea

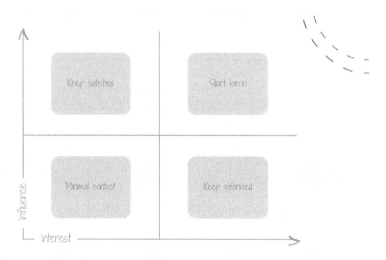

High Influence, High Interest

These individuals will be the easiest stakeholders to work with. Start here.

High Influence, Low Interest

Since these individuals have high influence but low interest, the most important thing is to keep them satisfied.

Low Influence, High Interest

Keep these individuals informed of what's going on. You want to keep them interested in your idea.

---

1. https://www.leadershipcentre.org.uk/wp-content/uploads/2016/02/The-Art-of-Change-Making.pdf (Starting at page 103)

Low Influence, Low Interest

Just ensure you're keeping these people informed on what's going on from time to time.

After building the Influence/Interest grid, you can start to determine which stakeholders are the ones you want to influence. If you find people with high influence and high interest, start there! If not, determine the communication and messaging you will use to build support from others on your grid.

Stakeholder mapping gives you the tools you need to better understand not only who to influence but also how to change your approach based on their stance vis-à-vis your change.

Change Your Response

Despite your best efforts to influence others, sometimes it's simply not possible to change "the system." When the issue in "the system" is unchangeable yet important, it can cause stress, sadness, and even anger. You might begin to perceive these issues as threats to your ability to do your job well, to your ego, or even to your job safety. This can be extremely frustrating, especially when the issues are brought up again and again during retrospectives without any perceived path forward.

And yet there is *always* a path forward. When you and your team can't change the external environment, the one thing you *can* change is your reaction to it.

To do that, the first step is to recognize you and your team are in a threatened state and to understand the implications. Psychologists and therapists have found that people who are in a threatened state *unconsciously* react in four ways:[2]

- *Fight* by taking aggressive action
- *Flight* by escaping or denying the situation
- *Freeze* by stalling until they determine what to do
- *Fawn* by pleasing the person threatening them

We want to emphasize that these responses are *unconscious*. They aren't choices. Nor are they good or bad. Don't judge yourself for reacting in one of these ways—it's simply human nature! You might feel your pupils dilating and your heart rate increasing. You might get "butterflies" in your stomach. Or perhaps your mind starts racing, making it difficult to relax or sleep.

---

2. http://pete-walker.com/fourFs_TraumaTypologyComplexPTSD.htm

And yet while these responses are natural, what makes us human is that we also have the ability to change them. Since the responses are unconscious, the first step is recognizing that you're having an unconscious response! This sounds trite, but we'd guess that you could point to many occasions when you respond in ways without realizing you're doing so. Once you've paused to recognize that you're having a reaction, the second step is to realize that it's *this* response that's causing you physical, emotional, and mental damage. It's not *them*—your boss, the market, or the system. It's actually *you*—or, more specifically, your unconscious response.

If fight, flight, freeze, and fawn are *unconscious* reactions, the way out is to *consciously* choose to change your response.

We admit that this is easier said than done. And in many cases, you won't be ready. It can feel good to relish in your anger and righteousness for a while! But at a certain point, most people and many teams reach a breaking point. Enough is enough. And that's when you and your team know you're truly ready to change your collective response to the situation.

If you find yourself in one of these moments, start your team's next retrospective by setting the stage with a simple group deep-breathing exercise. Research has shown that deep breathing relieves stress, reduces blood pressure, and even impacts your body organs including the brain and the heart.[3] Taking deep breaths with your teammates might feel "unprofessional" at first, but the science has shown that it really makes a difference. In fact, even the U.S. Navy Seals recommend a specific breathing exercise known as Box Breathing.

Now that your team is in a better mental state, it will be more ready to learn from asking "wonder questions" like:

- I wonder...what can we learn from this situation?
- I wonder...what would it feel like to be in their shoes?
- I wonder...how could the opposite of my beliefs be true?
- I wonder...in what way is this situation a gift?
- I wonder...what's my part in creating this?

You can use questions like these in your retrospectives to learn more about the situation, your team, and your collective behavior. You start to shift the locus of control for how you're feeling inwards. And in so doing, you can chart a new path forward for yourself and your team.

---

3. https://www.health.harvard.edu/mind-and-mood/relaxation-techniques-breath-control-helps-quell-errant-stress-response

Learning

Ultimately, retrospectives are exercises in learning. Some of the most memorable retrospectives we've been a part of haven't led to a specific action, but rather to the discovery of some new insight, a moment of reflection, or simply an increased awareness of the team's context.

Retrospectives like these don't necessarily end with a tangible output. But when asked, team members would likely be able to say they had an "aha!" moment in the retrospective that expanded their understanding of themselves, their team, or their environment.

These moments of whole-team learning can act as catalysts for change in and of themselves, even without a specific commitment to an action going forward.

Visualize Your Improvement Item

Regardless of whether you've picked an action item or experiment, decided to influence someone, or changed how you'll respond, your next job is to *actually follow through*. This is easier said than done! Far too many retrospectives have ended with good intentions that are followed with a lack of execution during the iteration.

To encourage follow-through, the first thing you will want to try is to make the change highly visible to the team. That's because the more visible something is, the easier it is to remember to work on it. Things that aren't immediately visible tend to be forgotten. This is a great example of a task for the Change Ambassador.

One way to make the change visible is to place it in line with the rest of your work. For example, if you're using Scrum, you might put the action or experiment in your Sprint Backlog. This approach works well when the change is task-oriented and time-bound. And of course, to put the change in the Sprint Backlog, the team will first have to prioritize it during Sprint Planning.

Another way to make your change visible is to track your progress using a big, physical visualization. Research has shown that your chances of success when trying to achieve a goal increase when you publicly or physically record your progress.[4]

For example, suppose your team has decided that the engineers need more regular interaction with the product manager. How might you create a big, physical visualization of your progress? One idea would be to create a board

---

4.   https://www.sciencedaily.com/releases/2015/10/151029101349.htm

where each column represents a day of the week and anytime an engineer interacts with the product manager, a check mark is placed underneath that day. It might look something like the following figure:

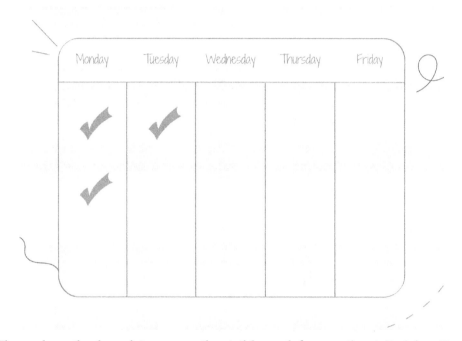

Then place the board in an easily visible and frequently visited location. Whether the change is on track or not, everyone will know. This creates accountability and enables the team to self-organize.

Monitoring for Results

Once your change is in motion, it's important to monitor it for desirable—and undesirable—effects. Occasionally, this is easy. But in most situations, determining the impact is not so simple, especially when the change you make has a delayed impact on the target outcome.

Here's an example. Suppose your team has chosen to introduce test-driven development (TDD) in an attempt to decrease cycle time (don't worry if these terms are unfamiliar to you—the point remains the same). Well, TDD takes time to learn and, like most complex changes, will likely have a *negative* impact on cycle time in the short run!

If your team is too quick to judge the efficacy of TDD, you might conclude that it's a failure. That's why it's important to recognize upfront that this change, along with many others, has a long feedback loop.

When faced with long feedback loops, the best option is to rethink the measurement by which you're judging the results. Rather than waiting for an impact on the outcome measure (in this case, a decrease in cycle time), look for steering signals.

Steering Signals

You can think of steering signals like guideposts to help you on your journey. If you're a hiker, you know to look ever so often for markers or blazes to keep you on the right trail. These indicators give you confidence that you haven't veered off course. And if you discover you *are* off course, you have the opportunity to correct your course well before it becomes difficult to do so! Steering signals serve the same purpose.

Steering signals tend to be subtle and hard to measure. But they *are* observable if you pay attention. For example, you might perceive small shifts in behavior. People might start asking you different types of questions. You might even notice a change in your own thoughts, feelings, or energy level.

When you start paying attention to steering signals, sometimes it becomes obvious that a change isn't working out *well before you see any changes in the desired outcome*. In other cases, the feedback from the steering signals might be more of a mixed bag. In those cases, the question becomes, "Should we invest more time into this change?" This might involve reassessing whether your steering signals have provided enough information. Or you might look at what you've learned so far. In either case, the steering signals have provided additional data you can use to make a call.

Supporting Larger Changes

When a change is perceived as small, people adapt without external support. For larger changes, the transition takes longer and happens at different rates for different people. Broader changes require more support and more attention to how people respond to change.

People experience predictable transitions as they let go of the old and take on the new, even when they've chosen and planned the change (*The Satir Model: Family Therapy and Beyond [Sat91], Managing Transitions: Making the Most of Change [Bri03]*. Those transitions occur in four phases.

Four Transitional Phases in a Change

Understanding the four phases of change will help you support your team. Every change is unique, and some aspects will be predictable. For instance, in Chaos it's typical for leaders to assume the change is failing. Messiness makes everyone uncomfortable. But similarities emerge in every change effort. Look for them in the four phases of change:

1. Loss

Starting something new always begins with letting go of the old. People experience loss of competence, territory, relationships, certainty, and so on. Excitement about the new may pull them through this phase quickly, or they may take longer to adjust. Either way, they can't, and won't, move forward until they let go.

2. Chaos

Letting go of the old doesn't mean we fully understand the new. People feel confused and strive to reorient themselves during a time of change. They explore how things will change and what this new way will mean for them. Along with confusion, chaos may spark innovation and creativity. People may invent new approaches because the rules aren't settled yet.

3. Transforming Idea

Eventually, people see or experience how this new way will work for them. Experiments and exploration lead them to a fresh understanding. An outside influence may bring a new perspective. Team members begin to try new behaviors and ideas.

4. Practice and Integration

An idea is not enough. People need to practice to learn a new skill or adapt to a new structure. Performance may drop initially but will improve with practice.

As people move through the stages of change, help them by attending to these three areas:

1. What People Value

Identify what team members valued in the old way. Look for ways to carry the value forward while leaving behind what isn't working. By acknowledging what was valuable in the old way, you recognize that people weren't stupid or wrong. At some time, someone thought it was a good idea, and it was, then. People move forward more easily when they believe that changing doesn't imply they've been stupid.

For example, during their release retrospective, Lakshmi and her team realized that they needed to increase their team size by 50% to keep up with demand for their product. They were excited their products were so successful, but they also felt the loss of their small, cohesive team. As they brought in new people, the team lead worked to clarify the team's values and the practices they wanted to keep. The original team prioritized what was most important to carry forward as they grew into a larger team.

2. Temporary Structures

Temporary structures help people navigate the chaotic phase between the old way and the new way. Temporary structures can be plans, roles, meetings, methods—any mechanism that bridges the current state and the goal state.

Here's how one team created a temporary structure: Franz and his team worked on high-tech medical devices. During the retrospective after a long, painful project, the team decided to manage risk by moving toward iterative incremental development using XP. They hired a coach and attended immersion training. The business, on the other hand, was skeptical of throwing away their requirements documents and relying on stories written on index cards—with reason. They were heavily regulated.

Rather than give up on XP or resent the business for not trying stories, the team devised a temporary structure. They gratefully accepted the business's requirements document and then turned the requirements into stories, one iteration at a time. At the end of every iteration, they showed the business the software they'd written and explained how the stories related to the requirements. After several iterations, the business people began to see the value of writing requirements as stories and devised a way to trace stories for regulatory purposes.

The temporary structure—translating requirements into stories—enabled the team to move forward toward a desired goal.

3. Information and Rumor Control

When something changes, people hunger for information about how the change will affect them. When people lack information, they fill in the gaps with their worst fears. Rumors start even on small teams.

Establish a regular mechanism to control rumors during the course of change. Offer new information, assuage fears, uncover rumors, and provide facts.

One team created a Rumor Control Bulletin Board. Whenever a team member heard a rumor, that person wrote it on a card and posted it on the board. Everyone could read the latest rumors and take responsibility for tracking down the facts. Once the facts were known, they were posted too, keeping the rumor mill under control.

In addition, the Rumor Control Bulletin Board telegraphed that much of what people were hearing simply wasn't true. People stopped overreacting to the latest gossip and checked out the facts before passing anything along.

Make It So

Retrospectives can be a powerful catalyst for change. A major transformation can start from a single retrospective. Incremental improvement is important, too. Celebrate it. It's more than many teams ever achieve.

CHAPTER 13

Elevating Issues Beyond the Team's Control

The larger the organization, the more likely it becomes that teams will bump into impediments that are outside of their control. Without a productive method to find a resolution, these "beyond the team" issues tend to resurface from retrospective to retrospective. Over time, this can lead to frustration and a sense of helplessness. Retrospectives devolve into gripe sessions and eventually become an energy drain.

Once that happens, teams come to accept that's "just the way we do things around here." Suboptimal processes and frustrating inefficiencies become the norm. People feel a loss of control, a lack of agency, and a decrease in autonomy.

You might think autonomy isn't that important at large organizations where it often feels like each person is just another cog in the machine. But autonomy *is* a big deal. It's one of the key elements of intrinsic motivation (*Drive: The Surprising Truth About What Motivates Us* [Pin09]). In creative industries like software development, intrinsic motivation is paramount to innovation and creativity and is a key driver of employee retention.

In this chapter, we'll discuss what to do when your team discovers an impediment beyond its control. We'll also share strategies that empower teams, even when they can't fix the problem on their own. The goal of this chapter is to help you turn these seemingly helpless situations into opportunities for improvement and growth.

Taking Responsibility

When something happens to you—whether it's a personal disappointment or a broken process outside your team that makes work harder—it's normal to feel a loss of control. Many things are outside individual and team control.

The response to this feeling of loss of control usually goes in one of two directions: either you shake your fist at fate or you passively accept the situation.

In an organizational context, shaking your fist at fate usually comes out as blame. It's not *your* fault since it wasn't you who caused the problem—so it must be *them.* You've probably overheard someone blaming "those people" (executives, managers, or other departments) for something going wrong, or when you feel like you have to jump over inexplicable hurdles. Blaming feels like being in control, but it isn't. We discuss the high cost of blame in Chapter 4, Managing Group Dynamics, on page 63.

The second response is the feeling of hopelessness like there's nothing you can do other than accept a bad situation. This leads to the "that's just the way it is" trap and the end of team-driven continuous improvement.

Both blame and hopelessness put the locus of control entirely outside the team.

But, here is a third option: taking responsibility.

At first glance, this may sound extreme, dangerous, or naive. If *they* created the mess, why should *I* take responsibility for it? In fact, taking responsibility might feel like making the victim accountable. This is far from what we are suggesting.

Instead, by taking responsibility we mean asking yourself what role you or your team may have played in contributing to the situation. That doesn't mean blaming yourself for causing the problem or making yourself responsible for its impact. It does mean recognizing that, by definition, everyone involved in the situation is playing a role in some way, shape, or form.

Here's an example of what this might look like. Imagine your team isn't getting timely feedback from critical stakeholders. Many teams would default to blaming the stakeholders for the lack of feedback. *They* aren't providing *us* with feedback, so it's *their* fault. Or perhaps the team would passively accept that this is just how things work around here.

Instead, we are suggesting stepping into responsibility by asking, "what did (or didn't) we do to co-create the situation we are in?" From this place of curiosity, it becomes possible to discover any number of things. For example, the team might realize that (surprise!) no one on the team actually ever *asked* the stakeholders for feedback in the first place! Alternatively, the team might realize that the method in which they've asked for feedback (by email, let's say) might not be the best for individuals with a busy inbox.

Taking responsibility in this way is empowering and is far more productive than blame or hopelessness.

Circles and Soup

Another way to step into responsibility is to use the Circles and Soup activity to help your team identify what actually *is* under their control (see our description of the activity on page 120).

The diagram will look like the following figure:

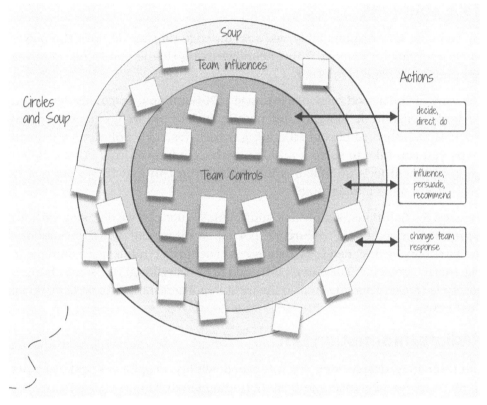

Then, explain we can take direct action over any issue in the inner "Team Controls" circle and influence others over any issue in the "Team Influences" circle. For the issues in the "Soup," first encourage the team to think creatively to find any way they might be able to move it into a different circle.

One way to do this is to flip the situation on its head. Ask the team: "What could we do to make the situation *worse*?" Not only is this often a fun twist on a familiar activity, but it also helps the team realize that in fact they *can* influence what's going on. If they can make the situation worse, it's likely they can also improve it!

Of course, some issues truly belong in the "Soup." For those, our best option is to choose *how we respond*. That's because ultimately there's only one thing you truly have complete control over: yourself. We acknowledge this takes discipline and is easier said than done. But simply discussing these issues *as a team* and deciding how we—collectively—will respond can help. It's certainly a first step toward taking responsibility.

15% Solutions

By stepping into responsibility, we acknowledge that we do have the power to choose "how to respond." But acknowledging this is one thing. Figuring out *how* to respond is another.

One way to find a good response is to use 15% Solutions. Originally developed by Professor Gareth Morgan and popularized by Henri Lipmanowicz and Keith McCandless as part of Liberating Structures, 15% Solutions are small steps you can take to solve a problem without approval from others. When an impediment feels outside of your control, you can use 15% Solutions to make it feel more manageable.

To use 15% Solutions, simply ask your team, "What can we do today without permission or additional resources?" It's important to note that 15% Solutions are intentionally designed to be baby steps. They aren't full-fledged solutions to big, thorny problems. They aren't intended to fix everything! But small changes can spark bigger changes, and so the most important thing is to do *something*. Just start.

Radiate Information Out

But ultimately, despite stepping into responsibility, despite our best attempts to manage our response and despite finding small wins via 15% Solutions, it's likely that systemic issues will remain that prevent us from reaching our full potential. What then?

Here's what you shouldn't do: stay silent. In fact, a common refrain we hear in the agile community is to follow the Vegas Rule of Retrospectives: "What happens in your retrospective stays in your retrospective." While the phrase is catchy and memorable, and the motivation behind the rule is a good one (to boost the team's psychological safety via privacy), it's more nuanced than that.

Here's why. Imagine your team has adopted the Vegas Rule of Retrospectives. In your next retrospective, you discover an impediment outside of your control. Since your team has agreed to "keep the retrospective private to the team," you're prevented from sharing what you discovered with someone who *can* make a difference without violating that agreement.

In essence, the Vegas Rule of Retrospectives prevents you and your organization from learning and benefiting from the valuable insights that teams discover in their retrospectives. Change will never happen this way.

That's why we'd recommend a different approach in your retrospectives: "Default to privacy; opt in to transparency."

Here's how this works. At the start of the retrospective, be explicit about two rules:

1. By *default* what goes on inside the retrospective stays private to the team. It's privileged information.

2. However, at any time, the team can *opt in* to share learnings, puzzles, actions, and other artifacts with people outside the team

The intention is to balance the benefits of team privacy and safety with the benefits of sharing and organizational learning.

Retrospective Radiators

One core aspect of agility is breaking down information silos via information radiators. Information radiators are big, visible displays of key information (think burndown charts, task boards, and incident reports). The intent is to openly convey the health of the team and promote transparency within the team and to any other passerby.

One particular instance of an information radiator is what we call a retrospective radiator. Retrospective radiators are big visualizations of the important information that *the team explicitly opts in to share from the retrospective*. Importantly, they are living documents and are updated as needed either during or immediately after many retrospectives.

What's amazing about information radiators generally, and retrospective radiators more specifically, is that they naturally promote "learning by osmosis." When information is hidden by default, one has to intentionally seek it out to learn about it. But when information is big, visible, transparent, and up-to-date, one learns simply by being a part of the organization.

For example, imagine if every team in your portfolio, product line, or even company placed a retrospective radiator outside their team room. What would that enable for you and your organization? Activities as mundane as walking from one conference room to the next would present you with opportunities to learn.

The next question, of course, is how to design a retrospective radiator to effectively convey information. Approaches vary, and there is no "one size fits all" here. There are only two rules:

1. Make it simple and clear. If it's not simple, your team won't update it. If it's not clear, others won't learn from it.

2. Ensure only the most important information is included. You don't need to radiate *everything*. In fact, this would be counterproductive. Information overload makes it harder to discover systemic insights, not easier.

One way we like to design retrospective radiators is to categorize our findings into topics like impediments (that are "out of our control"), learnings (things we discovered that have helped us in some way), and appreciations (what or who do we appreciate right now?). Here's an example of one team's radiator:

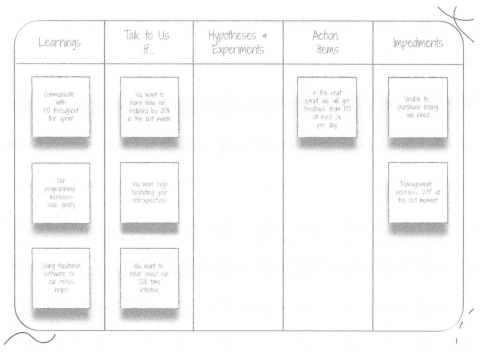

Other categories can work just as well. Virginia Satir, an early pioneer in family therapy, developed the Daily Temperature Reading, which can be done by partners together to strengthen their relationship. We've included this activity on page 97 as part of the Set the Stage phase of a retrospective. It's also useful here. The Daily Temperature Reading is made up of five parts:

1. Appreciations
2. New Information

3. Puzzles
4. Complaints with a request for change
5. Wishes, Hopes, and Dreams

We're big fans of these categories for retrospective radiators too.

David once worked with a company that took an even more systematic approach to using retrospective radiators. This company asked each of its roughly 100 teams to thematically tag the questions, actions, and blockers they had coming out of their retrospectives. Tags included communication, data, architecture, and so on. Importantly, this company—including management—respected the "Default to privacy; opt in to transparency" mantra previously discussed.

On a monthly basis, a group of agile coaches merged the retrospective radiators into a single, company-wide spreadsheet organized by tag. Then, the same group of coaches would look at the data and try to identify common themes.

Sometimes the coaches would discover that multiple teams were working on similar issues, which led the coaches to connect the teams so that they could tackle the problem together! Other times the coaches would learn that a large number of teams were struggling with a single blocker they couldn't solve on their own. In these cases, the coaches would bring their findings to management. With the knowledge that the blocker was impacting a large swath of the company, management was more inclined to take action.

The point is, there are an infinite number of approaches to developing retrospective radiators. Find one that suits you, your team, and your organization. We encourage you to be creative!

Getting Started with Radiators

At first, it might seem scary to radiate out information from your retrospectives. Couldn't it be weaponized?

Yes, it could. We recognize that. That's why we recommend starting small—perhaps with just a few teams that have a high degree of trust. In general, you don't need a manager's approval to do this!

In fact, this is a perfect example of both taking responsibility and finding 15% Solutions. Instead of blaming the organization for the situation you're in, you're taking responsibility for radiating your own team's information. And by starting small, you aren't waiting around for the organization as a whole to adopt the retrospective radiator concept. That's too big of a fish to fry. Instead, you're taking a small step that you *can* control.

If you're fortunate enough to have a good working relationship with your manager where sharing impediments would be appreciated and rewarded, then talk to your manager about this new initiative. Get their buy-in. More importantly, get your manager to commit to regularly inspecting their teams' radiators and find ways to help their teams become more productive.

Why Not Include Managers?

At this point, it's natural to ask why managers and other non-team members shouldn't be invited into the retrospective itself. Wouldn't that reduce the need for information radiators and eliminate the communication gap between teams and executives?

Perhaps, but in general, it's not the best idea. Why? (Note that we previously touched on this in Chapter 4, Managing Group Dynamics, on page 63, but it's so important we wanted to address it here as well.)

First, when individuals who aren't on the team participate in the team's retrospectives, psychological safety goes down. People stop being open and transparent and start shying away from saying what they really mean. That leads to less effective conversation, decreased potential for learning, and ultimately worse outcomes.

Second, people tend to share different things when managers are in the room. They might be less willing to bring up controversial or risky ideas. They might shy away from topics that don't "toe the company line." And they might be more interested in impressing the boss rather than discussing the issues the team is truly facing.

Third, remember that when managers attend retrospectives, they're likely to either dominate the conversation or, worse, not engage at all, leaving everyone wondering what they are thinking.

And finally, we've observed that when managers attend team retrospectives, they have the tendency to be over-eager to suggest solutions to problems, thereby unintentionally limiting the team's ability to self-organize and find solutions themselves. In the long run, this behavior creates an unhealthy dependency from the team to the manager.

For most teams, all of this tends to be intuitive. But for many managers and executives, we've found the opposite to be true! We can't count how many times we've heard managers argue that they should attend team retrospectives because they "believe in transparency" and just want to help.

Jenny Tarwater, Owner and Chief Agilist at Blueshift Innovation, ran into this issue. The CIO at one of her clients wanted to attend team retrospectives and felt that because he was cool and hip—he often had beers with the teams!—and wasn't like other executives, his presence would be beneficial. So Jenny went to her teams to get their feedback. She asked them whether they felt 100% safe with the CIO and wanted him to attend their retrospectives. Not one person agreed he should be there.

Retrospective of Retrospectives

What's worse than not sharing anything coming out of your retrospectives? Taking the time to share and then receiving no response. When nothing changes despite your good intentions, it can feel like a complete waste of effort.

That's why it's important for organizations to commit to making use of the information on the retrospective radiators. Change won't happen by default. Change only happens with intention.

One way to ensure your organization regularly inspects the retrospective radiators, discovers insights that apply across teams, and commits to some action in response is to organize a regular Retrospective of Retrospectives. You might have heard of a Scrum of Scrums, which is a cross-team standup. Similarly, a Retrospective of Retrospectives is a cross-team retrospective.

In a Retrospective of Retrospectives, representatives from each team meet to discuss what's going well and what's not going well at the program, portfolio, or company-wide level. The goal here isn't to help any individual team but rather to enable the group of teams to learn collectively and operate more effectively.

Since the group of individuals participating in a Retrospective of Retrospectives likely doesn't work together on a day-to-day basis, it's important to set some ground rules for the conversation (see our description of the Ground Rules activity on page 91). In particular, make sure there is a common understanding of who will make decisions and how those decisions will be made. This is important since in a Retrospective of Retrospectives we are discussing problems and solutions with the potential to impact a large set of teams. What if many managers are present? What if no managers are present? And so on.

When it's time to actually run a Retrospective of Retrospectives, follow the same five phases you always do.

Here's an example of how that might work.

Phase: Set the Stage

Activity: Reiterate the Goal

Instructions: Simply state the goal of the meeting.

Rationale: By reminding everyone of the goal of the meeting, we help ensure all attendees are on the same page.

Activity: Focus On / Focus Off

Instructions: See this activity on page 87.

Rationale: This activity encourages everyone to approach the dialogue from a perspective of curiosity rather than blame.

Phase: Gather Data

Activity: Review Retrospective Radiators

Instructions: If you're meeting in person, simply hang the radiators around the room. If you're remote, share links to the radiators ahead of the meeting.

Rationale: Retrospective radiators are a goldmine of information and the basis for the rest of the conversation.

Phase: Generate Insights

Activity: Pattern Spotter Questions

Instructions: See this activity on page 116.

Rationale: Pattern Spotter Questions can help the group discover what the radiators have in common and what they don't, what is surprising and what isn't, what is missing and what sparks your curiosity, and more.

Optional Activity: Fishbone Diagram

Instructions: See this activity on page 117.

Rationale: Sometimes the group will discover something from the Pattern Spotter Questions that naturally warrants a deeper analysis. In this case, using an activity like Fishbone can help the group discover the root causes of the issues identified.

Phase: Decide What to Do

Activity: Dot Voting

Instructions: See this activity on page 134.

Rationale: Now that the group has converged on a single issue, it's important to allow them to diverge on potential actions before committing to a single one. After listing the potential actions, evaluate options by using a technique like dot voting to get consensus or consent on the next steps.

Phase: Close the Retrospective

Activity: Recap Actions

Instructions: Simply restate the actions that the group has agreed upon.

Rationale: Even if the action is as simple as scheduling a meeting with someone, it's important to ensure everyone is on the same page with regard to whom will do what and by when.

Activity: Appreciations

Instructions: See this activity on page 151.

Rationale: Almost by definition, the problems discussed at a Retrospective of Retrospectives are challenging. (If they weren't, they would've already been solved at the team level!) As a result, holding space for the group to appreciate each other for their contributions can be especially important.

Closing the Loop

One important aspect of the Retrospective of Retrospectives is ensuring that whatever decisions were made (as well as those that were intentionally *not* made) are communicated clearly back to the teams.

Think about it. Imagine that your team took the time to add an important impediment they were facing onto their retrospective radiator. They knew that the next Retrospective of Retrospectives was scheduled for the upcoming week. But then the week goes by, as does the next, and they don't hear anything. Nothing changes.

This lack of feedback discourages the team from sharing their impediments in the same fashion the next time. That's why closing the loop is so important—even if a decision is made *not* to act on an impediment for some reason, the rationale should be clearly shared with the team so they know it was discussed. Teams need to *know* that they are being heard and that their ideas are, at a minimum, being seriously considered.

Returning to Circles and Soup

Remember the Circles and Soup activity? For many of us, especially those of us at larger companies, the initial assumption would be that the "Soup" (in other words, the items out of your control) would include a large percentage of items.

But imagine you work at an organization in which teams regularly radiate information out and managers regularly inspect this information to find improvements. Many of the issues you would have otherwise placed into the "Soup" would instead be placed into the middle "Team Influences" circle. That's because teams at these organizations have a productive method to speak up and influence change.

And ultimately that's the goal—to increase the team's span of control in order to provide it with greater autonomy and voice.

Subjective Impact Analysis

Once your team realizes that it actually can influence others in the organization, the next challenge it will face is figuring out *how* to do so. In Chapter 12, Catalyzing and Sustaining Change, on page 201, we discussed how Empathy Maps and Stakeholder Analysis can help persuade others.

Another approach is to use Subjective Impact Analysis, which helps you better understand the problem you're facing from others' perspectives. Here's how it works:

1. Identify the proposed course of action.

2. Determine what's important to the person who makes the decision.

3. Ask that person who they consider credible sources related to the issue.

4. Create a short interview protocol that reflects what the decision-maker views as important.

5. Interview the people the decision-maker identified as credible.

6. Summarize and present the results.

For example, a company that sold financial products had outsourced their IT operations as a cost-saving measure. Production handoffs between the developers (who were employees) and their partners at the IT operations company (who were not) were far from smooth. The most recent turnover had gone badly and resulted in an outage that affected their call center and thus thousands of customers.

As an experiment, the development team piloted a preproduction meeting to ensure everyone—on both sides—knew what was happening and what part they had to play. In the first joint meeting, the group discovered an error that could have caused another large outage.

Unfortunately, a VP got wind of the meeting and shut it down because the outsourcing company had billed for time spent in the meeting.

The team's coach set up a meeting with the VP to understand her concerns and what she cared about. He found out that downtime and customer responsiveness were at the top of her list. He also learned that she held three of the people who had attended the meeting in high regard.

So he interviewed those people and others who had attended the preproduction handover meeting. He asked them to consider the outage they'd avoided and estimate the impact on customers and the number of people affected.

While it wouldn't have been as bad as the most recent actual outage, it would have been bad enough. They extrapolated the number of customers who would've been told, "Sorry, the system is down." And that was enough to convince the VP that the cost of the preproduction turnover meeting was well worth the expense.

In our experience, teams that become practiced at Subjective Impact Analysis have greater success influencing the rest of their organization.

Scaling Frameworks

If your company utilizes an agile scaling framework, you're likely wondering how our suggestions apply to your day-to-day work. Will they work with your company's approach to agile?

Fortunately, yes. Our suggestions in this chapter are framework-agnostic. What we mean by that is they can be used at any company using any methodology. Here's how that might look using some of the more well-known agile scaling frameworks.

FaST

Of all the scaling frameworks, FaST is the least prescriptive when it comes to cross-team retrospectives. In reference to continuous improvement, the FaST Guide simply says, "Each Collective should experiment and discover what works best."[1] It does present a list of options to consider, one of which

---

1. https://www.fastagile.io/fast-guide

is forming a "guild that meets on cadence to reflect and tune." If you're using FaST, you can simply use the Retrospective of Retrospectives approach previously described.

LeSS

Part of the LeSS framework is the Overall Retrospective, which exists "to discuss cross-team, organizational and systemic problems within the organization."[2] The LeSS framework also describes an *improvement service* in which managers own an organizational improvement backlog that's populated, in part, by items coming out to team retrospectives. LeSS says that "managers review the Improvement Backlog in regular meetings and decide on actions to implement the improvement items."[3] If you're using LeSS, the Overall Retrospective is similar to the Retrospective of Retrospectives previously described.

Nexus

In the Nexus framework, a Nexus is "a group of approximately three to nine Scrum Teams that work together to deliver a single product." Nexus adds an event to Scrum called the Nexus Sprint Retrospective,[4] whose purpose is "to plan ways to increase quality and effectiveness across the whole Nexus." The Nexus Guide then says, "...the Nexus Sprint Retrospectives...[uses]...bottom-up intelligence to focus on issues that affect the Nexus as a whole." If you're using Nexus, the Nexus Sprint Retrospective is similar to the Retrospective of Retrospectives previously described.

SAFe

The SAFe framework includes Inspect and Adapt (I&A) as a significant event. During the I&A, teams hold retrospectives to "identify a few significant issues they'd like to address."[5] After the retrospectives are over, the Agile Release Train "holds a structured, root-cause problem-solving workshop to address systemic problems." SAFe recommends using Fishbone during the workshop (described on page 117) to do root cause analysis. The SAFe guide then goes on to say, "Often it is the Business Owners who can unblock the impediments that exist outside the team's control." If you're using SAFe, the Inspect and Adapt workshop plays a similar role to the Retrospective of Retrospectives previously described.

---

2. https://less.works/less/framework/overall-retrospective
3. https://less.works/less/management/improvement-service
4. https://www.scrum.org/resources/online-nexus-guide
5. https://scaledagileframework.com/inspect-and-adapt/

What all of these scaling frameworks share is an emphasis on collecting information from teams, analyzing it across teams, and committing to action to improve the whole. No different than our previous advice.

It Doesn't Have to Be That Way

Teams often struggle to effectively handle endemic or seemingly unsolvable issues. The default behavior for many teams is to simply complain and move on, only to have the same issue resurface at a later date. Almost all of us at some point in our careers will hear something to the effect of, "Well, that's just the way things are done here."

But things *don't* have to be done that way. We're the first ones to acknowledge that it's not easy to find solutions to problems that span multiple teams, a variety of product lines, or even the entire organization. But letting these issues fester has significant hidden costs that lead to a decrease in productivity, in employee morale, and even an inability to attract and retain talent.

That's why it's important to not accept the status quo when dealing with issues beyond the team's control. The path forward starts with teams who are willing to share, managers and executives who are interested in listening, and organizations invested in supporting change.

CHAPTER 14

Overcoming Objections

While we believe in the power of retrospectives, we've found that others are skeptical. Sometimes with good reason ("I've been doing retros for years and they've never worked before") and sometimes not ("Leave me alone—I just want to code").

Since retrospectives are most productive when the team is fully bought in, it's important to address these objections head-on. But how? How do you overcome individual—or even whole team—skepticism?

This chapter will help you effectively navigate these objections. We'll go over the most common reasons people are skeptical of retrospectives (or even disillusioned with them) and what to do about each one of them.

But first, let's start with why this matters in the first place.

The Vicious Cycle of Disillusionment

Imagine you're running a retrospective with your team. The meeting seems to have gone reasonably well, and by the end of the meeting, the team has committed to an action for the upcoming iteration or sprint. Everyone goes home happy for the weekend and comes back Monday morning ready to go. A few days go by. Then some more. And before you know it, the iteration is over and it's time for the next team retrospective.

As you walk into the conference room, you realize that you and the rest of the team forgot to work on the action from the previous retrospective. A knot in your stomach forms. "Oh no," you think! But you're able to release the tension and nerves, thinking to yourself, "No biggie. We'll just move on and try again."

As the next retrospective starts, you notice a distinct lack of engagement or enthusiasm from your team. To be sure, the usual suspects speak up. But others are actively disengaged and unafraid to show it—perhaps they are checking their email or looking at their phones. By the end of the retrospective, the team has nominally "committed" to a few action items, but deep down in your gut, you have a sense that the odds of anyone caring about them or working on them in the upcoming iteration are slim.

And sure enough another iteration goes by, and yet again, nothing changes.

Congratulations! You and your team have fallen into the Cycle of Disillusionment. Lack of engagement leads to a lack of follow-through which leads to a lack of engagement. And so on and so forth, until everyone (perhaps even you!) has become a retrospective skeptic. (See the following figure.)

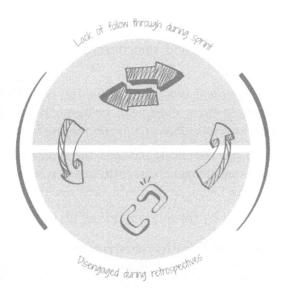

If this feels familiar to you, we feel your pain. We've seen it too and have some ideas on how to stop the downward spiral.

Start with Empathy and Curiosity

When you're responsible for—or simply passionate about—facilitating retrospectives, it's easy to lose sight of why others might not share your perspective.

You might think, "Can't *they* see we need to pause and reflect? Come on! It's obvious!" Or, "The only reason *they* don't believe in retrospectives is because *they* don't put their heart into it. If *they* would only care, it would be different...."

From this mindset, it's easy to cast judgment and blame. But the cost of blame is high, as we learned in Chapter 4, Managing Group Dynamics, on page 63.

The faster you can switch your mindset from blame to curiosity, the easier it will be to listen and learn. And it's only by listening and learning that you can help your team get out of the Cycle of Disillusionment.

While their perspective might not make sense to you, it certainly does *to them*. Your job is to approach the situation with genuine empathy, to ask questions, and to become an active listener. Remember, your goal at this point is not to convince or to argue—it's simply to understand.

When you take this approach, over time you will start to recognize patterns. People tend to bring up the same reasons for their skepticism of retrospectives.

We'll share some of the most common of them in this chapter.

Nothing Changes Anyway

Without a doubt, the most common reason why people become retrospective skeptics is because of a belief that Nothing Changes Anyway. It's the sense, grounded in that person's experience and reality, that retrospectives are a waste of time because they don't actually lead to real improvements and change. And it's the start of the Cycle of Disillusionment.

Here's the thing—this objection *makes complete sense*. One of the most important aspects of lean and agile is the removal of waste. It's the idea that anything that isn't providing value to you, your team, or your customers should be discarded.

If you run into someone who argues that Nothing Changes Anyway, it's important to realize that their objection isn't, in fact, about the *theory* of the retrospective itself. In other words, the person isn't disagreeing with the *idea* of regularly pausing to find ways to improve. What they are objecting to instead is a failure *in practice*—that the retrospectives they've actually run in the past haven't worked, and therefore they've found them to be a waste of time.

This is an important distinction because it allows you to find a common ground. It's likely the case that you both actually do believe in the idea of retrospectives as a driver of continuous improvement. Where you differ is whether you believe the ones you're running actually have value in practice.

With this recognition, it becomes possible to find a path forward. You might pose a question to the skeptic: "Let me offer up a crazy hypothetical to you. Imagine for a moment that I magically knew for a fact the next retrospective would lead to some meaningful improvement. Would you be interested in participating then?"

Almost certainly, the answer would be, "Well, yes of course. The problem is that I don't believe that's the case."

Your job, then, is to find a way to make sure the next retrospective leads to something that has real value. This was the approach that Senior Agile Coach, Ed Rowand, took. Rowand had taken over a team whose previous Scrum Master did 15-minute retrospectives, with no action items. As a result, he often heard that retrospectives were "a waste of time" leading many to want to skip the retrospective entirely as they saw no value in the meeting.

To combat this concern, Rowand "slowly added an interactive coaching segment and started tracking action items that led to gradual improvement for the team." With these incremental changes, Rowand was able to show his team the value of time spent in their retrospectives. "The tech lead told me that before I had become the Scrum Master, he thought that retrospectives were a waste of time. But now, he could see the value of them and could tangibly see the improvements in the team's performance."

Like Rowand, we suggest trying to build momentum by getting one or two small wins under your belt. Make sure to celebrate those successes at the start of your retrospective!

One of the best ways is to break down a large problem that everyone *wants* to fix into bite-sized chunks. While everyone would love to solve the whole problem right away, that's likely not realistic. In fact, chasing the big prize and not making progress on it is likely what got people into the Cycle of Disillusionment in the first place.

15% Solutions

We recommend finding 15% Solutions (which we described in Chapter 13, Elevating Issues Beyond the Team's Control, on page 219). As a refresher, 15% Solutions is a technique that helps you "discover and focus on what each person has the freedom and resources to do now."

This is the strategy Judy Graham, an Agile and Scrum Community Practice Lead, used when she joined an established team that had fallen into the Cycle of Disillusionment. "They kept running the same Mad/Sad/Glad retrospective. They only discussed the same issues as they had in previous retrospectives, and they kept moaning about the same things. Most of the issues being discussed were outside their control."

Judy helped them understand that they could instead focus on things within their control. Once that happened, they actually started to implement small changes, and over time, the team's resistance to retrospectives lessened.

Retrospectives Are Boring

Many of us have participated in more retrospectives than we can count. Let's face it, after a while, they can become a bit dry, especially when they are facilitated in a similar fashion from one retrospective to another. We also would be bored if every two weeks we asked ourselves the same two questions: "What went well?" and "What didn't go well?"

When people complain that their retrospectives are boring, we've found that a common response is to introduce retrospective games and activities that are specifically designed to increase the "fun factor." While there's nothing inherently wrong with having fun in a retrospective—in fact, all else being equal, the more fun the better!—having fun is not the actual goal of the retrospective. Rather, the goal of a retrospective is to encourage team learning and growth.

When retrospective games are picked solely to increase fun, they simply put a Band-Aid on the real problem—lack of effectiveness. And ultimately, it's the effectiveness that people are after.

Think about it—would you prefer a meeting that was fun but led to little to no meaningful learning and change, or a meeting that was relatively dry but made your job easier, your team more productive, and removed impediments to your success? For nearly all of us, the answer is clearly the latter.

There's nothing wrong with having fun. But, unless the retrospective actually helps your team learn and improve, eventually, the fun wears off, and you'll be left with the same ineffective, boring retrospective you started with.

Of course, the next question then is: "How do I make my retrospectives more effective?" Lucky for you, that's what this book is all about! Focus on effectiveness and the Retrospectives Are Boring objection will "magically" disappear. There's nothing boring about learning and continuous improvement.

No Difficult Conversations

Conflict is often uncomfortable. And since difficult conversations can lead to conflict and conflict can lead to difficult conversations, many people consciously or subconsciously avoid these situations. In fact, since it takes an intentional act to have these conversations, the default option is to avoid them!

But conflict avoidance is rarely the right strategy for people who work together for any meaningful amount of time. Rather than helping to find a resolution, it results in people holding on to their version of the events ever more tightly over time. Instead of bringing people together, it leads to people building evidence that further supports and cements their point of view. And in place of taking responsibility, it causes people to villainize and blame. What it *doesn't* do is help resolve the conflict.

Fortunately for us, one of the primary benefits of scheduling regular retrospectives is that they provide the time, space, and structure for direct conversations to occur *without* an intentional act. The flip side of this benefit is that *because* they provide the time, space, and structure for challenging conversations to occur on a regular basis, some people will want to skip the retrospective to avoid having them in the first place. That's when you know you have someone on your team who has a No Difficult Conversations objection.

In general, we've found that people who have this objection to retrospectives (whether explicitly or implicitly) have a low level of psychological safety with their team. Groups with high psychological safety feel comfortable talking about what makes them *uncomfortable*.

Model Better Behavior

When you come across the No Difficult Conversations objection, the best thing you can do is model the behavior you seek. Go directly to the person who is avoiding the difficult conversation and talk about what you see.

You could say something like,

> "Hey John, do you have a minute to chat? I noticed that our team hasn't run a retrospective for two months. I'm not sure if I'm right, but I suspect it might be due to all of us avoiding talking about X. That's making me feel frustrated and even a little sad because I believe that to get past issue X, we need to talk directly about it. I know I've contributed to this sort of avoidance, too. In fact, I hesitated even bringing *this* up with you!"

Let's break this down, because it is very intentionally worded.

First, by asking John, "Do you have a minute to chat?" you're showing respect for John's time and priorities and confirming now is a good moment to have a discussion. If not, it's better to try again later.

Second, you shared a fact ("Our team hasn't run a retrospective for two months"). This fact should be indisputable—either it's true or it isn't. It helps to build a shared mental model between you and John.

Next, you shared your opinion ("I suspect it might be due to…") and you made it clear that it was loosely held ("I'm not sure if I'm right"). This makes it obvious that you're approaching the situation with curiosity and gives John the space to disagree with your interpretation of the facts.

Then, you shared your emotions ("That's making me feel…"). This communicates to John another set of facts—how it's making you feel—and it enables John to build empathy for where you're coming from.

Finally, you shared how you're responsible for the situation, too ("I know I've contributed to this…"). This makes it clear to John that you aren't blaming or attacking him, and that you take your share of the responsibility for not talking about the issue.

By taking this approach, not only have you modeled the behavior you're looking for by directly addressing the issue with John, but you've also done so in a productive manner.

Use This Approach in Your Retrospective

This approach can be utilized with the broader team when you finally do run a retrospective on the topic. We call this activity "Facts, Stories, and Emotions", or FSE for short.

For more on this, see our suggested retrospective flow for "A Conflict on the Team" on page 176.

We're Too Busy

Has anyone on your team ever come to you and said something to the effect of, "I really don't have time for the retrospective today. Do you mind if I sit this one out or we reschedule?" If so, you've encountered the We're Too Busy objection. This objection often comes up for one of two reasons.

First, it can come up for legitimate reasons—perhaps there's a critical bug in production that needs immediate attention, for example. In these cases, the objection is worthwhile to consider. The team truly might be too busy for the retrospective *at that moment in time.*

Note that this doesn't mean the team should actually skip the retrospective. In fact, we'd strongly recommend running an "incident retrospective" once the critical bug has been resolved (for one approach, see our suggested retrospective flow for "After an Outage or Issue" on page 166).

But it's important to acknowledge that, once in a while, this objection can be a legitimate reason to *delay* running the retrospective until a more appropriate time. More importantly, this shouldn't happen on a regular—or even semi-regular—basis. If it does, it's indicative of a larger problem.

More commonly, the We're Too Busy objection comes up for less legitimate reasons. For example, the team might feel overloaded with work in general and is just "too tired and overwhelmed" to devote time to the retrospective. While on the surface this may seem like a good reason to skip the retrospective (more time to do "real work"!), it would be a much better idea to pause to retrospect on *why* the team feels so tired and overwhelmed. In fact, by doing so the team just might discover a long-term solution to its problem!

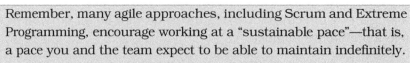

Work at a Sustainable Pace

Remember, many agile approaches, including Scrum and Extreme Programming, encourage working at a "sustainable pace"—that is, a pace you and the team expect to be able to maintain indefinitely.

If your team is doing so much work that it doesn't have time to pause to reflect and learn, it needs to slow down. Teams that learn how to do this will, in the long run, perform better and be happier.

Moreover, skipping the retrospective to do "real work" implies that the retrospective itself isn't "real work," which couldn't be further from the truth. In fact, if your job is to develop software, all of your work is learning work. That, of course, includes the technical aspects of your job like writing, debugging, and refactoring your code. But it also includes the nontechnical aspects of your job, like talking with stakeholders, capturing user feedback, and yes, running retrospectives. This is also true in any other creative industry.

We're Not Agile

For some people, retrospectives are something that only those "crazy agile teams do." For others, it's even more constrained than that: all retrospectives are assumed to be Sprint Retrospectives and since sprints are part of the Scrum Framework, retrospectives are something only Scrum Teams do. Under this belief system, if you aren't agile, or you aren't doing Scrum, then retrospectives are not for you.

The reality is that retrospectives are simply meetings that help groups of people learn together by reflecting on their experiences and constructing ways to become better going forward. As such, they can be helpful to any team in almost any context, whether agile or not.

To demonstrate this, imagine you work as an account executive for a large enterprise sales team. Over the past few months, you've noticed less collaboration and more tension on your team, but you're not sure why. Could you see how running a retrospective might help?

Or perhaps you work as a recruiter in an HR department and over the past two quarters, you've noticed a decreasing volume of candidates for your job applications. You wonder what your team might do to help fix this problem. Could you see how running a retrospective might provide an effective forum to discuss this situation?

More importantly, in neither of these simple examples are the teams "agile." There is no agile transformation. There are no Scrum Masters or Agile Coaches. There are simply people working together trying to solve hard problems. And retrospectives can help.

And yet, because the word *retrospective* has, for many people, become synonymous with agile, some people who work on non-agile teams resist running retrospectives. Fortunately, the fix to this problem is relatively simple: host a meeting with the same purpose as a retrospective, *just don't call it a retrospective*!

You can still follow the five phases outlined in Chapter 1, Help Your Team Inspect and Adapt, on page 3. Over time, as the meeting proves itself to be valuable, resistance to the idea will drop.

Retrospectives Only Lead to Blame

Retrospectives can turn ugly fast when they are used as an excuse to blame, shame, or humiliate. When this happens, it can understandably turn people off to future retrospectives, even after they move to other teams or begin working at other companies.

The best way to overcome this objection is twofold. First, empathize with the person who had this experience. You might say something like, "I understand you've had bad experiences with retrospectives in the past. You were blamed in front of your peers. I want to be clear—that would be awful, and I'd likely not want to participate in retrospectives either, were I the one to have that experience. Fortunately, it's not how we run retrospectives here."

Then, in the next retrospective, set the stage by sharing the Retrospective Prime Directive (which is outlined as an activity on page 92). As a refresher, it states:

> Regardless of what we discover, we understand and truly believe that everyone did the best job they could, given what they knew at the time, their skills and abilities, the resources available, and the situation at hand.

Notice how the Prime Directive prompts people to get out of a blame mindset. If you "truly believe that everyone did the best job they could," then it's hard to blame them for the results. Furthermore, if everyone did the best they could *given what they knew at the time*, the best question to ask would be, "What have we learned since then?"

Asking "What have we learned?" is the antidote to blame, and sharing that approach with someone who has this objection can help them overcome their resistance.

Unhelpful Manager Beliefs

On occasion, it's not the team itself that objects to running retrospectives, but the team's managers who claim they are a waste of time. How should you respond?

The first approach is to bring hard data that directly supports the value of retrospectives. Ideally, this data would be from previous retrospectives you've managed to run on the current team. If that doesn't exist, you could refer back to data from other teams you've been a part of in the past. If you don't have that either, you can always paint a hypothetical picture.

Here's an example of how you might use hard data to support the value of retrospectives. Imagine a situation in which it took one hour for your team's code to compile and build. (If this sounds extreme, consider yourself fortunate for never having experienced it!)

Now imagine you brought this to your team's attention during a retrospective, which would help the team discover a way to reduce the compile time and build time down to fifteen minutes. As a result, the team would find a way to save forty-five minutes every time it compiles and builds the code. Put another way, that's forty-five minutes of time the team used to be idle that can now be used productively. And since on average the team compiles and builds the code once a day, that translates to almost four hours of additional time each week...per person!

Armed with this data, you could go to your manager and explain how, thanks to a single one-hour retrospective, each person on the team has an extra four hours of productive time each week. Even better, this isn't a one-time benefit as it recurs each and every week. Armed with average salaries, you could even translate those four hours of savings into a monetary impact on the bottom line.

If bringing hard data doesn't work, the second approach is to agree to disagree. Your manager might have the *opinion* that retrospectives don't work, but it's unlikely he or she has *data* to back that up. Rather than engage in a debate about the efficacy of retrospectives based on opinions and beliefs, ask for space to run retrospectives as an experiment for an agreed-upon period of time (say, three months). Define a success criteria in advance that you both can agree to.

It's important to note that your goal here isn't to convince your manager that retrospectives work. Rather, it's to agree with your manager that they might be right, while also explaining that the best way to know for sure is to run a few retrospectives, collect some data, and see what happens.

This approach should lower your manager's resistance and provide you with some space for experimentation.

For more, see our description of FINE experiments on page 203.

Don't Be Deterred

A wide variety of objections exist to running retrospectives. Some people have formed these objections due to past experiences, while others are simply biased against anything that isn't hard technical work. In both cases, it can be challenging to know how to respond to these objections in a productive manner. This chapter presented some of the most common objections to retrospectives we've heard, along with the best approaches to dealing with them.

CHAPTER 15

Continuing the Learning Journey

We opened this book by claiming that retrospectives help teams—even great ones—keep improving. We believe this to be true because retrospectives encourage collaborative learning, and collaborative learning is essential to success in any creative industry.

Collaborative learning is only possible when teams are open and curious—not only with themselves but also with each other and with their environment. From that place of curiosity, it becomes possible to look at data in new ways, discover previously unrecognized patterns, and commit to actions that lead to radical improvements.

In the spirit of continuous learning, it's only natural that we conclude this book by sharing our recommendations on how you might continue on your retrospective learning journey. (Full disclosure: we are the authors of some of the resources below and have written introductions and recommendations for others—which shows that we believe they have good content!)

Retrospectives in General

Since the first edition of this book was released, there has been a beautiful blossoming of other helpful books on retrospectives. In no particular order, these include *Improving Agile Retrospectives [Loe18]* by Marc Loeffler, *Retrospectives for Organizational Change [Eck14]* by Jutta Eckstein, *Getting Value out of Agile Retrospectives [GL14]* by Luis Goncalves and Ben Linders, *The Retrospective Handbook [Kua13]* by Patrick Kua, and *Retrospective Antipatterns [Von21]* by Aino Vonge Corry. If you are looking for an online resource, David publishes his thoughts on Retrium's *Ultimate Guide to Agile Retrospectives.*[1]

---

1. https://www.retrium.com/ultimate-guide-to-agile-retrospectives/intro

Facilitation

Productive group conversation relies on effective facilitation. We've only scratched the surface of this critical topic in this book. For further learning, we recommend starting with *The Facilitator's Guide to Participatory Decision-Making [KLTF96]* by Sam Kaner et al. If you work in a remote environment, we recommend *The Remote Facilitator's Pocket Guide [CM20]* by Kirsten Clacey and Jay-Allen Morris.

Ultimately nothing replaces hands-on experience. Consider participating in experiential facilitation workshops that enable you to practice your facilitation skills in a fail-safe, risk-free environment. Or ask someone whom you respect and trust (and who understands facilitation!) to observe as you facilitate and provide you with feedback.

Finally, watch other people who are effective at leading meetings and working with groups. Watch how they interact with people and how they respond when a session isn't going smoothly. You may not end up using their exact words or actions, yet you can adapt their approaches to fit your own style.

Continuous Improvement

As we described in Chapter 12, Catalyzing and Sustaining Change, on page 201, even well-facilitated retrospectives can fail when the team doesn't know how to go about creating change. To learn more about fixing this common problem, start with Esther's book *7 Rules For Positive, Productive Change [Der19]*, which focuses on complex changes in complex environments, and Diana's book *Lead Without Blame [LB22]*, which provides a framework for cultivating workplace resiliency by moving beyond blaming and shaming.

Join the Community

Having collectively spent many decades being part of the broader retrospective community, we can say with confidence it's truly a wonderful group of people who are generous, kind, and open. We encourage you to join us. Every year, many of us participate in the Retrospective Facilitators Gathering, a week-long retreat filled with learning, laughter, and connection. Diana, Esther, and David are regular attendees and presenters at agile conferences across the world. We'd love to meet you at one, or many, of those. Lastly, if you prefer an online setting, simply join the Retrospectives LinkedIn community.[2]

---

2.   https://www.linkedin.com/groups/95111/

Continued Learning

We've learned a lot about retrospectives over the years. And yet, if there's one thing we're confident of, it's that there is still so much more to discover. We are delighted that so many of you have joined us on that learning journey and in so doing, have helped share the power of retrospectives with the world. Thank you for being part of that with us!

Now go forth, and retrospect.

Potential Prework Questions

Here is a list of questions we've found useful in several settings when preparing for large-scale retrospectives. Arrange the questions to flow from one to another and make logical sense for your interview or questionnaire. Grouping the questions, as follows, can help make the list seem shorter. Test the questions by answering them yourself before you try them with the group. You may not know the content of the answer; the point is to make sure the questions you send aren't so ambiguous that no one will be able to answer them. Be sure to let your participants know they can skip questions if they'd like.

- Focus Areas
  - What are three topics you think you must raise at this retrospective?
  - What other focus areas are of concern to you for team/organization learning and improvement?
- Appreciating what works
  - What do you value most about the contributions of others to teamwork, collaboration, and/or effective communication?
  - What do you value most about others' technical contributions?
  - What's working well today within and between teams that you'd want to sustain?
  - When you look back over the work we will consider, what do you consider to be the one or two high points or most energized times? Why did you choose those experiences? What made them memorable?
  - What do you value most about your contribution on this release?
  - What do you value most about the contributions of others?

- Moving to the future

  - Envision success for the work of the retrospective. Imagine you're in the future and this outcome has provided benefits for you, future efforts, and the organization. Describe a few things that will have changed for the better. What is the best possible outcome you can imagine?

  - What is the best possible outcome you can imagine for this retrospective? For yourself? For future efforts? For the organization?

  - What would have to happen during or after the retrospective to achieve those outcomes?

- Letting go

  - Everyone will need to let go of attachment to past concerns to move forward. What will be most difficult for you to let go?

  - What effective things (name one or two) could be done to "clear the decks" as far as challenges go in this and past efforts?

  - What has prevented even more of these things from happening up until now?

- Concerns

  - What other reservations, concerns, or worries do you have about participating in the retrospective?

  - Is there an essential issue that needs attention in order to reach a new level of effectiveness and productivity?

  - What puzzles you about the retrospective?

- What else?

  - What else do you think I should ask about?

  - If I asked that, how would you respond?

Explain that you'll use the information that you gather to design the approach to the retrospective. Assure people you will keep confidential the information they share and then be sure to keep it that way. If you do plan to summarize and share the information with the group during the retrospective, say so. Take care to protect individual identities.

Activities Reference Sheet

The table on page 254 and continuing on page 255 lists all the activities described in this book in alphabetical order. The checkmarks indicate which chapter(s) the activities are referenced in.

Use this reference table as a way to quickly locate where in the book you will be able to learn more about each activity.

	CHAPTER														
	Part I						Part II					Part III			
Activity	1	2	3	4	5	6	7	8	9	10	11	12	13	14	15
1-2-4-All										✓					
15% Solutions											✓				
Acknowledgments and Apologies												✓			
Aha!				✓											
Appreciations		✓							✓	✓		✓			
Art Gallery						✓									
Brainstorming/Filtering										✓					
Brainwriting and Evaluating Options										✓					
Cause and Effect Diagramming			✓												
Check-In Question (includes "One-Word Check-in")		✓										✓			
Circle of Factors										✓					
Circles and Soup					✓	✓		✓		✓		✓			
Compare Options										✓					
Constellations										✓					
Control/Impact Matrix										✓		✓			
Design Experiments										✓			✓		
ESVP	✓														
Dot Voting / Express Preferences					✓				✓	✓	✓				
Facts, Stories, and Emotions					✓			✓		✓					
Fill-in-the-Blanks					✓										
Finding Factors										✓					
Fishbone				✓		✓									
Fishbowl					✓			✓							
Fist of Five										✓					
Focus On/Focus Off		✓										✓			
Force Field						✓									
Gathering Data From an Improvement Action									✓						
Gradient of Agreement							✓		✓						
Helped/Hindered/Hypothesis (a.k.a. HHH)									✓	✓					
Hopes and Wishes								✓					✓		
Impact/Energy Decision Criteria	✓	✓													
Introduce the Focus Topic and Agenda										✓					
Keep Drop Add			✓												
Lean Coffee									✓						
Learning Matrix										✓					

Activity	CHAPTER														
	Part I			Part II							Part III				
	1	2	3	4	5	6	7	8	9	10	11	12	13	14	15
Mad Sad Glad										✓					
Meeting Ground Rules for Conflicts or Controversy				✓						✓					
More to Explore?			✓												
My Team Is Awesome									✓						
One "Now" Thing												✓			
Opportunities for Improvement		✓			✓					✓					
Pattern Spotter Questions		✓													
Patterns and Shifts		✓								✓					
Personal Insights and Resolves										✓					
Pleased and Surprised						✓									
Plus/Delta												✓			
Prioritize Issues												✓			
Proud and Sorry															
Recap Actions		✓								✓					
Reiterate the Goal				✓											
Report Out and Synthesis						✓				✓					
Retrospective Prime Directive										✓					
Return on Time Invested (ROTI)										✓					
Satisfaction Histogram		✓				✓									
Share the Agenda							✓								
Short Subjects		✓								✓					
Simple Objective Data Discussion	✓	✓								✓					
Simple Subjective Data Discussion		✓								✓					
Simplified Value Stream Map	✓	✓								✓		✓			
SMART Action				✓		✓				✓					
Story Cards (Retrospective Planning Game)													✓		
Team Radar	✓	✓								✓					
Temperature Reading		✓								✓					
Timeline				✓						✓					
What Has Shifted?										✓					
What I Hear You Saying Is										✓					
What Went Well / What Didn't Go Well				✓						✓					
Working Agreements	✓	✓								✓					
WRAP (Wishes/Risks/Appreciations/Puzzles)		✓								✓					

Bibliography

[Bri03]   William Bridges. *Managing Transitions: Making the Most of Change.* Da Capo Press, Cambridge, MA, 2003.

[Car21]   Dorwin Cartwright (ed.). *Studies in Social Power.* Hassell Street Press, , 2021.

[CM20]   Kirsten Clacey and Jay-Allen Morris. *The Remote Facilitator's Pocket Guide.* Berrett-Koehler, San Francisco, CA, 2020.

[Dav05]   Rachel Davies. Improvising Space for a Timeline. *Email.* personal, 2005.

[Der03]   Esther Derby. How to Improve Meetings When You're Not in Charge. *http://www.stickyminds.com.* online, 2003.

[Der03a]   Esther Derby. The Roti Method for Gauging Meeting Effectiveness. *http://www.stickyminds.com.* online, 2003.

[Der05]   Esther Derby. Helping Your Team Weather the Storm. *http://www.sticky-minds.com.* online, 2005.

[Der19]   Esther Derby. *7 Rules for Positive, Productive Change: Micro Shifts, Macro Results.* Berrett-Koehler, San Francisco, CA, 2019.

[DS06]   Esther Derby and Diana Larsen, Foreword by Ken Schwaber. *Agile Retrospectives (out of print).* The Pragmatic Bookshelf, Dallas, TX, 2006.

[Eck14]   Jutte Eckstein. *Retrospectives for Organizational Change: an Agile Approach.* Create-Space Independent Publishing Platform, Seattle, WA, 2014.

[Edm18]   Amy Edmondson. *The Fearless Organization: Creating Psychological Safety in the Workplace for Learning, Innovation, and Growth.* John Wiley & Sons, New York, NY, 2018.

[EH13]   Glenda Eoyang and Royce Holladay. *Adaptive Action: Leveraging Uncertainty in Your Organization*. Stanford Business Books, Redwood City, CA, 2013.

[GL14]   Luis Gonçalvez and Ben Linders. *Getting Value Out of Agile Retrospectives: a Toolbox of Retrospective Exercises*. Lulu, lulu.com, 2014.

[Hin05]   Siegi Hinger. Re: Improvising Space for a Timeline. *Email*. personal, 2005.

[Ker01]   Norman L. Kerth. *Project Retrospectives: A Handbook for Team Reviews*. Dorset House, New York, NY, 2001.

[KLTF14]   Sam Kaner, Lenny Lind, Catherine Toldi, Sarah Fisk, and Dwayne Berger. *Facilitator's Guide to Participatory Decision Making, 3rd Edition*. Jossey-Bass Publishers, San Francisco, CA, 2014.

[KLTF96]   Sam Kaner, Lenny Lind, Catherine Toldi, Sarah Fisk, and Duane Berger. *The Facilitator's Guide to Participatory Decision-Making*. New Society Publishers, Gabriola Island, BC, Canada, 1996.

[Kua13]   Patrick Kua. *The Retrospective Handbook: A guide for agile teams*. CreateSpace Independent Publishing Platform, Seattle, WA, 2013.

[LB22]   Diana Larsen and Tricia Broderick. *Lead without Blame: Building Resilient Learning Teams*. Berrett-Koehler, San Francisco, CA, 2022.

[Loe18]   Marc Loeffler. *Improving Agile Retrospectives: Helping Teams Become More Efficient*. Pearson Education, Inc., Hoboken, NJ, 2018.

[Pin09]   Daniel H. Pink. *Drive: The Surprising Truth About What Motivates Us*. Riverhead Books, New York, NY, 2009.

[RA22]   Karin M. Reed and Joseph A. Allen. *Suddenly Hybrid: Managing the Modern Meeting*. John Wiley & Sons, New York, NY, 2022.

[Roc22]   David Rock. *Leadership: Six Steps to Transforming Performance at Work*. Harper Business, New York, NY, 2022.

[Sat91]   Virginia Satir. *The Satir Model: Family Therapy and Beyond*. Science and Behavior Books, Palo Alto, CA, 1991.

[Sch90]   Johanna Schwab. *A Resource Handbook for Satir Concepts*. Science and Behavior Books, Palo Alto, CA, 1990.

[Sch94]   Roger Schwarz. *The Skilled Facilitator*. Jossey-Bass Publishers, San Francisco, CA, 1994.

[Von21]   Aino Vonge Corry. *Retrospective Antipatterns*. Pearson Education, Inc., Hoboken, NJ, 2021.

[Yur16]   Adam Yuret. *How to Have Great Meetings: A Lean Coffee Book*. Create-Space Independent Publishing Platform, Seattle, WA, 2016.

Index

Thank you!

We hope you enjoyed this book and that you're already thinking about what you want to learn next. To help make that decision easier, we're offering you this gift.

Head on over to https://pragprog.com right now, and use the coupon code BUYANOTHER2024 to save 30% on your next ebook. Offer is void where prohibited or restricted. This offer does not apply to any edition of the *The Pragmatic Programmer* ebook.

And if you'd like to share your own expertise with the world, why not propose a writing idea to us? After all, many of our best authors started off as our readers, just like you. With up to a 50% royalty, world-class editorial services, and a name you trust, there's nothing to lose. Visit https://pragprog.com/become-an-author/ today to learn more and to get started.

Thank you for your continued support. We hope to hear from you again soon!

The Pragmatic Bookshelf

SAVE 30%!
Use coupon code
BUYANOTHER2024

Liftoff, Second Edition

Ready, set, liftoff! Align your team to one purpose: successful delivery. Learn new insights and techniques for starting projects and teams the right way, with expanded concepts for planning, organizing, and conducting liftoff meetings. Real-life stories illustrate how others have effectively started (or restarted) their teams and projects. Master coaches Diana Larsen and Ainsley Nies have successfully "lifted off" numerous agile projects worldwide. Are you ready for success?

Diana Larsen and Ainsley Nies
(170 pages) ISBN: 9781680501636. $24
https://pragprog.com/book/liftoff

Behind Closed Doors

Great management is difficult to see as it occurs. Great management happens in one-on-one meetings and with other managers–all in private. It's hard to learn management by example when you can't see it.

Find out what goes on *Behind Closed Doors* and see how a skilled manager turns around a tricky management situation in seven weeks. You'll learn how to provide and use feedback effectively, and become a better coach and mentor peers and team members. As you begin to build a cohesive, "jelled" team you'll learn how to use your influence across the organization and make better choices daily to survive and thrive.

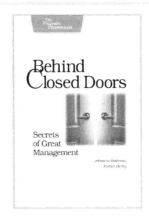

Johanna Rothman and Esther Derby
(172 pages) ISBN: 9780976694021. $24.95
https://pragprog.com/book/rdbcd

Competing with Unicorns

Today's tech unicorns develop software differently. They've developed a way of working that lets them scale like an enterprise while working like a startup. These techniques can be learned. This book takes you behind the scenes and shows you how companies like Google, Facebook, and Spotify do it. Leverage their insights, so your teams can work better together, ship higher-quality product faster, innovate more quickly, and compete with the unicorns.

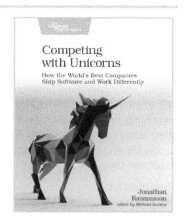

Jonathan Rasmusson
(138 pages) ISBN: 9781680507232. $26.95
https://pragprog.com/book/jragile

The Agile Samurai

Here are three simple truths about software development:

1. You can't gather all the requirements up front. 2. The requirements you do gather will change. 3. There is always more to do than time and money will allow

Those are the facts of life. But you can deal with those facts (and more) by becoming a fierce software-delivery professional, capable of dispatching the most dire of software projects and the toughest delivery schedules with ease and grace.

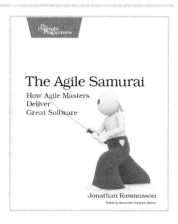

Jonathan Rasmusson
(264 pages) ISBN: 9781934356586. $34.95
https://pragprog.com/book/jtrap

Your Code as a Crime Scene, Second Edition

Jack the Ripper and legacy codebases have more in common than you'd think. Inspired by forensic psychology methods, you can apply strategies to identify problems in your existing code, assess refactoring direction, and understand how your team influences the software architecture. With its unique blend of criminal psychology and code analysis, *Your Code as a Crime Scene* arms you with the techniques you need to take on any codebase, no matter what programming language you use.

Adam Tornhill
(336 pages) ISBN: 9798888650325. $53.95
https://pragprog.com/book/atcrime2

Programming Ruby 3.3 (5th Edition)

Ruby is one of the most important programming languages in use for web development. It powers the Rails framework, which is the backing of some of the most important sites on the web. The Pickaxe Book, named for the tool on the cover, is the definitive reference on Ruby, a highly-regarded, fully object-oriented programming language. This updated edition is a comprehensive reference on the language itself, with a tutorial on the most important features of Ruby—including pattern matching and Ractors—and describes the language through Ruby 3.3.

Noel Rappin, with Dave Thomas
(716 pages) ISBN: 9781680509823. $65.95
https://pragprog.com/book/ruby5

Text Processing with JavaScript

You might think of regular expressions as the holy grail of text processing, but are you sure you aren't just shoehorning them in where standard built-in solutions already exist and would work better? JavaScript itself provides programmers with excellent methods for text manipulation, and knowing how and when to use them will help you write more efficient and performant code. From extracting data from APIs to calculating word counts and everything in between, discover how to pick the right tool for the job and make the absolute most of it every single time.

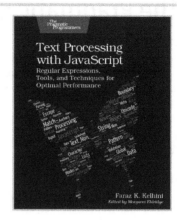

Faraz K. Kelhini
(240 pages) ISBN: 9798888650332. $51.95
https://pragprog.com/book/fkjavascript

A Common-Sense Guide to Data Structures and Algorithms in Python, Volume 1

If you thought data structures and algorithms were all just theory, you're missing out on what they can do for your Python code. Learn to use Big O notation to make your code run faster by orders of magnitude. Choose from data structures such as hash tables, trees, and graphs to increase your code's efficiency exponentially. With simple language and clear diagrams, this book makes this complex topic accessible, no matter your background. Every chapter features practice exercises to give you the hands-on information you need to master data structures and algorithms for your day-to-day work.

Jay Wengrow
(502 pages) ISBN: 9798888650356. $57.95
https://pragprog.com/book/jwpython

The Pragmatic Bookshelf

The Pragmatic Bookshelf features books written by professional developers for professional developers. The titles continue the well-known Pragmatic Programmer style and continue to garner awards and rave reviews. As development gets more and more difficult, the Pragmatic Programmers will be there with more titles and products to help you stay on top of your game.

Visit Us Online

This Book's Home Page
https://pragprog.com/book/dlret2
Source code from this book, errata, and other resources. Come give us feedback, too!

Keep Up-to-Date
https://pragprog.com
Join our announcement mailing list (low volume) or follow us on Twitter @pragprog for new titles, sales, coupons, hot tips, and more.

New and Noteworthy
https://pragprog.com/news
Check out the latest Pragmatic developments, new titles, and other offerings.

Save on the ebook

Save on the ebook versions of this title. Owning the paper version of this book entitles you to purchase the electronic versions at a terrific discount.

PDFs are great for carrying around on your laptop—they are hyperlinked, have color, and are fully searchable. Most titles are also available for the iPhone and iPod touch, Amazon Kindle, and other popular e-book readers.

Send a copy of your receipt to support@pragprog.com and we'll provide you with a discount coupon.

Contact Us

Online Orders:	*https://pragprog.com/catalog*
Customer Service:	*support@pragprog.com*
International Rights:	*translations@pragprog.com*
Academic Use:	*academic@pragprog.com*
Write for Us:	*http://write-for-us.pragprog.com*

Milton Keynes UK
Ingram Content Group UK Ltd.
UKHW051018010324
438541UK00001B/1